Continuum

Continuum

How science, psychology, and mysticism
point to a life beyond . . . and to an
extraordinary kind of God

by Robert C. Casselman

Richard Marek Publishers, New York

Library of Congress Cataloging in Publication Data

Casselman, Robert C
    Continuum.
    1. Faith. 2. Casselman, Robert C. I. Title.
BV4637.C35   248'.246 [B]   78-7670
ISBN 0-399-90017-9
Printed in the United States of America

To Dorothy, who probably made this book inevitable the day she married me; and to Norm, who pushed me in ways he never knew; and to Ross, who must have known he was pushing me, but not where.

Acknowledgments

I won't try to name all the people who have patiently tolerated my arguing and probing all through the many years I was seeking answers. They will see themselves in here, and they should; they made this book possible, and I am grateful.

To Carl Hermann Voss, who had more to do with my searching than he ever guessed, and whose books *The Universal God* and *Quotations of Courage and Vision* left an impress on my mind and some words in this book, I give special thanks. To my children, whose encouragement never flagged, and especially to Carl and Fritz, who wouldn't let me write as badly as I might, I am particularly grateful. And finally, I remind my perceptive, tactful, and patient wife that this is her book as much as mine.

I am indebted to several publishers for permission to use material:

Harper & Row. *Nothing So Strange.* Arthur Ford and Margueritte Harmon Bro. New York. 1958.

Mockingbird Books. *Life After Life*. Copyright © 1975 by Raymond A. Moody Jr., M.D. A Bantam/Mockingbird Book.

Doubleday. *The Other Side*. Excerpts from THE OTHER SIDE by James A. Pike. Copyright © 1968 by New Focus Foundation. Used by permission of Doubleday and Company, Inc.

Garrett Publications. *Awareness*. Published by Garrett Publications. Copyright © 1943 Eileen J. Garrett. Copyright © 1971 Eileen Coly. Reprinted with permission.

Holt, Rinehart & Winston. *The Link: Matthew Manning's Own Story*. Copyright © 1974 by Colin Smythe Ltd. Published in the United States by Holt, Rinehart & Winston.

Also, I want to acknowledge the particular helpfulness of several sources not quoted in the book that added special insight and direction along the way: The International Journal of Parapsychology; Proceedings of the Society for Psychical Research; Lawrence LeShan's *The Medium, the Mystic and the Physicist* (Ballantine Books); Ostrander and Schroeder's *Psychic Discoveries Behind the Iron Curtain* (Prentice-Hall); the U.S. Department of Commerce Joint Publications Research Service, for Russian research transcripts.

Contents

PART II After Discovery

PART I

The Search

"Science without religion is lame, religion without science is blind."

—Albert Einstein

Chapter 1

Simply Stated. . . .

For years I used to sit in church and wonder if I were the only one there having such difficulty buying what I was hearing, and what I had been hearing since I was a child. Did the rest of these nice people around me have some sort of pipeline to God that I'd somehow missed? Did they know something I didn't know that made them believe they could call on God to help them straighten out their problems? Some of them would tell me just that, when I found myself in prayer meetings or got talked into going on retreats to ponder God and life.

Only some of them, though. Most of the people I knew in my church, when I could get them to talk at all candidly about it, seemed to be almost as fuzzy as I was about the whole God thing. Even the true believers seemed to be selective about what they accepted as literal truth and what they chalked up to legend—and each one's list was different.

On balance, my impression was—and still is—that most Christians are very unclear about what they believe and why they believe it. I certainly was. And I don't think I was alone. I also suspect that very large numbers of us have no deeply felt religious convictions at all.

That's a big statement, and it's not meant to be critical. What many of us have, if we've been brought up in the church, is a "belief" in God and Jesus Christ that was instilled in us throughout our childhood years, but whose substance we have rarely tried (or dared) to question or examine in depth. We cannot for the life of us articulate this programmed belief in words other than those we have learned in church. We don't know what it is we are trying to say.

In times of great crisis or sorrow, we do find ourselves groping for ways to use God to ease our pain or bewilderment, but for most of our days he remains forgotten. And though it's true that when we go to church, many of us do in fact get a great deal out of it—perhaps a sense of uplift, a feeling of comfort from being with people who are trying to be better people—few of us *know,* when we leave, that we have been in touch with a real God and that our lives will somehow be different because of it.

Yes, I had a problem, and I think it was not mine alone. Simply stated, it was this:

> Is there something there to believe? If there is, and if I did in fact believe it, would I become a better human being? If a great many of us believed, would we collectively make a better world?

I spent the better part of my life trying to answer those questions. Why? Because I also knew some people who did not have this problem. They had a faith that was unmistakable, and their lives shone because of it. Did I envy them? Perhaps. But beyond any envy was sheer curiosity: what did they know that I didn't know? They could not tell me. I had to find out for myself.

Now, years later, I can say, without the slightest question in my mind, that there is powerful reason to believe. The answer to all of those questions is: yes.

This book is written to tell where that "yes" came from. It came from sources far from organized religion. Modern physics, for one. The mind sciences, for another. Psychic investigations, for still another. The church played but a small part, serving largely as the springboard for this search for meaning.

I write this book for others who have not yet found the assurances they would like to have as they try to cope with the problems of living. It tells, as plainly as I can tell it, how I got from where I was—an uncomfortable, churchgoing near-agnostic—to where I am today—a deep believer in a hereafter and in something I can readily call God. I can now pray, I can occupy a pew in relative comfort. I can also be a stay-at-home with no sense of guilt when I choose to do something else on Sunday.

You may not like or agree with what I found, but you will be along during every step of the way, and you can match your insights to mine on the journey. This is not a tale of sudden conversion, of a laying-on-of-hands that breathed fire into my soul. With a single exception, nothing extraordinary ever happened to me.

What happened happened because over twenty years ago I found myself having to make a choice between remaining a part of a church whose teachings I didn't really believe, or simply abandoning a longtime association with the church because of the increasing discomfort it was causing me. In these days when organized religion seems to have such a tenuous hold on its adherents, you may wonder why the problem was in any way an acute one.

It was acute because I had spent my whole life deeply involved in the church. I liked it. I liked the music, the mystery, the people. I liked the idea that there was an order, a purpose, a divine intent for us that could be discerned if we worked hard enough at being faithful. Working hard meant going to church, studying the Bible, believing what the Bible told us about the person, or power, or spirit named God.

I did work hard, all my life to my mid-thirties. But I could never fathom God. Maybe it was because I was part of his cast for too long, starting back when I was a choirboy in a wealthy Pittsburgh Episcopal church. We weren't all that wealthy—my

mother ran a tearoom downtown and my stepfather was a
chemist who helped himself squeak through the depression by
testing other people's bootleg booze for a fee. Calvary Church
didn't insist that you be well-to-do, but I got the impression
God liked it if you dressed up a little for church. So we looked
as classy as we could afford to, on Sundays anyway.

Choirboys don't have much to do in church when they're not
singing, so they play all kinds of little games. We used to count
the gulps it took for the minister to polish off the communion
wine, and trade wisecracks over the fat behinds that stuck out
at us as their owners knelt at the communion rail. As our voices
changed and new chemistries began stirring, the games we
played during the sermon became more adult, and included
speculation on who was doing it with whom. The younger boys
were never quite sure what "it" was, but that didn't slow the
whispered chatter. Revelation came with time, and thus was the
sex education of the choirboy begun. And all of this in church,
right in front of God and everybody.

Maybe singing in the choir, carrying the cross, swinging the
incense, counting the house, and fighting weekly with the
Catholic choirboys from the church across the street is what
schooled me to look on church as theatre and God as the far
away producer of the show. Certainly, we all had to go to
Sunday school, study the Bible, memorize the prayers and
countless bits of ritual we were involved with as acolytes. We
knew full well there was a God, that he knew what you were up
to, that it was better to do right than wrong even if you didn't
get caught. But we never *knew* God.

I don't know of a one of us who went all the way through this
experience, right up to the time we went away to college, who
ever had "religious" thoughts. We had a code, of sorts, that I
distinctly remember kept us from doing really bad things most
of the time. But this was hooked up only in the loosest sort of
way with God, and was concerned mostly with what he would
do to us if we were bad. The big thing we worried about was
getting caught.

There was one expectation, and one only, that I can recall
being left with from my ten years of bit-playing in God's

company at Calvary Church. And that was the conviction that *someday* I would have a religious experience—I would hear God or see him or in some way know that he was for real and then all that I had been taught would become truth to my own eyes. In a vague sort of way, I felt that if I kept at it, such an experience would indeed come and that's why it was so important to keep going to church. I bought that because it made eminent good sense. Lord knows I'd put in a lot of time, as had all my teachers and everybody else. There had to be something to all this to make it worthwhile, because it had been going on a long, long time. But that "religious experience" never happened.

College years turned out to be not well suited for continued Christian nurture, perhaps because I was attending M.I.T. and there was precious little time for speculation on matters of the spirit in a scientific institution. For that matter, there seemed no real need for looking into unworldly matters when there was so much we had yet to learn about things we could look at, and measure, and find causes for and effects of. One studies the world and finds it an exceedingly ordered world, one that can be counted on to reveal its truths to a diligent searcher. At a technical school, one develops a feeling that understanding the most baffling and complex aspects of *everything*—from our own human selves to the organization and future of the universe—is simply a matter of time and patience. Maybe hundreds more years of time and billions of hours of patient investigation, but we human beings will someday surely *know*.

They didn't teach it *exactly* that way at M.I.T., and none of my professors was arrogant enough even to suggest that all the answers would be found in science. But that's the effect the place was apt to have on us. Yes, we had courses in English and the "humanities" (the term always disturbed me because most of my time was spent studying what had to be the "inhumanities"). We even read poems and plays, listened to good music, and had the TCA (Technology Christian Association) at hand to remind us that God was working our part of the Charles shore, too.

Not that I doubted it. God was just what he had always been, for me: there, somewhere, keeping score, obviously not upset enough with me to make his presence known and probably preoccupied with problems far more complex than any I was creating for him. I happened not to run across anyone during those years who had a really passionate belief in God, yet neither did I encounter a genuine atheist. Our bull sessions did not include him (for which, were I God, I should have been grateful) and maybe that says something about the way *all* of us looked on religion. We were perhaps a little ashamed, budding technologists that we were, to try to discuss things that came terribly close to being superstitions when looked at with the scientific method. And we were just as afraid to say we *didn't* believe in all this, brought up as practically all of us were, in good homes that paid attention to church or synagogue.

During the war, the problems of just coping with the pressures of living and raising a family doubtless interfered with whatever revelation might have been in store for me. I can remember, though, periods of some bewilderment over the paradox of a kindly, protective, omniscient supreme being permitting young men by the thousands to be killed in a brutal war. I wondered how prayer could possibly do any good when God had to choose between a German and an American boy's plea to have his life spared. As a boy, I wondered about the same problem when Pitt used to play Notre Dame in my home town and the Notre Dame boys prayed and we didn't. They usually won, and that kept me off-balance about the power of prayer in those days.

Women, it seemed, were much more at ease with church and the idea of God than we young men were. My wife, Dorothy, a minister's daughter, seemed to have things figured out perfectly well for her own needs—she *believed* in God, she felt refreshed after church, she had great faith in prayer. She had been as much a part of church theatre as I had been, growing up in a minister's family and watching organized religion deal so imperfectly with its imperfect clientele. But those shortcomings didn't seem to bother her. She knew there was a God and that if you believed in him, one way or another you would be helped in the ways you really needed help. She didn't pray like the Notre Dame football team; she wasn't looking for a win, or even a tie. She just needed to feel that she was not all alone.

She couldn't talk about God with me other than to say she just knew he was there. She couldn't describe him or even her view of him. She wasn't at all sure there was a life after death, and it didn't really bother her because the only life she knew was the one she was living right now, and that was sometimes tough enough. I'd point out that if there were no life after death, then the only reason to behave in a particular way in this life would be to get the most out of it and that either the Rotary Club or Hugh Hefner could point the way. This neither amused nor concerned her. She was programmed solidly, and no rational probing was about to rattle her anchor chain or blunt her conviction that the God she knew was real and on call.

I knew several others who had the same kind of solid belief, the kind I had always expected would come if I worked at it. And I did work at it. I taught Sunday School, read the Bible fairly thoroughly, sang in the choir, even became a deacon in my church. And I discussed, and probed, and argued endlessly with my fellow churchgoers, seeking to find what it was that made them as they were. I never found it.

I learned that there was no way to take a belief apart and weigh each morsel of faith. Some believe in the resurrection, some don't (if you push them hard enough). Some believe in Christ's miracles, some don't. Some think the Old Testament is largely legend, some view it as pure history, some aren't at all sure what it is. Belief in the Bible is pretty selective, it seems.

This ability to believe, albeit selectively, was something I could not seem to acquire, and this is where a technical mind and education do not help. There was no way I could find to handle the problem of dealing with several highly improbable events described in the Bible, selecting one or two to believe while rejecting the rest. Yet the people whose faith I admired seemed to be able to do just that: each seemed to have his own set of accepted Biblical "facts"; the others were called legend. If that was what I was to have to do to have my long postponed revelation of God, I was increasingly dubious it would ever come off.

So here I was, wanting to believe and unable to. Wanting to be a part of a church that had meant a great deal to me, but becoming increasingly uncomfortable as I sat as a hypocrite in its pews. I had to find a way to believe, or move on. Yet I knew that sermons and scriptures weren't going to make the difference, no matter how long I heard them. I had to find another way to learn whether there was indeed a God and a life beyond, and I had to find it outside of church teachings. Church history seemed the obvious place to begin, since it was in its pews that my discomfiture was most acute and my questions most pointed. I started with one of the most basic beliefs, the existence of a "place" where we spend eternal life. What do we know about it? Where did our ideas come from?

Chapter 2

God and the Gods

In 1961 the Russian astronaut Yuri Gagarin pushed our heaven a little further out when he told the world, as he returned from his epochal space flight, that he looked around while he was up there and didn't see God anywhere. His little dig at Western religion surprised no one, but it did remind us that we had some problems.

One problem, for those who would believe, is having to describe a kind of heaven that isn't "up there" and that the average twentieth century mortal can believe in. This has not been easy for the theologians of recent years. But a more awkward problem of having our upstairs heaven shot down is that it raises similar questions about a great many more items of our religious faith.

At least it did with me. If a heaven "up there" was merely an understandable superstition of our forebears, who knew no better, how much more of our religious teaching must be filed in the same folder? Is that same kind of superstition the origin of *all* of what we have been taught to believe?

How *did* Christianity happen to come up with its particular set of beliefs? Where did its ideas about God and Jesus and eternal reward and punishment come from?

Right here let me sum up briefly the key elements of the religion Christians grow up in, and I apologize to those who have spent their lives trying to prove you can't do that.

Here goes: Christianity says there is a single, omnipotent being (God) who resembles us (or we him), who knows of our needs, thoughts and deeds in this life, and who judges our merit and determines what our circumstances will be in an assured life to come. He aided us in preparing for that life (and living this one fully) by providing us a Savior who lived among us and showed us the way. The Savior, Jesus, was born of a virgin, conceived by God in a virgin mother, and thus distinguished from ordinary mortals. He was born not as a king with secular powers (though this is what most of the people of the age were expecting) but as an ordinary child of poor peasant stock. His birth took place in a stable, with animals as his attendants. The occasion was marked by prophecies and visitations of prophets, who followed a star to the infant's birthplace. The event was further marked by a recognition on the part of the local ruler of the possible threat the child presented to his throne. Thus, shortly after his birth, the child Jesus had to be spirited away to a foreign land to escape the butchery of all male babies ordered by the king.

Jesus returned to his people in his late twenties, and after a very brief ministry during which he taught, healed, performed miracles, and preached a code of behavior based on love of one's fellow man and preparation for a final judgment, he was betrayed and denied by his friends, convicted of blasphemy, and nailed on a cross until he died. Two days later he rose from the dead and appeared to his disciples (there were twelve of them), imploring them to carry on the teachings in his name. He appeared to others, also, and by his reappearances and the words he said, inspired them to extraordinary demonstrations of loyalty and faith.

It was on the work and the faith of these few people that the Christian church was based, and their recitals and writings form much of the New Testament Bible. Jesus is "one" with God, and is our help in the world to come. The Holy Spirit is the manifestation of God in our daily lives, guiding us in unseen ways. There will be a reappearance of Jesus, as well as a day of judgment, in which the entire world as we know it will come to an end.

Thus endeth the scripture according to me, and I apologize once again for my temerity in attempting it.

Now, what of this, if any, came from earlier religions that may have been based largely on superstition, and what of it is unique to Christianity? The story of the early church gives some surprising clues.

The faith would almost certainly have died out had it been confined to the tiny areas of Judea and Galilee, where the original followers lived. But Paul, a devout and highly educated Jew, was bowled over by a reappearance of Jesus in the desert and became an impassioned follower of the resurrected Christ.

It was Paul who could reconcile Jewish teachings with the Greek philosophic thought which dominated the civilized world at the time. It was Paul who was able to instruct and encourage absent followers by letter. It was Paul's zeal, resulting from the power of his conversion, that gave the church the impetus it needed in its very shaky first century.

The going was tough then. One man kept the feeble flame alive. One man preserved the faith that was to rule—and sometimes tyrannize—the world for the next 2,000 years.

Because of Paul and others who followed, the Christian sect by 300 A.D. was perhaps the most popular one in the entire civilized world—"civilized" being that world principally dominated by Rome, but affected by Greek and Egyptian thought.

During those first centuries, the interesting thing to note is that though Christians had indeed been fed to lions from time to time, they had also enjoyed over long periods a surprising freedom of thought and expression. In part, they can thank a precursor philosophy, that of the Stoics, which originated in Greece some 300 years before Christ and which spread widely over the civilized world. The Stoics (who originally were teachers who frequented the "Stoas" or cloisters of the temple courts to discuss philosophy and ethical conduct) held that virtue is the chief good in life, and its achievement life's main aim. Consideration for others, love for one's fellow man, patient acceptance of adversity—these were some of the basic tenets of their philosophy. There is a close correspondence between these Stoic teachings and the ethical code that Jesus laid down. Marcus Aurelius, the Roman emperor who ruled between 160 and 180 A.D., was the most famous of the Stoics and was so adored by his subjects that they revered him along with the other household gods of Rome. Some of his followers even claimed that he reappeared after his death to his faithful, though no lasting Aurelian cult seems to have followed that event. His short reign was a golden age for Rome, and the tolerance of that day, stemming from the Stoic code, greatly helped to pave the way for the spread of the Christian faith— and for the ultimate extinction of the noble Stoic culture at the hands of militant Christians.

There was another contributor to the fortuitous climate that aided the spread of Christian thought—Mithra. This was a cult imported into Rome about 60 B.C. from Persia and which for a time became the most popular faith in Rome. "Truth," it seems, was the basic tenet of this religion, and the ethical teachings it offered were very like those of Christianity. But beyond its ethical concepts the Mithraic faith possessed some legend remarkably similar to the descriptions of Christ's life.

Mithra is an old, old Persian deity, already ancient by the time of Christ. He was born on December 25 in a cave, and his mother was a virgin. He traveled widely as a teacher, and gathered beside him twelve companions who carried on his teachings after he died. His death was a violent and tragic one, but after it he reappeared to his followers and exhorted them to carry on. For many centuries his worship festivals were held at the time of the winter solstice and the spring equinox, just as our Christmas and Easter celebrations are timed.

Another Persian religious figure, one who long preceded Christ, was Zoroaster (Zarathustra), said to have lived about 1800 B.C., but probably more accurately placed about 300 years before Alexander the Great (600 B.C.). He was born of a virgin, but his conception was not commonplace: it was occasioned by a ray of light which entered his mother's bosom. (There *is* this constant problem with virgin births: what starts things going?)

Zoroaster was sought out by the king to be slain when he was a babe, but escaped to live for thirty years. He was tempted by the devil on a mountain, and on another mountain he received, in Moses' fashion, the word of God. He died a violent death, including piercing with spears, and trampling by oxen and horses, and burning in a fiery furnace, where his image "shone like brass." Zoroaster was a teacher and writer and preached of one God who struggled for men's minds with a devil, and who demanded a code of behavior very similar to that of the Stoics and, later, of the Christians.

The cults of Mithra, Zoroaster, and other "pagan" gods coexisted in the Roman Empire for 300 years after Christ, some of them aiding the growth of Christianity, some impeding it. All of the religions were marked by alternate periods of acceptance and repression, usually in accordance with the whims of the emperors. Constantine (250 A.D.) was the first Emperor to become a Christian himself, and it was his conversion that assured the ultimate stability of the church. It is said that he made the choice during a battle in which he saw a vision of a cross in the sky, on which were the words *"in hoc signo vinces"*—by this sign thou shalt conquer. I find it dismaying to note how quickly after the death of Jesus his teachings were perverted into righteous militancy. Constantine, perhaps unwittingly, assuredly paved the way for the vengeful and cruel clerical regimes that were to follow, all seeking victory by the sword in the name of the gentle man from Nazareth. But Constantine did legitimate the faith, which was kept alive for the early centuries by the zeal of its followers and aided importantly by the tolerance preached by Mithra and by the Stoics.

Looking back beyond Mithra and Zoroaster in the gathering haze of history, there appears another God by name of Krishna, who appears to have been for India a close counterpart of Mithra and Zoroaster for the Persians. (Indian religion is a complicated one in comparison to our simple Christian concept of the Holy Trinity. Ours is certainly simpler in numbers, though some of us do have difficulty defining that Holy Ghost part.)

Indian gods number in the thousands, a fact which presumably traces to the very numerous tribes and settlements in India which have existed for so many millennia. In India, useful gods don't just die out; they find themselves wedded to other gods from adjoining provinces in a continuously complicating heavenly family.

Krishna was one of eight sons, and I wasn't able to pin down exactly what happened to the other seven, or even whether they made it as gods in their own right. But Krishna did indeed become a god, one of the most popular ones, with a large following of Indian believers spread all across the subcontinent many centuries before Christ. Krishna was born of a virgin mother and, like Mithra, entered the world in a cave, the most humble of surroundings in those days.

His birth was announced by a star that led worshippers to the cave from great distances. Probably because of these strange circumstances, the local ruler became unnerved and sent out orders to destroy "every strong-looking male child." Krishna escaped by being carried across a river out of the reach of the murderers, and was thus able to start a life of teaching and healing. Unlike Jesus, he demonstrated a considerable sexual prowess as a youth, but he did find time to argue with learned elders and to amaze them with his knowledge. He became noted, apparently not for his miracles, but because he slew demons, which was probably a pretty close equivalent in those days. Several stories surround his death, one of them attributing it to crucifixion (which was a widely used form of torture and execution for many centuries), after which he first descended into hell and then rose again to appear before his followers in the flesh. He is still venerated in some parts of India, and his name is attached to present-day cults.

As with Mithra, the Krishna legend is difficult to pin down as to dates of origin, although scholars do tell us that Krishna had obtained a substantial following as early as the seventh to fifth centuries before Christ. What is clear is that the strange parallels between his life and that of Christ were not borrowed from Christianity, because writings accurately dated as far back as the fifth century B.C. describe what you have just read.

Leaving the Indian legend to look at some from perhaps even earlier times, we meet Adonis (or Tammuz) who was originally a Syrian god, later woven into Greek mythology. Adonis was also born of a virgin, though with presumably greater difficulty than Mithra or Krishna in that his mother had been changed into a tree because of some aberration of conduct before Adonis' birth. Adonis was worshipped as a god of the sun, particularly the summer sun. He was killed by a boar in the autumn, and he rose again in the spring. His resurrection was annually celebrated, even by the Hebrews.

I should also note another God—Attis—a deity of ancient Phrygia, located in what is now central Turkey. He, too, was born of a virgin, but in his case there was better knowledge about the precise means of conception. His mother simply placed a ripe almond (some say pomegranate) in her bosom, and after the required interval Attis was born. Like Adonis, he was killed by a boar, though some legend holds that he castrated himself. In any event, he bled to death but was later resurrected. In the ritual celebration of his death and resurrection, which came at the spring equinox, his image was fastened to the trunk of a pine tree, in fashion suggestive of the Christian crucifixion symbol.

There are numerous other gods (such as the Greek Hercules, who was a savior for the common man, miraculously conceived by a divine father and virgin-born) and as one probes each for antecedents, the very earliest recorded civilizations begin to appear. Of all of them, the most fascinating has to be that of the ancient Egyptians.

There is so much that amazes in ancient Egypt, so much that remains mysterious, that it is a place, a story, an age we would do well to know more about. I found myself making a visit there to see with my own eyes some of the magnificence of which I had read, and came away with very deep and strange feelings about this ancient land and the people who made it what it was.

In much of Egypt the twentieth century loses 5,000 years.

Modern man feels himself watching a culture and a terrain that have changed little since the earliest records on earth. The feeling is an eerie one, aided in no small part by the remarkable state of preservation of the buildings and artifacts of this ancient age. The temples are there, the desert is there, the burros and peasants of antiquity are there.

Some messages about life here and life hereafter are there, too. Not all of their miracles did the Egyptians leave to their gods.

Chapter 3

Egypt: The Teacher

The story of Egypt is the story of the Nile River. Without this mighty source of water, the land could not have existed. Egypt is desert, with the Red Sea to the east and the Sahara to the west. Only the Nile, flowing northward from its origins deep in Africa, makes the land habitable, and the ancient Egyptian kingdom was in fact a narrow strip of land, averaging little more than twelve miles in width and hundreds of miles in length. Since time immemorial the Nile has annually overflowed its banks, depositing a rich effluvium in the narrow flooded area and providing water for a lush agriculture. Rainfall is practically nonexistent. The merciless sun can be the implacable enemy, and from earliest times the sun was the greatest of gods, to be worshipped faithfully and feared mightily.

The first king of Egypt ruled about 3400 B.C. (some historians say 4500 B.C.) and the succession of kingdoms flourished right up to Roman times—over twice as long as the entire span of

Christianity to date. Though Egypt's fortunes waxed and waned, depending on the genius of its long succession of kings and the greed and military might of its neighbors, it was probably the most powerful civilization, and certainly the longest-lived one, the world has ever seen. Where Greece and Rome count their glories in centuries, Egypt counts hers in millennia.

But the extraordinary fact of Egypt is not her longevity but the accomplishments of her culture. We are inclined today, technologists that we are, to look on the early Egyptians with a smug condescension, a little impressed that a primitive people could have done all they did, but nevertheless sure that they were indeed primitive by our standards. When I visited Egypt ten years ago, I found almost unbelievable what this ancient people had accomplished. To this day we do not know how they did some of the things they did. I'm more careful about that word "primitive" now.

Fifty-five hundred years ago they performed one of the great engineering feats of all time—the diversion of the mighty Nile from its natural bed to create a dry-land plateau on which the city of Memphis was built. This bit of engineering and building would sorely tax our own skills today, and would literally make Aswan look simple by comparison.

The pyramids are doubtless the most impressive reminders of Egyptian building skills, and to this day we are not quite sure just how or why they were built. That they were intended as tombs of the pharoahs seems obvious, but we are less sure that that was *all* they were. There is some dispute about how they were constructed, one that is not yet resolved. The Great Pyramid at Gîza contains about 2,300,000 stone blocks, none less than two and a half tons in weight and many topping fifty tons. Each was so carefully cut and fitted to its neighbor that even today, thousands of years later, many of the joints are so tight that I could not slide a business card between them.

We know of no power available to the Egyptians other than muscle power, and that appears to have been limited to the use of levers and wooden rollers. So how did the stones get cut, transported hundreds of miles by water and over desert sands, and piled with such extraordinary accuracy? My own probings tell me that we simply don't know. None of the technical hypotheses I have read really satisfy my analytical nerve ends. There are just too many glib spots.

The Great Pyramid is also a symbol of Egyptian mathematical skills, a masterpiece of geometrical precision in many ways. For one, the base area divided by twice the height yields the familiar *pi*—3.14 etc., though mathematical scholars place the first use of *pi* no earlier than 1700 B.C., ages after the pyramid was built. The very shape of the pyramid incorporates accurately the "Golden Mean" ratio that mathematicians, architects, and sculptors have relied upon for centuries to obtain pleasing proportions.

The mathematics the Egyptians developed were sophisticated enough to allow them to predict eclipses and to chart the precise tracks of the sun and planets. They could even add and multiply fractions in order to carry out trade, which you and I can't do, and neither can most modern mathematicians without their calculators. To the Egyptians we owe our twelve-month calendar and the twelve signs of the zodiac, which accompanied each of their months. They gave us our 365 day year, complete with leap year. They divided the day into twenty-four hours, and they invented the first clocks—water-operated—of exceptional accuracy.

They were talented in medicine, performing successful cranial surgery, to say nothing of setting broken bones and repairing teeth. It is thought they were well-informed about hypnosis, and probably used it for anesthesia. They were the first people we know of to develop a written language. They established schools for the teaching of letters and mathematics. The schools were run by the priesthood (just as they were here in New England 150 years ago). They were great boat builders and sailors, roaming the Red Sea and the Mediterranean in boats nearly 200 feet long, sailing by the stars and the sun. Their architecture, paintings, sculpture, and carvings must be seen to be believed. Some of the work is much more exquisite than early Greek works done a thousand years later.

There is just no way this ancient people can be termed primitive. There can be no doubt that their minds were every

bit as sharp as ours, their knowledge of their world and how to
control it uncomfortably close to our own. And in the achievements of their culture and their demonstrated ethical standards
one is strongly tempted to say that they outshine us.

Women, for instance, had equal rank with men, and in fact
formed the genealogical line through which family inheritance
was carried out. Women had the right to own property and
could buy and sell goods, a right which most of the Western
world blotted out for thousands of years. Though most of the
people of old Egypt were poor (as are most of the people in our
twentieth century world) there were no caste bars to individual
progress. Persons of the poorest origins could and did rise to the
highest offices in the land. The Egyptians practiced slavery, but
unlike our early customs, the slaves were in time absorbed into
society and accepted as members of it.

Egypt's rule and Egypt's religion were nearly one and the
same. The head god was Amon, the sun god. He was to be
feared and respected, equally for the famine he could cause and
for the good life he could bring. He ruled the living and the
dead. The dead did not die: the soul continued to live after
death for thousands of years until the time when it would re-
enter its earthly body. This was the core belief of Egyptian
religion. The afterlife was as real, as unquestioned, as breath
itself.

Amon was by no means the only god. There were thousands
of them, and one of the reasons for the huge numbers was the
Egyptian practice of deifying the ruling monarch (and even
some of his relatives, occasionally). The king-gods—pharaohs—
were assisted by a powerful priesthood, but their rule seems not
to have been wholly despotic. There appears to have been
genuine concern on the part of the pharaohs for the welfare of
even the humblest Egyptians.

Undoubtedly this concern derived from the conviction of the
pharaohs that their fate in the afterlife would be determined by
their performance in this one, and many of them seem to have
worked hard to follow precepts of truthfulness and virtue. This
may seem hard for us to believe, schooled as we are by grade B
movies of Egypt, showing cruel priests, tyrannical monarchs,

and armies of slaves building pyramids at the ends of long whips. But the proof of their ethical concerns is found in the longevity and elegance of their culture. Prolonged tyranny does not beget progress, as we have seen time and again throughout the ages.

We get a clue to the culture's commitment to fairness and truth from an inscription on the tomb of a warrior who rose to the rank of governor of one of the provinces sometime around 2000 B.C. Remember, as you read it, that this man was completely convinced that the gods knew his every thought and deed and would judge him when he died. Presumably, he caused the inscription to be written on his tomb as a friendly reminder to his gods as well as to the family and friends he left behind. This is what it says: "Giving justice to the palace, his virtues made the people happy in everything. He is a sage nourished with knowledge, judging exactly that which is true. Holding his heart in great perfection, he applies himself to hear each in his place. Exempt from all vices, virtuous in all his thoughts, his heart is right. No crooked way is in him ... he renders justice to the poor, he is severe upon the fraudulent. Applying his heart to make peace, he makes no distinction between the unknown and his familiars." Would that our own public servants all merited this epitaph.

Is there a connection between the extraordinary longevity and cultural achievements of Egypt and the religion that existed for those thousands of years? I'm urged to say yes. For one thing, most of the mighty feats of engineering and architecture the Egyptians performed were for religious purposes of one sort or other. The motivation was obviously powerful. And as we've seen, the impress on their ethical behavior, stemming from their certainty of judgment in the hereafter, was profound. It undoubtedly accounted for their tolerance and enlightenment much more than merely the good hearts of a few kindly disposed rulers.

As I've noted, the Egyptians held their kings to be actual gods, and worshipped them as such throughout the thousands of years of the kingdom's existence. Other gods crept in, too, as each of the initially strung-out tribes and settlements gradually cohered into a single kingdom, bringing their separate gods with them. Interestingly enough, there seem to have been few wars of note fought over this multitude of gods. In a manner quite the reverse of the Christian way of doing things, strange gods were readily accepted and the legends surrounding them were neatly woven into a continuously changing but acceptable theology, all based on an afterlife.

It took a highly trained priesthood to master the resulting clutter, and partly for this reason and also because of the deification of the ruling monarch, the priesthood was powerful indeed, standing side by side with the pharaohs.

The masses, though, were largely excluded from the royal observance of religion, from the temples, and from the ministries of the royal priests. Their favorite god was Osiris, and his worship seems to have been the first religion to gain wide acceptance by will of the masses rather than by imposition by a king or a priestly hierarchy. The Osiris cult began to thrive about 2500 B.C., and it continued to be a strong force not only in Egyptian religion but in Greek and Roman cultures right up to the era of Christianity. There are some remarkable traces of Osiris in all the religions I have noted—most particularly, our own.

Osiris was said to have been an ancient king, born a god as were all other reigning monarchs. He was a great-grandson of mighty Amon (Ra), the sun god and the omnipotent being. His father, Geb, was king of Egypt before him, and when Geb died, Osiris took over as king of Egypt and took Isis, his sister, as queen. He was a skillful and loving ruler who united his kingdom, gave it just laws, and civilized the country. With his country at peace, he left the reins with Queen Isis and set out on the conquest of Asia. But while he was away from the palace, he was betrayed by his brother Set and tricked into capture. He was killed, and his body dismembered into fourteen pieces, which were scattered far and wide. His anguished wife Isis set out in search of the pieces and succeeded in finding just thirteen of them, the fourteenth being the phallus, which fell into the sea and was devoured by a crab.

Isis, being a goddess in her own right, put the remaining

pieces back together again and Osiris came back to life. He settled things amicably with the treacherous brother Set—Osiris was not a vindictive man—and conceived a son in Isis in order that the family line might live. His son, though technically not born of a virgin (we can assume Isis had lost her virginity long since) was nevertheless miraculously conceived, in view of that missing member. The three—Osiris, Isis, and the son Horus—are often shown as a "holy trinity" in Egyptian paintings and sculpture, and Isis and Horus are seen painted or carved in a pose that inevitably suggests the Madonna and Child.

(Set, by the way, became a god himself, and a fairly important one. He is usually depicted with the head of an ass, which, to the Egyptians, was a reverent, not demeaning, representation. Indeed, the ass was venerated by many ancient peoples as a wise, patient animal with god-like qualities, including an oft-demonstrated talent for finding water in arid regions. Thus, when Jesus chose to ride an ass into Jerusalem, by this earlier tradition it was an act not of humility but one of mystical significance, implying triumph.)

Osiris resumed his rule briefly when he returned from the dead, but having now sampled the joys of heaven—which he entered through hell—during his brief time of death, he elected to return to the other world and preside over the souls of the dead. He had twelve companions in his life, and twelve servant-disciples bore him to his funeral ark and rowed it to the tomb of hell. Some historians suggest that he boarded his ark for that trip on the same day that Genesis tells us that Noah boarded his ark to ride out the flood.

Osiris' birth date is held to be December 25, and he is said to have died on either December 25 or 27. Both events are tied to the winter solstice, which occurs a few days earlier and which marks the point of lowest descent of the sun in the southern sky. The sun was then feared to be "dead," in earliest times. Three days after it had reached the lowest point and begun to climb, there were celebrations held in thanks for its safe return. In Osiris' cult, there was annually a three-day period marking his death and resurrection, the latter celebrated on December 25. His worshippers used a sacred wine and unleavened cake in these rituals, the cake very much like the Hebrew "massoth," which traces to the Christian communion ritual.

And although the cross as a religious symbol was not reserved exclusively to Osiris, it had wide use in his worship, usually in the shape of a "T", sometimes in shapes quite suggestive of the one common in the Christian church. Another cross shape particularly associated with Osiris is obviously phallic in design and traces directly to corcern over his lost penis. Like it or not, many of our familiar designs and symbols have a similar origin, including the highly decorative fleur-de-lis.

Perhaps the most distinguishing thing about Osiris was his appeal to the masses of people, to whom he was their savior and intercessory in this life and the life beyond. When pharoahs died, their priests made elaborate preparations for their journey to the beyond, including the most extravagant means for the preservation of the mortal remains. It was universally believed that there would be rebirth at some distant time in the future and that the dead body would be re-entered by the spirit. If it took a massive tomb—even a pyramid—to assure the safety of the body, so be it. The pharoahs went out in style.

But the high cost of pyramids ruled them out for everybody else. The average Egyptian could not have been happy at being excluded from this kind of insurance of a safe return. Osiris was the god to whom he turned. He was the common man's savior, much as is Christianity's Jesus. Though Osiris was called the God of the Dead, he apparently was regarded not with dread but with affection, because the Egyptians did not fear death. For them, physical death was not the end. It was through Osiris that the great masses of Egyptians were able to fulfill their belief in an afterlife. And all this without much encouragement from the priesthood, who seemed more concerned with power and kingly ritual than with the needs of the masses.

The necessity to preserve one's mortal remains for later re-entry of the soul accounted for the widespread practice of mummification. One scholar estimates that some 420,000,000 Egyptians were preserved in this way, each in the expectation that his body would be ready and waiting for reincarnation between 3,000 and 10,000 years hence. Some of the results, as we know from direct observation today, were startlingly successful, even though the rebirth the Egyptians looked for has not yet been noted.

There seems no question but that Osiris and his worship had a profound effect on the conduct of the masses of Egyptians. Their conviction in a life after death was complete. Osiris' codes of goodness and love of one's fellow man were demanding. The Egyptians seem to have responded in a way unparalleled for so long a time in any other part of history. Certainly, there were times of tyranny and war and greed, and Egypt was always marked by slavery. But there were long stretches of harmonious, fruitful, golden years which saw the Egyptians flourish in the arts, in medicine, in science, in philosophy, and in architecture to a degree and for a span of time which today's world, for all its knowledge and skills, cannot match in any relative sense. I cannot ignore the Egyptians' religious convictions in assessing their accomplishments: we could wish for something like them today.

*   *   *

Egypt ... India ... Persia ... Greece ... What does this collection of familiar beliefs tell us? Look at them again: a God who is human in form and appearance; a divinely conceived child born of a virgin mother; a birth in the humblest of surroundings, marked by a star which guided important visitors; escape from the murder of male babies ordered by the king; the repeated number 12, as with the disciples; temptation by the devil; betrayal and violent death, descent into hell, and reappearance a few days later to the faithful; symbols—the cross, the ass, the bread and wine; the promise of an afterlife, and of judgment based on one's thoughts and deeds in this one: and a code of behavior that teaches a love of truth and of one's fellow man.

Is there anything left that can be called uniquely Christian? Not much, unless it be the particular miracles Jesus is said to have performed—and even here, ancient religions are so replete with strange happenings (we call them myths) that the idea of divinely inspired "miracles," to use our Christian term, was old long before Jesus' time. One is left with the disturbing impression that Christianity is very little different from many other faiths that have come and gone over the ages, borrowing liberally from them and adding little new except for the particular timing, the location, and the personality of its named deity.

Christianity's survival and growth appear to have stemmed not from its unique message and the unique nature of its beliefs but from a very large collection of happenstances—something akin to having the right idea in the right place at the right time and with the right people behind it. I won't trouble you with a recital of the excesses and brutality that have marked most of the centuries of the history of the church. Let's just say that, however good and noble were the teachings of the early faith, they have obviously been unable to influence man's actions significantly for the better over the 2,000 years of the existence of the Christian church. The Egyptians, it seems, behaved at least as nobly as we.

Now, all of this may prove a little distressing to Christians who have been taught since childhood that Christianity is the one way, the only way to salvation. Given its origins, and noting the rise of other compelling faiths such as Islam hundreds of years after Christ, it's clear that Christianity shouldn't have been making those claims. And it certainly shouldn't have been dispatching so methodically over the centuries all those who disagreed.

Yet there is nothing in what you have read about these ancient beliefs that makes the whole idea of gods, or a God, or a life beyond unconvincing. Indeed, the story of Egypt showed that out of a fierce and universal conviction about the reality of judgment and a hereafter could come strange and wonderful things. Nothing yet says that *all* of man's gropings for meaning, his beliefs over the ages, were mere superstition without truth. We haven't proved that either way.

Though some of the things the ancients had to explain through religion can now be explained by science, we all know there is a great deal more remaining that *neither* they nor we have yet been able to explain. For these, one first turns to mysticism—which I did—and then to psychology, physiology and physics, because I had to.

Chapter 4

Brush with the Other World

Life after death—an idea as old as all history. Did man have to invent it because he couldn't bear the thought of an absolute end? Or is there reason, some evidence, to suspect an existence beyond?

Any probing for life's meaning must quickly come to this point. Christianity has no Christ, no Easter, without that eternal promise. The great religions of the world are empty of mystery and hope without the survival dream.

There are thousands and thousands of books and treatises on the subject, and one need read relatively few of them to obtain an exhaustive—and exhausting—impression of what is reported and claimed about survival after death. These books are apt to leave one with a strange ambivalence, difficult to describe.

On the one hand, I found that the extensive reports of communication with the dead and of glimpses of their condition in the afterlife created an increasing credulity in the conscious, rational corners of my mind. The instances reported are so numerous, so widely scattered in time and place, so impressively attested to by people of high reputation, that I could not, having read, and read, simply refuse to believe everything I had read. The evidence adds up almost to the point of being overpowering, and not to believe it would be akin to not believing that water was made of oxygen and hydrogen atoms, just because I couldn't see the atoms.

Yet, convincing as my rational thinking made these reports seem, there was something missing. I didn't really believe them with the *rest* of my mind, the part that contains the deep convictions and the intuitions. I didn't believe these reports down in my gut, where some of my strongest feelings seem to reside. Though I was intellectually persuaded by the facts I had read, I was a long way from acquiring an intuitive conviction that when my number was called I would pass into a new existence, and still be the *me* I knew so well.

Whether you're a skeptic or a firm believer in the hereafter, I think you may enjoy reading a couple of examples of "other world" stories to see what we're up against. They're quite typical of hundreds you can find by yourself, and I've selected them not only because I found them particularly interesting, but because they have some of the more impeccable credentials surrounding the participants of any stories that you're likely to come across. When you have finished reading them, you will understand better the ambivalence I am trying to describe.

The first sample involves Arthur Ford, a widely known American psychic and medium, taken from his autobiography published in 1958. Ford discovered his strange psychic gifts while in an Army camp in New Jersey in World War I. One night he dreamed of a roster of names of soldiers who had died of influenza during the night and, on checking in the morning, found to his consternation that his list was absolutely correct. The dream recurred many times, and Ford began to recite each night's newly-dreamed list to his buddies in the morning, before the official list was published. Word of his strange powers quickly spread, and Ford became a local celebrity and curiosity. The dreams persisted and ultimately came to include the names of men killed at the front thousands of miles away.

Ford was alternately frightened by his powers, ashamed of them, and fascinated by them. He did not decide to become a full-time medium and psychic investigator until many more years had passed. One of the tales he relates is of unusual interest because of the wide publicity that greeted this particular encounter with the next world.

Arthur Ford was the medium who claims to have received a message from Houdini two years after the death of the famed magician. Throughout his life, Houdini had shown great contempt for spiritualists, mediums, and all others who claimed to be in touch with the supernatural. He exposed many frauds and claimed (and frequently demonstrated) that all of the "mystical" happenings that took place in darkened seance chambers could be done by him, using just the illusions and tricks of a skilled magician.

But as he grew older, he may have begun to have some doubts about the finality of death. He vowed to his wife that if it were possible to get through to her after his death he would do so, using an elaborate code which she alone would understand. Before he died, in 1926, he publicized widely his intent to determine once and for all whether there is life after death. If the great Houdini could not get through, we could all be assured no one could, that the grave was indeed the end.

In the months following Houdini's death, many mediums in all parts of the world claimed to have received the secret code, but Mrs. Houdini disclaimed them all. It was more than two years after his death that the first "real" contact was made, and it was through Arthur Ford during the course of a private sitting he was holding. None of those in attendance had ever met Houdini, and none had asked at the sitting to be put in touch with him. It just happened, and it happened through the "control" with whom Arthur Ford had worked for years. (A "control" is a departed person who somehow seems able to use the physical body—voice, fingers, arms—of a medium in a trance, and to relay messages through the medium to those gathered for the sitting. The medium is, for all intents and purposes, unconscious throughout the sitting, and has no recollection on awakening of what he has said or done.)

Ford's control, "Fletcher," said he had a message from Ehrich Weiss (Houdini's real name) and that he was having great difficulty getting it through. Only the first word—ROSABELLE—came through in that first sitting, and it took seven more sittings, spread over two months, to obtain the rest of the words. All of the eight sittings were held for small private groups, a few for single individuals (one a New York physician, one an editor of *Scientific American*). None was held with the idea of contacting Houdini.

Here is the complete message Ford received during the several sittings: "ROSABELLE * ANSWER * TELL * PRAY * ANSWER * LOOK * TELL * ANSWER * ANSWER * TELL." Fletcher went on to say that Houdini wanted the code written down then and there, signed by all in attendance (it was), and then taken to his wife. Houdini said the code was known only to his wife and that when she had read it and pronounced it genuine, she was to arrange a sitting with Ford, during which Houdini would explain the code to all and decipher the message it contained.

Mrs. Houdini, on receiving the message, at once pronounced the code as authentic and signed a public affidavit to that effect. A session with Ford was scheduled for the following day, to be attended by three members of the group who had been present at the previous sitting plus a reporter from United Press. When they had all gathered and Ford had gone into his trance, Fletcher again came through, saying that Houdini was there and would proceed. The dead Houdini and his living wife, talking through Ford and Fletcher, then proceeded to corroborate the validity of the code and the messages. Houdini broke down the code to reveal what the ten words actually said: "Rosabelle, believe." The code was one which the magician and his wife had used in their mind-reading acts, and it was in fact known only to the two of them, according to Mrs. Houdini. "Rosabelle" was an intimate name Houdini used for his wife, taken from a song she frequently sang early in their marriage.

Houdini's parting words to her through Fletcher were: "Tell the whole world that Harry Houdini still lives and will prove it a thousand times more. I was perfectly honest and sincere in trying to disprove survival, though I resorted to tricks to prove my point for the simple reason that I did not believe communication was true, but I did no more than seemed justifiable. I am now sincere in sending this through in my desire to undo. Tell all those who lost faith because of my mistake to lay hold again of hope, and to live with the knowledge that life is continuous. That is my message to the world, through my wife and this instrument." Thus, it is claimed, did Harry Houdini, consummate magician and lifelong skeptic, make his demonstration to the world, in the presence of persons of high integrity, of his survival beyond death.

Another interesting case, made particularly strange by the collection of circumstances surrounding those involved, is that of Episcopal Bishop James A. Pike and his son Jim. Jim took his own life in a New York hotel room in February, 1966, at the age of twenty. The preceding years had been difficult ones for the boy, as they had been for many youngsters of the time. These were the peak days of student discontent, of LSD, of war, of fast-changing moral standards. Jim was one of the many casualties of the times and of the culture, and his death was a numbing shock to his parents and friends. And though Pike had been preaching Christian doctrine for years, he was, as he says, "unable to offer comfort to the family on the basis of belief in life after death. Elemental honesty ruled out offering solace on the basis of what I felt then was an insufficiently supportable ground of hope."

Two weeks after Jim died, Bishop Pike decided to resume the work he had been carrying on in England during a sabbatical and returned to Cambridge with two church colleagues, David Barr and Mrs. Maren Bergrud, who had known Jim and who had helped in his work. In England they planned to occupy the same flat that Pike and his son had shared for several months, and which they had left only a week or two before Jim's death. During that previous stay in England, though father and son had become closer than at any time before, Jim had continued to use mind-altering drugs and had become increasingly uncertain about himself and about life in general. It was with some apprehension, then, that Pike returned to the Cambridge flat to greet powerful memories of those turbulent but loving months.

Within a few days of their occupancy of the apartment, they began to notice odd happenings. Postcards and books were moved from their customary places and placed in careful arrangements corresponding to the exact angle of clock hands at 8:19, the hour of Jim's death. Maren's hair, on three successive occasions, was found in the morning to have been singed away at the bangs (which Jim never cared for) without any recollection on Maren's part of any sensation or feeling. Nightmarish dreams afflicted all three of the flat's occupants. Manuscripts disappeared and turned up later in unexpected places.

These, and many other occurrences like them, persisted for so long and were so disquieting that Pike finally sought out Canon Pearce-Higgins, an old church colleague, and asked to be put in touch with a medium who might be able to help explain things. And so a sitting was arranged with a Mrs. Ena Twigg, a respected medium known to Canon Pearce-Higgins. Pike and the canon went to her house, the canon agreeing to be the note-taker.

Pike's detailed recital of the preliminaries to the sitting, the surroundings at Mrs. Twigg's, and of his own feelings at the time makes most interesting reading, for here was a man who had never experienced anything like this before and who all his life had been a non-believer in life after death. What transpired at the sitting is indeed startling, unless one chooses to doubt everything Bishop Pike, the canon, Mrs. Bergrud, and Mr. Barr have reported. There was far too much communicated to repeat here, but some excerpts of what Jim seems to have said through Mrs. Twigg will give an idea of what is reported to have taken place:

Mrs. Twigg (in trance): "He's here—he's working hard to get through." Then she began to speak as if for another—Jim.
Jim: "I failed the test, I can't face you, can't face life. I'm confused. Very sudden passing—have had to do this—couldn't find anyone. God, I didn't know what I was doing. But when I got here I found I wasn't such a failure as I thought. My nervous system failed ... I am not in purgatory—but something like hell, here. Yet nobody blames me here ... I hope nobody

blames me *there* ... I came to your room, I moved books, I knocked on the door—came to your bedside—you dreamt about me and spoke to me."

Mrs. Twigg: "Send his love to the family—two girls, one boy." (That was the correct makeup of the Pike family, unknown to Mrs. Twigg.) "He is saying something about a gate—golden ... a golden gate. He says he's glad about that. Does that mean anything to you?" (Jim's ashes had been scattered on the waters at San Francisco's Golden Gate—a fact not known to Mrs. Twigg or the canon.)

Bishop Pike: "... I'll be calling your mother to tell her about what's going on here now."

Jim: "Good. I want her to know—to know I really love her—that I'm alive."

Bishop Pike: "She believes that, Jim—she did all along. By the way, about things in your new situation: are you ... alone, or—"

Jim: "I have masses of people around me, and hands lifting me up, as it were ... I was so unhappy until I could make you know."

Mrs. Twigg: "Someone with a foreign accent—German, I think—is speaking ... wait ... Paul, there is a Paul here. He says, 'Don't worry about the boy. He's in safekeeping. He is surrounded by our love.' He sends you his love, Bishop, and shares a common bond. He says, 'Thank you for dedicating your new book to me.'" (Pike had dedicated his book *What is This Treasure:* "To Paul Tillich, Principal Mentor and Dear Friend Much Missed." Tillich had died the previous winter.)

Jim: "That reminds me that nothing I've seen over here makes me any more inclined to believe in God."

Tillich: "Well, he hasn't been here very long. *I* still hold the belief, but I now conceive of it somewhat differently—"

Jim: "Give my love to Mom ... We've all got to grow. Be kind, be gentle. Tell her I've been back. Give her a kiss from me. I'll be with you in June. We are beyond grief—we've defeated the last enemy. And, by the way, Dad, there'll be no more disturbances now, no more movements."

Bishop Pike was to have many other experiences involving Jim, and his whole life was changed because of them. Pike's book *The Other Side* is one of the more readable and appealing documentations of this sort that I've come across in my wanderings.

For a final example of reported communication with the dead, I give you an account taken from a book written by Matthew Manning, an English lad twenty years old as I write this, who began having strange experiences in his early teens. His book *The Link* was published in 1974, and its recency and the fact that some of the contributors are well-known and highly respected contemporaries may attach additional credibility to the incident I shall relate. (Many of the books one reads in a search like this date back many years, and I know in my own case I was somewhat less ready to accept as true accounts those which came from writers or noted people who lived well before my time. There's probably some unwarranted twentieth-century conceit showing there.)

Mathew Manning is not and never has been a medium. He is a quite ordinary schoolboy of promising intellect, considerable shyness, but with one extraordinary difference from his fellows. When he was only twelve, he and his family fell victim to a very active poltergeist, one who made their lives increasingly miserable by breaking objects, moving furniture, spilling the contents of sealed cans, and causing other endless nuisance. Poltergeists, according to those who have studied the phenomenon closely, are not "ghosts" themselves who invade homes on their own and do their mischief, but are a manifestation of some supernatural influence which uses the psychic powers residing in a living individual—in this case, Matthew—to cause objects to fly about. The individual is not in control of the actions, and indeed need not always be close to the place where they occur. With Matthew, the incidents followed him. for years, wherever he went, and at one point he was almost sent home from the English boarding school he attended because of the severity of the disruptions he (or, rather, his poltergeist) caused there.

In his late teens, Matthew discovered that by engaging in "automatic writing" he could redirect the psychic forces that were causing him so much trouble, and he began to do this extensively in order to lay the poltergeist to rest. Automatic writing differs from seances and mediumship in that the writer does not appear to go into deep trance and then communicate by voice, but rather seems to let his mind wander at will while he holds a pencil over a paper. When the writing begins (and he can never be sure that it will happen at any given time) the writing usually bears no resemblance to his own—indeed, each time a "message" is written, the handwriting is apt to change markedly. The message always purports to be from the other world, and the handwriting style is presumed to be that of the departed spirit who wrote that way while alive on earth.

In Matthew's case, the handwriting was highly varied and frequently took place in languages and even in letters and symbols that he did not understand and could not translate. In addition to the automatic writing, Matthew discovered that he created "automatically" quite remarkable drawings, and in his book are reproduced several superb ones signed by noted masters such as Albrecht Dürer and Goya, each of them in the particular and unmistakable style of the departed painters. (Matthew has never had formal art training and was considered by his schoolmasters to be only an average drawer and sketcher.)

Shortly before his book was published, Matthew received a call from his publishers: "Do you know anyone named George Laing? Have you ever received an automatic message from him? Do you know anything about this man, or is that name known to your father?" Matthew replied that he didn't recall that name, and knew no one by that name. Why was it important?

"We have one of your messages here and a George Laing appears to be connected with it," was the reply. The name meant nothing to Matthew and he tried to forget about it. Only later did he learn that, included in the mass of material he had given to his publishers were two sheets of writing, done in what appeared to be Arabic, and one striking picture of a beautifully drawn eagle carrying what was thought to be Sinbad in his talons. In the corner of the picture was a signature in an Eastern or Arabic script. The publisher had sent all of this to Professor S. Bushrui at the American University in Beirut to see what he could make of it. The professor succeeded in translating the writings, but they appeared to make little sense. Furthermore, various parts were written in different handwritings, ranging from a well-educated, literate hand to a style that seemed to have come from a poorly educated man. One thing, though, was baffling. The writing in the corner of the picture was, in fact, a design that incorporated the name "George Laing." And in one of the messages there was a series of disconnected words that did not make up a coherent sentence: "Kingdom of Saudi Arabia," "slopes," "build houses," "ports," "buildings," "hiding," "rocks," "rubble." In both messages the name "George Laing" appeared.

Not knowing any of this, but aware from the telephone call that George Laing was proving to be of interest to somebody, Matthew tried to communicate directly with "George Laing" through automatic writing. No writing appeared when he tried, so he asked anyone in the next world for information about this man. Within thirty seconds, he says, his hands began to move and the following message appeared:

> "George Laing asks me to tell you that he was murdered by a servant of the king's household and not many know because the police were no good and his body was buried on the slopes. He wants to know why he died when he was trying to help to build houses and develop the ports. He was hit on the head and died in the Kingdom of Saudi Arabia. Poor George, how is his building? Carry him through and hoist the flag. We are only simple because you are stupid and we have many barriers to cross.
> —Monique Vanderhout"

Matthew put this in the mail to his publishers, who called back immediately on receiving it: "This message is just too good to be true. In fact it's so remarkable that I can't help being suspicious of it. It's like finding a murdered man and discovering that the picture of his murderer is still visible in his eyes." Only then was Matthew told all of the details leading up to this last message, including the fact that the disconnected words of the previous Arabic message all appeared in Monique's message. He immediately set about asking the communicator, Monique Vanderhout, if she could tell him when George Laing died. Here is the reply, written through Matthew's hand:

"Here is poor Monique who was killed by her loving husband's bullets, to tell you that George Laing joined us in 1943. This is odd, why must you put us off with the radio? It makes it so difficult for us in a small space. . . .
—Monique Vanderhout"

Matthew notes that he was doing his automatic writing with the radio on.

Little else had been discovered about George Laing by the time Matthew's book went to press, other than the name of a man who was said to have murdered him at Sakaka, with a blow on the head. Perhaps at some point there will be further attempts to trace the story out, but for now it rests as Matthew tells it—a dead name appearing in a script Matthew could neither write nor understand.

Matthew Manning participated in a two-week seminar in Toronto in July, 1974, in the company of twenty-one scientists of the western world. The subject was psychokinesis—the movement of material objects by forces not understood—and Matthew was the subject of experiments which caused one of the participants, a physicist, to say this:

"We are on the verge of discoveries which may be extremely important for physics. We are dealing here (with Matthew) with a new kind of energy. This force must be subject to laws. I believe ordinary methods of scientific investigation will tell us much more about psychic phenomena. They are mysterious, but they are no more mysterious than a lot of things in physics already. In times past, 'respectable' scientists would have nothing to do with psychical phenomena; many of them still won't. I think the 'respectable' scientists may find they have missed the boat!" The man who said that is Dr. Brian Josephson, a professor of physics at Cavendish Laboratories at Cambridge University in England. In 1973 he was awarded the Nobel Prize in physics.

*   *   *

You've now read three samples of "survival" accounts, and you can read three hundred more and come out about where you are now. If you're at all like me, you'd like to believe them, but you can't really do so wholeheartedly. They're probably not faked—the people involved seem to be honest, intelligent, responsible people, and they stand to gain nothing by putting us on. And yet ... the whole thing seems so incredible that there must be some other explanation—perhaps mass hypnosis, or some strange dream mechanism that affects several people at the same time. There's *got* to be something, something we don't know about and they're not telling us about, that will explain these things in a plausible, scientific way. You can't quite believe in these things, you can't quite not believe in these things. Finally you put them out of your mind.

If that's where you come out, join the club. You're like most people I've talked to about this, and I've talked to a lot. There's just no way to get our hands around ideas as bewildering as this. Part of the problem is simply the habit of being skeptical about things we haven't experienced at firsthand. And, I suppose, there is also considerable resistance to appearing gullible, out of step with modern scientific thinking. We are taught to live with reality from the time we are born, and we unconsciously equate reality with what we can know from our five senses, nothing more. Alas, we're trained to be realists—all of us.

As I was reading accounts like these, I also kept looking for clues that might link the kind of life one gets dealt over there with one's behavior patterns during life here. Eternal reward and punishment are basic to most beliefs, and it would be helpful to get a line on how that works out.

But not much came of that. As far as I could tell from the books I read, the afterlife was pretty much the same for everybody. Christians got there, Moslems got there, shoemakers got there, statesmen got there, and thieves and murderers got there, too. If I took all the reports as true (and in this field it's pretty hard to draw lines between the true and the not-so-true) the moment after death is not one that begins with an interview. There's no mention of grand juries being called up to review our earth lives and decide on the kind of eternity we shall have. The reports all say the same thing—the person who passes through death feels very much as he did before, except that there is "peace." There is some talk of God in a few of the reports, but most of the ones I read did not mention him. Even the departed Paul Tillich, one of our greatest modern theologians, came through, as we've just seen, with the statement that though he still believes in God, he now conceives of him somewhat differently.

I concluded, when I had read enough of the survival books, that if we do indeed survive, we survive with everything we had when we left, including a belief in God. If we didn't happen to have that belief, we'd survive anyway—maybe to acquire it in the hereafter, maybe not. The books are pretty fuzzy on that, as they are on a lot of other things.

So I didn't find any clues about reward and punishment. There was nothing said that should cause us to alter our earthly conduct to get a better deal over there.

I did learn that I was not alone in finding little use in my everyday life for the knowledge that there may be a life after death. One famous contemporary churchman, John Haynes Holmes, stated long ago that he had an absolute belief in the survival of individual personality after death, having made his own investigations and having had personal experiences similar to those I have recounted. But, he said, that was as far as he could go; those convictions brought him no more perfect understanding of God.

That statement discouraged me when I came across it. Here I was, attempting to put the pieces together in ways that had either eluded or did not interest an eloquent and scholarly churchman. But then, I didn't know John Haynes Holmes, and I didn't know what his needs were. I told myself that his Christian programming was vastly different from mine—I hope it is for ministers—and, as I know in my own case, the programming can get in the way.

For me, this sampling of the eternal scene produced pretty vaporous results. I likened this first sortie into the world of the mysterious to reading the last chapter of a novel first. You learn how it comes out, but you have no idea how the book got there. I had to start nearer the beginning of the book, taking much smaller steps, in hopes that I might thereby be able to put together better the parts of the puzzle.

I turned to matters that, though mysterious, were more closely connected with *this* plane of existence than with the next—things like mindreading, prophesying, dowsing, flying saucers and the like. Maybe understanding of smaller mysteries closer to home could bring understanding of the greatest mystery of all.

Chapter 5

First Encounters with Things Psychic

I knew so little about "unknown" phenomena when I began that I couldn't even make a halfway complete list of them, let alone use accepted terminology. To me, the words all meant the same thing—"paranormal," "psychic," "extrasensory," "supernatural," "parapsychological," "occult"—they all described the spook world, the one science knows does not exist.

I was starting an inquiry—this was over twenty years ago—at a time when only the most gullible of us, or the least scientific among us, or the most fanatically religious of us could with any aplomb confess that we were seriously interested in things like this. Even today, when some genuine scientific interest is beginning to be evidenced, one still risks smart remarks and sidelong glances from friends if he confesses belief in one or two of the aspects of the "unexplained."

Now that I have boned up on these things, I can identify the different kinds of phenomena and even put names on them that have some currency among the investigators in this bizarre field.

The kinds of "unexplained" happenings are so numerous and so varied (at first glance) that even a listing of the more important of them is apt to affront your credulity, but let me take that risk. I could add some more, but the list is overlong as it is, and I don't want to overburden you. However, if you want to add things like palm reading, tea-leaf reading, phrenology, numerology, ouija boards, and crystal-ball gazing, feel free to do so. They're all valid mysteries for some of us.

I've tried to arrange the phenomena in what was for me, looking back to when I first began probing these things, something of an increasing order-of-difficulty of belief. As you read it, you may find it interesting to make your own mental check marks beside those that you presently view as *genuinely* real phenomena:

Total-recall Memory, in which every detail of a scene that took place in the far past is summoned up in one's conscious mind.

Hypnosis—access (usually through a trained hypnotist) to the subconscious by shutting off conscious control of the mind and permitting the subconscious to respond to external suggestion.

Drug-induced visions—(hallucinations?) of other worlds of the mind, closely akin to worlds described by mystics and religious fanatics.

Bio-rhythms—cyclical physical processes in our bodies, controlled by solar, planetary, or stellar rhythms.

Déjà-vu—a strong sense of having previously experienced a situation one is in the midst of.

Clairvoyant Dreams, in which information unknown to the dreamer reaches him, such as that of an actual, recorded happening that took place, is taking place, or will take place somewhere.

Acupuncture, either as a cure for disease conditions or to bring about anesthesia.

Animal homing under conditions that exclude use of the known senses.

Firewalking, and other demonstrations of willed immunity from pain or injury.

Eyeless sight, such as reading with the fingertips.

Flying saucers—unknown objects in the sky that defy our physical laws of motion.

Dowsing (divining), to locate water or minerals underground.

Mental telepathy—communication between two persons without the use of any of the five senses.

Clairvoyance—conscious awareness of actual happenings or circumstances that are beyond the reach of the senses.

Pschokinesis—movement and control of objects with no known physical force applied.

Precognition—foreknowledge of future events.

Postcognition—knowledge of past events completely outside of the experience of the knower.

Plant sensitivity and response to human thoughts or emotions.

Thought photographs—creation of images on unexposed photographic film by mind action alone.

Astrology—use of star and planet position, beginning with the exact time of one's birth, to accurately forecast future events.

Faith healing, (and prayer) that brings about actual, measurable improvement in circumstance or in physical condition in self or others.

Auras—glowing patterns, invisible to most of us, that surround parts of human beings, animals, and plants.

Poltergeists—Entities that cause movement of objects or creation of sounds without any human or other natural participation or intervention.

Levitation—lifting of material objects by a trance medium, using no known physical force.

Possession—the taking over of a human body and psyche by malevolent spirits, causing profound changes in personality and great distress to the subject.

Astral projection—the existence of a "second body" in each of us, containing our personalities, memories, and physical characteristics, and which can be released from our primary, physical bodies and become visible to others great distances away from our physical bodies.

Ghosts, apparitions, hauntings—the visible or audible presence of persons known or presumed to be dead.

Communication with the dead, through mediums, automatic writing, dreams, or conscious experience.

Reincarnation, transmigration—the re-emergence of a departed soul in a new life—human, animal, or plant.

If you're like most, your mental checkmarks may be pretty sparse, provided you checked off only those where you have an *absolute* conviction in their reality. In my own case, before I began seriously studying these things many years ago, I believed in almost *none* of them except for five or six scattered near the top of the list. Even for some of those, I believed only in the fact that they did exist, and had not paid much attention to the implications their existence held.

Hypnosis, for instance, was simply the unconscious mind revealed in a wakeful trance, and dreams were the same mind operating unchecked by our sleeping conscious control. I was pretty sure we had an unconscious (or subconscious) part of our minds, but I'd never been particularly curious about it. It was the sort of thing one didn't need to pay too much attention to unless something got out of kilter, and then the psychiatrists went to work on it.

As for almost all the rest of the phenomena on the list, they were all part of the spook world—I certainly didn't believe in them, but I can't say I had worked up a strong disbelief in them either. They just weren't part of my ordinary life.

But now I had to learn about them. The dead-ending of my religious wanderings, including my look at the afterlife, left me with the choice of either boring into all of these to see if they held some meaning or giving up the whole idea of finding some route to understanding. I started, but it sure wasn't easy.

It wasn't easy because the same thing began to happen here that happened in my little sortie into the spirit world. I read book after book about clairvoyance, telepathy, psychokinesis, astrology, and other weird things, each replete with remarkable tales of happenings that were impossible to explain by any known physical laws. Some of the books (not all of them, by any means) are quite plausible in their recounting of these happenings—the observers seem to be responsible people, the conditions under which the happenings take place are well-documented, the accounts are dispassionate and are related without evidence of exaggeration or naive credulity. Taken all together, they are very hard to disbelieve—in a rationally examined intellectual sense.

But the mere reading of them left me in about the same state I arrived at in my readings about communication with the dead.

All by themselves, read as one reads any book or article about matters foreign to one's own experience, these accounts of supernatural happenings did not create in me any deep-seated, intuitively based *belief* in the reality of the phenomena, the kind of belief and conviction I was searching for.

It began to dawn on me, as I went through gee-whiz book after gee-whiz book, that a few things were missing in my near random approach to these mysteries. For one thing, when I started all this, I knew so little about the workings of the mind, about suggestion, and hypnotism, and the subconscious, that it was all too easy to write off these accounts of mysterious happenings as "hallucinations," or some form of "self-hypnosis." Someone once said: "Whatever you are *totally* ignorant of, assert that to be the explanation of everything else."

That's exactly what I was doing when I relegated these things to the mysterious realm of the subconscious. That sweeping solution didn't solve anything, of course, but it helped defend my credulity for a while.

So I had to learn something about that subconscious. I had to try to find out whether our present-day knowledge of the mind and of matter held any valid explanation—or even a hope of a future explanation—for the strange happenings I was reading about.

There was a second thing that was missing, something I now know was probably the most important ingredient of all. It was the complete absence (I thought) of any direct experience with the mysterious phenomena I was reading about. I had never taken drugs, never been hypnotized, never been to a seance, never had a vision, never seen a flying saucer—indeed none of the really amazing things I was reading about had ever happened to me, as far as I was aware. Nor had they happened to anyone else I talked to, with very few exceptions (most of which I could readily write off as "coincidence" or, again, "the subconscious at work").

Tempting as it might have been to try a firsthand experience with hypnosis or LSD or a seance, I never did. Some of them made me nervous; the tamer ones were still so different from normal living routines that I wasn't interested in them. If this is indeed a world in which we are allowed to find some beliefs, we shouldn't have to resort to drugs or spooky practices that take things out of our own conscious control. (I confess that I did buy a ouija board, but I could never get it to do anything but just lie there.)

A third thing that was missing was what I considered an almost complete lack of scientific documentation of almost all of these phenomena. Knowing of that lack, it was easy to retain lingering doubts even though I was reading very credible accounts that my rational mind could accept readily. None of us likes to be fooled, and the knowledge that charlatans, quacks, and conjurors have been preying on our human gullibility since time began made me keep my guard up. Science would have explained these things by now if they were true, I told myself.

Unfortunately for the kind of task I was undertaking, there had been programmed into me some confidence in and belief in science, one that said, in effect, that if science has proved it, it is probably so. There also existed that devastating corollary that shouldn't follow, but does, for many of us: *if science hasn't proved it, it probably can't be so.*

I should have known better, and I did, yet I still fell into that trap. We all know that science has erred in the past, that some of the basic scientific truths we were taught have had to be replaced by new theories and new hypotheses. I knew as well as anybody that science was neither perfect nor omniscient.

Yet, the stamp of truth that science can apply to explanations of natural phenomena is powerful indeed, and its absence is almost equally convincing. You and I will never see an electron, nor will any man ever. Yet we believe without a doubt that they exist. (Some eminent physicists today, though, will tell you *they're* not so sure anymore.) We have never seen inside an atom, and never will, but we're sure all matter consists of atoms, and that atoms consist almost wholly of empty space. I know that this typewriter in front of me is only a specialized arrangement of trillions and trillions of near-voids, as is the organization of cells and chemicals that is punching its keys.

How strange that I can believe and trust atomic theory so readily, yet reject things labeled "supernatural"!

Or take another scientific truth, one that Hiroshima taught us all to believe. Until 1945, "mass" was "mass" and "energy" was "energy"—two separate and totally dissimilar physical entities we could measure and manipulate (but not quite explain). Now we live, uneasily, it must be said, with the knowledge that mass and energy are the same thing.

Who says these things are so? Science. Who believes it? Everybody. Many times I found myself wishing that science had been trying as hard for the past fifty years to explain the supernatural as it has the atom.

Actually, I was aware of some very small-scale and limited scientific research that had been underway in the spook world for a number of years, because many of the books I read referred to it in their efforts to make all occult phenomena believable. The references were all the same, describing some work with card-guessing experiments during the late twenties and thirties. Most of it had been done by an obscure professor at Duke University named J. B. Rhine, and some more had been done by English investigators. (The English seemed to be much more enthusiastic about psychic phenomena than the Americans were, and they had some pretty heavy names associated with their inquiries. But I was an American boy, and America was where the real science was being done. Besides, I was M.I.T., and Duke was a tobacco college.)

It had been very easy for me to read right past those meager reports of scientific experiment and discount their significance. Eventually I was obliged to go back to that work and study it much more carefully. Limited as it was, it turned out to be the only aspect of the psychic world that appeared to have had any scientific rigor applied to it. And, as I've said, my kind of mind felt it had to have a little scientific proof before it was about to believe anything.

First, though, I had to get that "subconscious mind" idea in some perspective if I were to stop using it as a catch-all for my doubts. I had to learn what I could about our minds and our brains in hopes I'd come across some modern knowledge about how they work, something that might explain at least a few of the puzzling things on that long list of spooky phenomena. Psychology should have some answers. After all, the word itself derives from the Greek *psykhē*—"breath, life, soul"—and that's just what I wanted to find out more about.

Chapter 6

What Psychology Has to Say

For someone who hasn't spent a lifetime in the study of psychology, the task of getting one's arms around this massive field is formidable. There just aren't any compact little books that cover the ground—there's simply too much ground.

The problem is not just that of the mind's complexity, though I guess everything in the last analysis stems from that.

The practical difficulty arises from the fact that no one scientific discipline seems to be able to look at the thing as a whole. The psychologist does his thing, the psychiatrist his, and the psycho-biologist something else. They need the help of the neuro-anatomist, and the neuro-anatomist needs the bio-chemist to poke around in the brain cells. And a bio-chemist these days had better have a bio-physicist by his side, and what physicist can do without a mathematician? On and on. Mind-science is like a lot of little streams flowing into one big river, each bringing its quota of clear water, eddies, currents, and murk.

Still and all, I was not trying to become a psychologist; I was simply looking to see whether there existed plausible scientific explanations for some of the things I had read about.

I also knew very well that my own mind from time to time behaved in odd ways—not "supernatural" ways, of course, but in ways certainly not controlled by my conscious mind. I knew my subconscious was responsible for those commonplace quirks, and they became my reference points as I pursued my studies.

For instance, I have noted that I can be glancing idly through the pages of a newspaper, not really paying much attention to or caring about what I am reading, when a particular word— usually a name—will pop out at me from some obscure part of the text and make me go back, search for it, and read that part carefully. It's a mental counterpart of the comedian's double-take. What causes that? Obviously, my eyes printed more of the page on my brain than I chose to examine consciously. But my other mind had its own ideas and examined the picture more closely. How long did that picture last in my mind? Could it still be there?

Something of the same sort happens occasionally when I write letters, or talk to my wife, or engage in spirited discussion, only then the effect is apt to be more positive. I sometimes find myself writing things or saying things I didn't know I knew how to write or say, shaping ideas and concepts that I had never consciously thought about before. As a matter of fact, I've learned over the years to use this strange source of insight in a very helpful way, by talking about or writing about things I had never talked or written about before, just to find out what I really think about them. I must admit that some of the significant positions I've taken on major issues I've had to meet, and most of the *good* decisions I've made, were reached by forcing myself to talk or write about them *at length*. I knew what I really thought only after I had heard myself *say* what I thought, and not before. I've always felt it strange that the mind should work this way. Is this what we call "inspiration"? Does it come wholly from information I had already stored in my mind, or could it come from some other source, in part?

A final example. Pungent odors have an unusual way of triggering recall from distant corners of my mind and pushing aside whatever the conscious part was doing at the time. There's a particular kind of paint whose smell has taken me way back to my boyhood and to a shack our gang had built out of scrap lumber, old packing cases (those were the days when they shipped refrigerators in gorgeous wooden boxes), and odd bits and pieces liberated from local construction projects. The paint smell doesn't just remind me of the *fact* of having built the shack; it makes me relive the scene in extraordinary detail—the site on a hillside, the secret meetings, the stuffy, airless enclosure with an overpowering smell of the fresh paint we used on the walls, paint I can remember borrowing from my father's workshop. The rush of memory-image is powerful but fleeting, for when it passes I can't pump up any more images no matter how hard I try. Why is this memory so extraordinarily complete? Can it be that *everything* that ever happened to me is similarly stored? If so, why do I have such trouble remembering what I *want* to remember?

In all of these quirks, we're dealing with "memory," a word we use so often we forget it is but a word, not an explanation. Thanks to the patient work of many decades, psychology knows a good deal about the varying ways in which memory manifests itself, though it is absolutely unable to tell us what memory *is*. Nonetheless, the mind-sciences can teach us quite a bit about memory, and through examination of memory, something about the subconscious mind that is its storehouse.

The "imagery-memory" of my paint smell works differently from the kind of memory that tells me what my phone number is or what my wedding anniversary date is. The "image" kind provides nearly total recall of a scene in unbelievable detail, not triggered because I willed it (as I do with my telephone number) but completely without thoughtful action on my part. And both my telephone-number memory and my boyhood-recall memory differ, in the way they respond, from another kind of memory that I use all the time, as does every human being in the world.

That's the kind of memory on which we rely when we want to move a finger, or scratch a nose, or say "hello," or do any of the things we must do thousands of times a day to stay alive and functioning. Watch yourself wiggle your big toe sometime—the part of you that's furthest from your brain—and ask yourself "how can it be that it moves just the way I want it to without any thought process of which I am conscious?" You just "will" it to move, and it does. And moving a toe is a pretty simple trick. Think of what has to happen when you say "hello." And then think of a soprano singing the whole of *Aïda* without a single piece of music to guide her. Or consider an outfielder who takes off at the crack of a bat, somehow calculating the trajectory of the ball so as to catch it on a dead run over his shoulder.

The conscious mind simply doesn't work fast enough to handle these kinds of trained motor-response tasks. They must be entrusted to that marvelous part of the mind that operates by itself, sometimes on the command of our wills, sometimes capriciously. This is where all the mysteries reside.

One of the tools which has been of enormous importance in the past few years in charting the unknown corners of the subconscious is hypnotism. This strange key to the door of the inner mind has had a stormy history over the past 200 years, since Anton Mesmer, an Austrian physician "discovered" it and used it to "cure" his patients of many kinds of disease. Inevitably, there followed abuse and fraud, and Mesmerism languished in disrepute for 150 years. It has only been fairly recently that the phenomenon—now called hypnotism—has regained the good graces of legitimate science and medicine.

What is hypnotism? We don't know yet. But we know what it does. It places a suitably receptive mind into a state of greatly reduced awareness of its surroundings and permits the subconscious, or unconscious (we won't quibble with semantics here) part of the mind to surface. Our subconscious minds are continually suppressed by our sensory and conscious thinking processes while we are awake; hypnotism shuts off this suppression and lets the hypnotized subject have direct access to some of the unconscious workings of his mind. The state resembles sleep, but the subject is fully awake and alert. The difference is that he will respond with his subconscious mind to suggestions made under hypnosis, and those suggestions will stay with him when he leaves the trance-like hypnotic state.

Hypnotism has provided psychologists and psychiatrists with an extraordinary tool for probing the inner recesses of the mind. We now know that the mind can be instructed to blot out pain sensation, and hypnotism is today widely used as an anesthesia in dentistry and minor surgical procedures. ("Deep" hypnosis will permit painless major surgery, but only a small fraction of human beings can be put into a deep hypnotic state.) We know that in the hypnotized state we can be made to recall in vivid detail scenes that we had long forgotten and were unable to dredge up consciously from our memories. Our bodily rhythms— heart rate, blood pressure, respiration—can be altered by hypnotic suggestion in ways that most of us cannot duplicate consciously. Through hypnotism we have been able to document very powerfully the fact that mind can indeed control matter, at least the matter in our bodies, and the processes our bodies perform without our conscious knowledge.

We also know that hypnotism does *not* require the services of another person to put us into a trance and to make suggestions to our subconscious. We can do it ourselves, by and to ourselves, and many people have learned to do just that. I get the strong feeling that most, if not all, of the mind/body cults we hear so much of today—Yoga, transcendental meditation, kung fu, T'ai chi and all the others—have their basis in self-hypnosis. Perhaps the hallucinogenic drugs operate in much the same way. Calling all of these things "hypnosis" doesn't explain anything, of course; it merely links them all together in the common mystery of the subconscious mind.

The simplest way to look at the subconscious is as a giant reservoir that retains in some way not yet understood a record of everything that has ever happened to us. *Not quite* everything, say some; it's just too much of a strain on their imaginations to believe that every card we ever played in all our bridge games, every move we ever made on every chess board, is stored away in our skulls. *More* than everything, say others—knowledge of our ancestors' lives, knowledge even of our origins before man became man. Take your pick. What is inescapable is the fact that the subconscious mind is an astounding reservoir, wherever you choose to draw the line. It lies there, full of stored information, pressing always on the sluice-gates of our conscious minds to let the information flow through.

The *conscious* mind is a kind of three-way control valve. It lets us put selected things into the subconscious for later use; it lets us recall information from the subconscious when we want to have it; and it helps us keep the subconscious subdued when we don't want it messing up our checkbooks. It works in all three directions, and if it were not always on guard during our waking hours, we would be so overwhelmed by information reaching our senses from outside, and by random bubblings-up from inside, that we would be unable to function.

All of our sense organs that tell our brains what's going on are carefully designed to bar information that would be confusing or useless to us so that we can handle adequately the information that we need to exist in our world. There are sounds we cannot hear, radiations we cannot detect, smells we cannot smell, sensations we cannot feel—all of them just as real in nature as those our senses tell us about, but screened off from us.

For that we can be thankful, because most of us have enough trouble handling the torrent of information that *does* reach us every minute of every day in this modern world.

Our conscious minds, like our sense perceptors, also screen off, tune out, turn down unwanted "noise"—information that reaches us with a confusing or unwanted signal—and let us maintain our sanity in a world full of ambiguity, intrusion, and contradiction.

A simple example of this screening ability, one that has been a matter of serious study by psychologists, is the "cocktail party" phenomenon that all of us who are suitably sociable have experienced firsthand. Somehow we can single out one lone voice from an overpoweringly noisy babble and hear what it is saying, if we try to. (I sometimes wonder, at cocktail parties, why we try.) A microphone over our heads will record only a noisy babble, yet we are able to select out what we want to hear just by intensely concentrating our senses. We are using a *consciously applied* filter; we use it all the time.

We use this kind of filter not just to detect audible signals in a noisy background, but—for instance—to sort ideas that interest us from the competing and sometimes unwelcome ideas that constantly bubble around us. That's probably how some of us become Republicans and some Democrats. We pick and choose ideas throughout our lives, just as we pick and choose what we will see or ignore with our eyes and hear or ignore with our ears. In that way we use our conscious minds to help shape our personalities and our lives. We are constantly making these "filtered" choices in accordance with a pattern which we help weave with our conscious minds, even though we are not always aware of the fact that we are doing it.

This "unconscious" conscious selection importantly affects our ability to recall from our subconscious those things that we desire to remember or think about. It seems that the material stored via the conscious route is usually more readily available to us than the images or impressions that reach our subconscious without our being aware of them. The kind of memory we rely on for telephone numbers and for getting us places on time is ordinarily quite accessible, though it becomes less so with time and disuse. So with repeated practice with arithmetic tables, spelling books, finger exercises on the piano and all of the other things we teach our minds and bodies to do because we want them to. How much information we can recall readily depends on a number of things, but mostly our stored-memory recall abilities will match pretty closely the general state of our prior awareness of the things we are trying to remember. If we are never consciously aware of and never think about flowers, we'll have some difficulty tuning in on the garden club meeting, no matter how many thousands of flowers have passed under our eyes and noses and into our deep mental reservoirs. In this way, our conscious minds still further shape what we become: they not only tune down what we choose to ignore, but they place at a less accessible level the information we might want to call up from our memories.

We should expect exactly these same processes to apply to exposures we have had to things of a psychic nature. Our conscious minds, if we are skeptics, will filter out for us and will affect the storage levels and recall ability. If we're *convinced* we're not psychic, our conscious minds will be glad to oblige.

What this boils down to is a confirmation of a somewhat unnerving suspicion that most of us have held from time to time; that each of us is the kind of person he is largely because he made himself that way, certainly in non-psychic matters, and probably in psychic ones as well.

True, there are inherited traits and talents built into us, and there are differences in our individual chemistries that make us tend to behave in individual ways. But the old adage that *what we think, we are* contains more than just a suggestion of truth. We do shape our views of the world, of others, and of ourselves in ways we consciously control, and we become over the years of our lives pretty much what we have made ourselves become. I can't blame my problems with God on God, or on my parents, or on my church, or on anybody but me. I'm the one who chose to think as I did, to ask questions I knew nobody could answer.

It's not particularly comforting to have to acknowledge that. Most of us would prefer some more remote scapegoat for our difficulties, though we'll gladly take credit for the beautiful aspects of our personalities.

This fact of personal, conscious accountability for the kind of person we are was one of the more rewarding of the findings I made in my foray into psychology, because there's an obverse side of the self-responsibility coin: If I've made myself what I am, I can change myself into what I want to be. The books don't tell us exactly how to go about it, but they allow a perfectly clear inference that it can be done. Perhaps the most important factor is the extent to which we train our two minds to respond to our wishes. We can, if we choose to, discipline our conscious and subconscious minds to serve us better, just as we can train our muscles and their controlling brain and nerve networks to paint pictures and ride bicycles.

Western psychology doesn't seem to have paid too much attention to the business of training healthy minds to serve their owners' conscious processes better. I get the distinct impression that most of the weight of psychological research, and practically all of psychiatric research, has been directed toward the "abnormal" mind, the misbehaving mind that gets so many people into trouble and pays so many psychiatrists' bills. I suppose that is completely understandable, given that the universal desire for good health, mental as well as physical, is what powers the medical industry.

But, today, there are signs that Western psychology is indeed becoming more interested in tapping the latent powers of the mind. It is turning, of all places, to what it terms the "traditional" psychologies, a neat euphemism that embraces the hitherto disdained teachings of "Eastern," or "mystical," or "occult" psychologies. All of these have for the millennia of their existence taken a quite different view of man's mind, one that centers on his subconscious mind and stresses control of the conscious mind to let the subconscious function at its highest and most useful level. Yes, Yoga, Sufism, Zen and many other ancient and mysterious schools of thought are beginning to be looked at seriously now as Western mind-science strokes its chin and reflects on how far it yet has to go in understanding the enormous powers of this hidden part of man's mind.

I'm going to leave it at that, resisting the temptation to provide a short course in Eastern mysticism. The point to be made is that this is where our psychologists appear to be heading, though many will still hotly deny it. I suspect that those who continue to resist will be heard from less and less, because their classical approaches seem not to be getting very far. For all of the work that Western psychology has done over the years, we are really not close at all to understanding what our minds actually are and how they work. And we know nothing that lets us explain the mechanisms of psychic phenomena. There is even no way yet of proving that such phenomena do not exist.

I learned what I had to know: that I could not look to the mind-sciences to provide acceptable, conventional "scientific" explanations for the goings-on in the psychic world.

I also learned that classical, twentieth-century psychology

must redirect itself if it is to provide us with any new insights. Not only will our psychologists have to start paying attention to what the mystics have been saying; they'll have to use quite different approaches from the ones they are using now. Let me tell you why I say that.

Chapter 7

What Do We Mean When We Say "Probably"?

We'd all be lost without the word "probably" in its many forms. We'll probably vote Republican. We probably won't like oysters. We'll probably tangle with our mother-in-law. We use this handy word endlessly to express uncertainty about almost anything.

So do our scientists. So do our psychologists who are trying so hard to fathom the mysteries of the human mind and personality. In the realm of mind-science it is rarely possible to conduct experiments that can be repeated with the surety of an electric-light circuit. Yet some measured kind of surety is what modern science demands of all experimentation. That measure is summed up in a code science uses to express just how sure it is of what it is saying, and that code is called, understandably, "probability theory." We use it all the time—must use it—if we are to get anywhere at all in most of our scientific pursuits.

When Western scientific man seeks to account for things he doesn't understand, he relies on modern "scientific method"—a process of experimentation, observation, and deduction. If a phenomenon a scientist is seeking to explain can be made to happen with unfailing regularity when all conditions are kept uniform, he can accept the validity of the existence of the phenomenon and begin to search for cause and effect. When he alters a single condition of the experiment and the phenomenon changes in some way, he can infer that the condition affects the phenomenon—again, only if it always happens.

Or almost always, that is. He has to say "almost" because he can rarely control all of the conditions that surround an experiment—indeed, he can't know in most cases all of the possible conditions that might affect it. He defines "almost always" by employing probability theory, and every modern science in the last analysis relies on it to state a case and support a theory.

Scientific method requires that "chance" be ruled out of any experiment designed to establish a cause-effect relationship. Only if chance *is* ruled out will the experiment produce predictable results that can be duplicated by others, and only then does the experiment finally carry any weight.

Probability theory is the basis on which all of modern physics rests; it is the only way science can make order out of the natural chaos that surrounds us—in minute, atomic form, for example. We can use carbon dating of archaeological specimens because we know that all radioactive materials decompose at a precisely predictable rate; yet the disintegration of any *one* atom in a radioactive mass is a matter of purest chance, not in any way predictable. Probability theory tells us that we can be absolutely *sure* of the combined rate of decay of *all* atoms taken together, but not of each one in turn. Probability theory predicts accurately when the numbers are large, and it predicts exceedingly well.

This "law of large numbers" is the cornerstone of probability theory. Simply stated using a familiar example, it says that the longer we keep trying to guess the turn of a card or the roll of a die, the closer we'll get to a purely "chance" result—if *only* chance and no other factor is present. If we call for a "3" and immediately get it when we roll a die, we impress no one; that's mere chance. If we get it three times in a row, we may feel good about it, but we have not really defied the laws of probability. There's still a pretty big likelihood that the three-in-a-row was just chance. But if in 6,000 rolls we turn up 2,000 "3's" instead of the 1,000 that chance would explain, the odds are several million to one that the result is not pure chance. Something else, something other than chance, must be at work.

You and I, not being physicists or mathematicians whose life work is based on probability theory, may still choose to call such exceptional dice-rolling "chance" (and wish we could take it to Vegas). But the fact remains that we really mustn't do that unless we are also prepared to throw out *all* of the basic theories on which modern physics depends. We can't be choosy about when we believe in probability theory and when we don't.

Back to scientific method as applied to studies of the mind. Everything we know about the mind's behavior, and all of the speculations that psychologists today indulge in when they seek to account for what the mind does, are based very directly on the scientific method: experimentation, observation and deduction, all supported by probability theory. That's the only way we yet have to find explanations, make diagnoses, and predict outcomes. Modern psychology insists on large numbers of cases added to large numbers of similar cases to support its theories, and those theories are accepted only when they can predict outcomes satisfactorily—again in numbers large enough to carry convincing statistical weight.

But most *paranormal* or "unexplained" phenomena simply don't behave frequently enough or repeatably enough to lend themselves to classic scientific method. That is one of the reasons they have been ignored by most psychologists.

Little wonder you and I have difficulty accepting as genuine fact, and certainly as predictable phenomena, those occurrences which are unusual or unexpected—a lost dog trailing his owner over two hundred miles of unfamiliar terrain, a wife who utters the very same words her husband was about to say, the phone call that comes from a long forgotten friend that you just happened to be talking about that very day. We call such things "coincidences." Actually, they are events that take place with such infrequency and with such a low order of possibility of duplication by controlled experiment that we don't look on them as susceptible to "scientific" examination as we know it. Their repeat predictability is of a very low order.

What we have to recognize is that this low predictability may be the *only* way in which they differ from scientifically confirmed and accepted phenomena. Though science can investigate and confirm readily the existence of things that can be made to happen over and over again in the laboratory, scientific method begins to flounder when things can't be made to happen on command, in a laboratory, under tightly controlled conditions. That doesn't mean these infrequent, unpredictable phenomena don't exist. It just means it is not at all convenient to investigate them in the classical manner.

Thus, when I state that we won't begin to make the strides we need to in understanding the human mind until psychological science looks far beyond where it is now looking, and uses tools it is not now using, I am neither deprecating classic methods nor rooting for blind acceptance of any explanation someone offers for phenomena science does not now understand. I am simply pointing out some limitations of modern scientific method.

There is one very firm conclusion I have reached, one I would like to leave with you as you read further about the mind. Given that we know almost nothing about how the mind works, we must avoid, if we are to learn more about ourselves, the notion that if there's no universally accepted "scientific" proof of something, that something doesn't exist. That caution may seem perfectly reasonable as you read it, but you'll find it's hard to continue to heed as we probe deeper and deeper into the strange and unknown processes of the mind. I know that I had to keep reminding myself of that, and I suspect that you will, too. Remember that as we take a brief look at the machinery part of the mind, the human brain.

Chapter 8

Are the Answers in the Brain?

We have made enormous strides in understanding the physical functioning of the human brain, that organ most of us tend to equate with "the mind." We are so aware of our brains, and science knows so much about the anatomy and physiology of the human brain that it is perfectly natural for most of us to assume that the brain is not only the *location* of the mind, but that it indeed *is* the mind—that it is not only the storehouse of all of the information the mind uses to do its thing, but is also the switching center that uses that information for thinking, for sensing our surroundings, and for control of our physical functioning. But when one studies what we know about the brain, one concludes that that is not so. We can explain *some* of what we loosely call "mind" by our modern knowledge of brain function—but we cannot explain *most* of it. We cannot yet explain thought, we cannot yet explain memory—two of our most commonplace faculties.

The human brain is almost as incredible, as a mass of living tissue, as is the mind which it seems to serve. It has been only within the last couple of decades that science has had the instruments with which to study this three-pound mass—electron microscopes that reveal the structures of molecules; chemical analyzers that detect minute changes in the chemical composition of sites in the brain while it is being stimulated by one of the senses, or by thought itself; extremely tiny electric probes that can be inserted into the brain tissue to excite it or to detect its electrical currents; wave analyzers and computers that can make meaning out of bizarre electrical signals flowing through the brain. With these tools, with endless animal experiments, with medical and surgical skills, man has learned an enormous amount about the way the brain is put together and how its tissues function.

You have seen pictures of the human brain—a large wrinkled mass perched atop a smaller supporting stem. Making up most of the upper mass is the *cortex,* and the stalk on which it rests is the *brain stem.* Each is made up almost wholly of brain cells and nerve cells—billions of them—and each cell is connected to other cells by tails which are nerve fibers. Each nerve fiber branches at its end many times, and each of the ends of these branches is joined eventually to another cell. A particular nerve fiber may in some cases be connected to as many as twenty thousand other cells, and all told there are estimated to be some ten thousand million such connections. That is a perfectly staggering number of connections, but even more staggering is the fact that with such a huge number of pathways available, the patterns of interconnection between several cells—two, ten, two hundred, two thousand, two million—are infinite. A single brain has incomparably more "power" than the very largest computers. If it were as easy to program as a modern computer, we would never have had to invent that machine.

One of the greatest breakthroughs in brain research occurred when it was discovered many years ago that tiny electrodes may safely be inserted into human brain tissue (which is insensitive to pain) and current passed through them to stimulate the brain cell pathways. The fact that electricity was involved in nerve-pathway transmission had been known for years, since the time in 1770 that Galvani attached wires to the nerve fibers of a frog's leg and caused the leg to twitch when voltage was applied. Over the years since then it has been shown that all nerve fibers conduct electricity—those that connect our sense organs to the brain, those within the brain itself, and those that operate all of our muscles. Our nervous system, including the brain, is a bundle of living wires of sometimes microscopic size and widely varying lengths, and these wires appear to do just what ordinary wires do—conduct electricity to cause things to happen.

When small electrodes are inserted into particular areas of the brain and tiny currents caused to flow through them, things do indeed happen. The subject can be made to hear sounds that aren't there, to see nonexistent lights and other visual images around him, to move various muscles he didn't try to move, to talk without any conscious effort of will, to forget or be unable to say his name, to feel pleasure or pain—even to lose consciousness momentarily when either of two (and only two) tiny areas are stimulated. In this way, the human brain has been "mapped" to identify the portions of it that control various emotions, and sensory and motor processes.

And in this way, also, human beings have been artificially stimulated to experience things that are suggestive of the supernatural—fleeting visions of scenes and places unknown, voices from a past not remembered or a present unknown. Where do they come from? Are they already stored in the brain somewhere, or does stimulation simply make the brain a better antenna for picking up information originating somewhere else? Nobody knows for sure.

Let's look at some of the principal parts of the brain—not to try to become expert about this intricate organ, but at least to develop a proper sense of wonder. The *brain stem* is the more ancient, primitive part of the brain, and the less mysterious in the view of modern neurology. Among other things, the brain stem appears to be in charge of the automatic processes of our bodies—heart, lungs, digestive tract, and so forth. It also appears to be the seat of our emotional and sex drives (though not without control and monitoring by regions of the cortex, thank heaven). Animals possess primarily a brain stem, with a far more limited cortex than man has developed, and this undoubtedly helps to distinguish man in his intellectual powers from his animal precursors.

The cortex is where more of the action that interests us as people takes place. This is where sensations received from our eyes, ears, and skin wind up and are processed. And here also is the part of our brain that sends out commands to our muscles to make them do, consciously or unconsciously, what we wish them to. The amount of brain tissue devoted to the various motor functions varies with the complexity of the function—the hands and lips have exceptionally large areas associated with them. The cortex is divided into two halves, each half controlling the opposite side of the body. It has been known for thousands of years that this division of our brain is nearly absolute as far as our left-right muscle control is concerned, and the fact was largely viewed as just another of nature's remarkable safeguards against injury. If half of our brain is injured irreparably, we still retain muscle function of the opposite half of our body.

Much more recent is the knowledge that the right and left halves of our brains are quite different in the way they control our thought processes and our mental states. We now know that the left half is largely responsible for our rational, intellectual, verbal processes, and our right half dominates our sense of space, our aesthetic sense, our artistic and crafts endeavors.

The separations are not absolute, of course—nature always provides some redundancy. But it is clear that the two halves do tend to specialize as we mature. Damage to the left brain in adults can produce irreparable loss of speech, whereas the same order of damage in the same place in children will in time be overcome by the right side's taking over the speech function.

The left brain (right hand) appears to process information sequentially, as it must in solving problems in mathematics or logic or in communicating ideas through the sequential words of human speech. The right brain, on the other hand, appears to process many inputs at once, to tell us instantly whether we are in a round or square room or whether that face belongs to mother or Aunt Minnie. The two halves work together, receive common inputs and produce combined outputs that make us behave in particular ways. Ideally, we use both halves in a balanced way, but the balance alters from situation to situation and varies widely from individual to individual. This variability accounts for some part of the great differences in human personality, from the coldly logical, positive, verbal, "unfeeling" left-brain types to the flighty, warm, unpredictable "artistic" right-brain types that we can all identify in mental caricature.

Psychology can't tell us much about how we go about strengthening one half and weakening another if we wish to alter our personalities a little. Really, all it knows from modern brain research is that the two halves, though interconnected, do specialize in the way described, and do account for at least some of the differences in what we call "personality."

The frontal region of the cortex (also split), called the frontal lobes, positioned above and behind our eye sockets, contains about half of the total surface area of the cortex. This is the least understood part of the brain. It seems to have little if any direct involvement with our sensory, motor, or ordinary intellectual processes and is thus difficult to map by electrical stimulation. There have been numerous cases of destruction or disconnection of the frontal lobes without noticeable loss of functioning, in the everyday sense. What does happen in such cases is a change in personality, sometimes a drastic one. Modern psychosurgery is occasionally used to carefully alter the brain paths in the frontal lobe area to calm highly agitated patients or patients in extreme, intractable pain from disease. The frontal lobes are held by some scientists to be the "seat" of human personality, if indeed any such precise locus can be held to exist for such a complex collection of traits and characteristics.

Far back from the frontal lobes which are so especially human, where the overhanging cortex joins the brain stem, are located some particularly highly interconnected regions which seem to affect, very importantly, our emotions. Here is found, for instance, the hypothalamus, a very small region that regulates our breathing, heart rate, and blood pressure; it controls our desires for eating and drinking, and is a center for our sense of temperature and the body's response to temperature changes. All of these regulatory functions are linked with our emotional state—anger, fear, desire—to arm our bodies in preparedness. Also, in this region, deep in the center of the brain, is a strange glandular body resembling a pine cone. Its function is understood hardly at all—the only gland in the body, I believe, of which this is still true. It is called the pineal body, and it exists in all invertebrates, lower-order vertebrates, mammals, and man.

In the lesser animals, some of the pineal cells are photosensitive, and the pineal is believed to influence reproductive functions in those species whose sexual cycles are associated with seasonal changes in the earth's light. In man's pineal there appear to be no such cells, and the gland is considered to be exclusively a secretory organ, producing an enzyme necessary to the synthesis of serotonin and melatonin, two compounds of whose exact roles in human physiology we are still unsure.

We do know that the pineal gland is relatively large in children and begins to shrink before puberty. In adults, the gland begins to calcify as the years progress, and by the time we are in our sixties, the pineal body is apt to be almost wholly calcified and (presumably) essentially inoperative. I mention all this not only to show that we still have things to discover about the physiology of the brain, but for another reason closely associated with part of the thrust of this book. Eastern mysticism has since the beginning of time viewed the pineal body as the physical connection point between the brain and supernatural influences. It is called "the third eye" in these ancient cults, and we shall be looking at it a little later on.

Mapping of the electrical circuitry of the brain (and I have described only a small part of what we know) is only one aspect of modern brain research. Much progress is being made in identifying the *chemical* processes that take place in the brain, each cell of which is a tiny chemical processing plant in itself. Because cell chemistry is expected ultimately to hold the answers to cancer and most other diseases, understanding of the intricate chemical processes that go on in human cells is being energetically sought and gained by cancer investigators all over the world.

Cell chemistry research has importantly aided efforts to understand the role of the brain in one of the most elusive processes of the mind: *memory*. Brain cells and nerve cells not only synthesize complex chemicals that control various bodily functions; they produce electro-chemical energy that is the basis for all nerve impulse transmission and that seems to underlie the very functioning of the brain. Just as artificial electrical stimulation can cause the frog's leg to twitch, so a special stimulus can produce a bizarre effect on human memory.

This discovery came about almost by accident many years ago when a Canadian neurosurgeon, Wilder Penfield, was undertaking pioneering studies of electrical stimulation of the brain. Penfield's experiments arose out of his work as a surgeon treating patients with brain dysfunction such as epilepsy. Epileptics are frequently known to have strange thoughts and mental sensations just before the onset of a seizure—dreamy feelings, sharp recollections of fragments of childhood, strong feelings of being somewhere else or of knowing in advance what is about to happen. All of these are well outside of the patient's normal experience and are suggestive of disturbances in his psychical makeup.

Penfield used electrical stimulation of areas of the brain to try to locate and to correct surgically if possible the precise portions of the brain that were involved in seizures. It had been fairly well established in the forties and fifties that epileptic seizures were triggered by spontaneous "showers" of electrical discharges in the temporal lobes of the brain. It was thus a logical step to utilize controlled electrical stimulation of these areas to try to track down the origins of the problem and look for surgical correctives. In these procedures the patient was conscious at all times, able to speak without inhibition, and feeling no pain from the electrical probings.

What Penfield discovered by accident in his work, and reported on in 1958, was an extraordinary capacity of the human brain to remember clearly and in rich detail things that had happened many years earlier in the patients' lives. Not just the traumatic events that psychiatrists and hypnotists can sometimes pry out of us, events that our conscious minds had repressed because we didn't care to think about them. No,

Penfield's needles produced vivid recollections of perfectly trivial, insignificant happenings that none of us would deem worth remembering even if we could recall them. Happenings like this:

A twenty-six-year-old woman with electrodes in her brain hears a neighbor woman she knew as a child calling her little boy; when the electrode is turned off, she hears nothing and recalls no more—no name, no place, nothing. When restimulated, she hears exactly what she had heard at the first stimulation and she redescribes the scene just as she had before. As the stimulation this time continues for a little longer, she begins to sense exactly where she was: "down at the lumber yard ... I've never been around the lumber yard much." Further stimuli let her revisit a scene down by a river which she visited as a child, where she clearly hears the voices of a man and a woman; she lives again a scene late at night at a traveling carnival and hears the voices and the noises that went with it. But after about forty minutes of stimulation in the same area of the brain, the recall becomes weaker and finally disappears. The woman senses and remembers nothing when the electric current is reapplied.

Penfield has reported many similar cases of total recall—patients hearing and singing along with orchestras throughout entire tunes and placing the event years back in their childhood or teens. Restimulation of the area always seems to start the recollection at the same instant that the patient reported on the first stimulation—the orchestra begins each time as it did on the first occasion. And when the electrode is withdrawn, the orchestra stops instantly and cannot further be recalled.

This remarkable capacity for *total* recall cannot now be explained by any of the theories that have been offered by scientists seeking to fathom the mysteries of the brain. Even given the billions of cells and their interconnections that exist in the brain, there is nowhere near enough storage capacity, in the computer sense, to handle this incredible amount of detail. Penfield's work suggests that *everything* that ever happened to us is somewhere stored in our minds. Most of it is not subject to our willful recall, but nevertheless there it is, waiting for us when the right stimulation is presented.

Because brain cells, for all their numbers, can't explain this capability, science today looks to much smaller structures in its search for the mechanism. It looks at the very molecules of brain cells, and centers its attention on the most fascinating one of all. This is the "master" molecule that was created when our father's sperm cell met our mother's egg and formed the first cell that was "us." That molecule has faithfully replicated itself in every one of the billions and billions of cells that comprise each of us. It makes each of us unlike anybody else in the world since the beginning of time.

This individual blueprint molecule, called DNA (deoxyribonucleic acid), indeed "remembers" for us, in that it has been shown to account for the nose that looks like father's, for the haircoloring and eyes that are mother's, for the musical gifts that seem to stem from grandpa, and for myriad other family resemblances of which we are all so aware. We know for a fact that this enormously complex molecule that exists in every cell nucleus accounts for hereditary traits. Is it also the storehouse of our living memories?

Maybe it is, maybe it isn't, says science. All we're sure of is that the DNA molecule, and its cousin RNA (ribonucleic acid), can be shown to affect our memory processes when we deliberately alter the molecules or interfere with their normal supply or functioning. We learned a few years ago, for instance, that we can train a simple form of worm, when stimulated either by light or by an electric shock, to move his head in particular directions. If we then cut him in half, this particular kind of worm will grow a new head, and the new worm with the new head will exhibit the same training (in a statistically satisfactory sense) as the old, whole, trained worm. His "memory" is apparently stored in his tail as well as his head.

We further know that if we grind up the poor worm and feed him to another, untrained worm, some training is passed on to the new worm. (This is precisely what the cannibals of old contended as they selected particularly valiant victims for supper.) It has been established that DNA and RNA are involved in this memory transfer, at least to the extent that the transfer will not take place if the molecules are absent or altered in particular ways.

But all we in fact know today is that these marvelous molecules play *some* role in memory. We are not sure what the role is, nor do we know how it is played. Most importantly, we are obliged to say that, whatever role that might turn out to be, it can be only a part—and perhaps a very small part—of the total process that we call memory. One of the reasons why we must say that, is that, though brain cells do not die and get replaced as do other cells in the body, the very atoms that make up the cells are continuously being replaced by new atoms. The old ones move on, as they finish their roles in the unceasing chemical change in the cell. Our brain matter is continuously changing, though the structures and pathways remain the same. Yet memory—detailed, intricate, living—persists throughout our years, unchanging except for the annoying fact that as we grow older we seem a little less able to remember whether we've told that story before or to attach a name to a face that turns up from the past. Yet, strangely, as we enter our late years, we can relive with what seems to be increasing clarity events that took place decades ago. Science does not know why.

Though there are mountains more of knowledge about the mind and the brain, more than my own or anybody else's can possibly hold, I found not so much as a hillock more than I have reported about the basic mystery of thought and memory, nothing that explains how they really work. And just as there is no physiological knowledge today that can account for memory, there is none that accounts for psychic phenomena. I could not find even a suggestion that the future of brain research will hold the answer to that one. If we are honest with ourselves, and particularly if we fancy ourselves scientifically inclined, there's no basis on which we can presently choose to disbelieve in all psychic occurrences simply because science hasn't yet got around to proving that the psychic world is one large hoax.

That's not to say we won't continue to hear pronouncements to the contrary from our friends who are doctors or psychologists or researchers. I found few (two to be exact) of the dozens of such people I talked to who were in any way prepared to look on psychic phenomena as worthy of discussion. Most professionals simply don't believe in them, and if you try to force the argument, you get the feeling you're being looked on as a clinical case yourself.

I have no wish to belittle such people, some of whom have been important contributors to man's knowledge and improvement. They are only doing what the rest of us do all the time—filtering out the things they don't want to hear or have to cope with. I'd feel more kindly about them, though, if they took their mortarboards off when they say things like that. When they talk as scientists and then say very unscientific things, they get us all off-balance. We tend to believe them because of who they are, even though they're talking about things they know little about.

But then, we've seen scientists do that in other fields, too, and they have sometimes led us into trouble when they do. Maybe the key thing to remember is that they are, after all, just people. People who pull their smocks on one arm at a time, just like you and me.

On the encouraging side, there are now a handful of "legitimate" scientific centers in the United States, most of them only a few years old, engaged in the serious study of psychic phenomena. They are seeking to apply scientific method to the spook world we've so long been taught to feel uncomfortable about.

As that work grows, more of us will be able to shed our hang-ups because of what I hope will result from responsible, credible research in this field in America. Institutions as prestigious as the University of Virginia, Stanford Research Institute, the Menninger Foundation, and Maimonides Medical Center in New York, are already investigating matters as diverse as altered consciousness, out-of-the-body experiences, and life after death.

Perhaps the best thing for all of us, while we wait for better understanding, is to wait with an open mind.

Chapter 9

The Turning Point in Science

What you have read about our current state of scientific knowledge of mind and brain can scarcely be called comprehensive. It's pretty much bare bones, but I think the main bones are all there. I've left nothing out that might explain psychical phenomena.

At least one thing is clear. We cannot bury our doubts about psychic happenings beneath that arcane word "subconscious." The long list of paranormal phenomena is still there, and must be dealt with.

I'm not going to take each of them in turn and cite examples to make you ooh and ah over these weird manifestations of the supernatural. There are plenty of books that will do that for you, most of them to the point of anesthesia. This book isn't intended to be an anthology of the occult. It tries merely to track one man's passage from nonbelief to belief.

Looking back, I now know that my own turning point—once I had ruled out "the subconscious" as a handy explanation for everything—came in reading and rereading accounts of the exceedingly few scientific investigations of paranormal phenomena attempted by the time I began this search. I say rereading because that's exactly what I found I had to do in order to grasp the significance of these investigations. They were largely ignored by the scientific world twenty or thirty years ago, and they dealt with only a tiny portion of the list of things supernatural. But in that portion I began to find some of the proof I was looking for, and the rest of the slow building of some belief followed.

The earliest American work in parapsychology was done by Dr. Rhine at Duke University beginning in the late 1920's. Rhine is a botanist turned psychologist, one who was dissatisfied with the basic premise that all of man's awareness of himself and of his surroundings is obtained through the known senses of sight, touch, hearing, taste, and smell. He was unwilling to deny, simply because it had never been measured or explained, the existence of other nonsensory methods of communication and perception. He strongly suspected from his knowledge of behavior that other, unidentified, forces of the mind existed. He set out to establish by credible scientific experiment that these forces were real.

Rhine succeeded. He did it by repeating a simple experiment thousands and thousands of times until he had compiled some impressive statistics that showed a clear ability on the part of *some* human beings to transmit their thoughts to others telepathically. His experiments were based on a card-guessing game, using special cards with simple and distinctive shapes printed on them. The "sender" turned the shuffled deck, card by card, while the "receiver," placed some distance (sometimes miles) away, recorded his impression of the image on each card as the sender concentrated on it. Probability theory can predict what the mere guess or "chance" score will be in such an experiment; the proof of telepathy that Rhine was seeking had to be found in scores that far exceeded the chance level.

He succeeded in startling fashion, but only with some of his subjects. He found some whose correct guesses were so far above what chance would explain that the mathematical odds against the scores being correctly ascribed to chance were not just a million to one, but as high as 1-with-35 zeros after it.

Rhine's work for many years caused great controversy in scientific circles, even leading to intense argument by mathematicians as to whether probability theory (on which all other science leans, as we've noted) could appropriately be used in experiments like this. Rhine's experimental techniques were exquisitely probed and criticized. Some shortcomings of his early methods were pointed out, and for a long time these served to discredit his work. But even though they were corrected and his later work finally came to be viewed as impeccable, without any apparent chance of conscious or unconscious fraud, there was great unwillingness on the part of most classical scientists to acknowledge his findings or even to keep abreast of his work. Such inertia delayed for years the acceptance of extrasensory perception (ESP—Rhine's term for telepathy and related phenomenon) as a legitimate field of scientific inquiry.

Not all of the argument about Rhine's ESP work centered on his methods and statistical techniques. There was a respected body of scientists who refused to accept his findings because the results were so highly variable from subject to subject. Even the *same* subject's performance varied in repeat experiments.

Most of Rhine's subjects scored merely at the level of chance. Relatively few scored at even modest odds of a few hundred to one. Only very rarely did he find people who could score in the billion-to-one range, and they were not consistent. The absence of predictable repeatability of the phenomenon made it easy to reject Rhine's work out of hand, because of that unwritten law of science that says that nothing is proved until it can be demonstrated at will, *ad infinitum,* by any investigator making the same experiment. Rhine's work was not *an* experiment. It was thousands of tests, on hundreds of people, all designed either to prove or deny the existence of an elusive, undependable, unpredictable faculty that he suspected lay in the mind of man. *Occasional* proof he did find, and though some scientists even today may refuse to view his findings as valid because of the erratic scores, most students of the field now accept ESP as an established fact.

As long ago as 1955, in a symposium on ESP hosted by the Ciba Foundation (a research foundation created by the Swiss pharmaceutical firm), a courageous American biophysicist from the University of Pittsburgh, Dr. R. A. McConnell, had this to say: "It is my conviction that anyone who is familiar with the striking results obtained in the better ESP experiments, and who also knows how dependably binomial [probability] theory has proved itself in the orthodox branches of science, will unhesitatingly reject the idea that there is a feasible counter-explanation to extra-sensory perception." That, in lay language, says: you'd better believe.

And I do. Anyone can. It is an established fact, now beyond denying, that *sometimes, some* human beings can communicate with each other by mind alone. Not just images on cards, but far more complex images and sensations. Human beings can receive telepathic images not only from senders near them but at distances of thousands of miles. Of course, the further one gets from simple card games, the more difficult it becomes to conduct convincing laboratory experiments. When one experiments with the transmission of abstract thought, it becomes much harder to know what the exact thoughts of the sender are and how well they correspond with the impressions picked up by the receiver. Nevertheless, a very large amount of serious, careful experimentation has gone on in these more sophisticated areas in recent years and the evidence seems to be gathering that this remarkable capacity is in no way confined merely to guessing card images in another's mind. It has even been shown that ESP is not limited to the communication of presently existing images or facts. *ESP can tap a small slice of the future.*

This incredible fact came out almost by chance from examination of some ESP experiment results conducted by a British investigator, Dr. S. G. Soal, in the late thirties. He was engaged in research paralleling that of Rhine's. In reviewing some disappointing results of card-guessing from a subject whom he knew to be highly gifted with an ESP faculty, Soal was startled to discover that there was a high percentage of hits shown when he matched the receiver's results not with the card the sender was viewing at the instant, but with the next card waiting to be turned! This led to a number of experiments which were constructed to rule out any foreknowledge of the card sequence on the part of the sender. The results were the same—correct guessing of the next card, with better than a billion-to-one odds against chance.

This happened with only two of the hundreds of subjects Soal employed in his work at that time, and the reproducibility of their scores was at an even lower level than it was with straight ESP tests not involving precognition. Yet the rigor of the experiments seems not to have been effectively challenged; the results are there for all to see.

Soal's work did not necessarily establish the fact of *precognition* (knowledge of future events) in the way that the ESP experiments proved that ESP exists. All it did was show that, within a randomly arranged pack of cards, it was possible for some human beings to predict the next card that would be turned. It did not prove that man's mind could predict events in future time, because the cards did of course exist in a given order in present time.

The convincing laboratory work on precognition didn't emerge until many years later, and it was done by Dr. Rhine's successor at Duke University, Dr. Helmut Schmidt. Schmidt is a physicist who was for a number of years affiliated with the Boeing Scientific Research Laboratories. He brought to Duke the disciplines and tools of modern physics to aid in the exploration of the paranormal. In his tests for precognition, he sought to rule out not just possible foreknowledge but the·very *existence* of a forthcoming event.

He did that by employing the randomness and unpredictability of the decay of radioactive materials, using the radioactive emissions of a strontium-90 source to cause a set of four colored lamps to light in random sequence. The subject was asked to predict which lamp would light next by pushing an appropriate "guess" button. The guesses were scored in essentially the same manner as in other ESP experiments.

The results were of the same order as all of the rest. Some subjects scored as high as 2,000-million-to-one odds against chance. Schmidt's work seems to have carried some added weight with scientific skeptics, possibly because more "scientific" gear was employed in the experiments. In any event, the ability of the human mind to predict a near-term event which had not yet happened has been demonstrated without room for doubt.

For me, the work that Rhine, Soal, and other more recent investigators have done proved many times to be the key to a more open review of the reports and descriptions of supernatural phenomena that I had read on my first trip through this mysterious other world. The ESP work was for me exciting, not mystifying. I enjoyed reading the arguments that boiled up around the ESP work, and learning of the painstaking precautions that the investigators took to rule out fraud or deception.

Though there's nothing particularly exciting in the cards themselves or in the statistical procedures used, the effect on me of reading and rereading the experimental details was one of exhilaration: here was careful, patient, scientific investigation breaking out wholly new ground, opening up for all of us to see a capacity of the mind that only the mystically inclined could have believed in heretofore.

The fact that card-reading was of no practical use, and that only a small portion of human beings scored well bothered me not at all. The exciting thing was to discover that a mysterious and unknown faculty of the mind had been shown without question to exist. That knowledge makes it much easier to examine other kinds of phenomena with a mind less skeptical and tentative than it tends to be on opening the first of the gee-whiz books.

Not that I found myself instantly and totally converted. I hadn't bought the whole crazy store just because I had bought one package. But I did find myself paying more attention to things around me, to coincidences that I would earlier have brushed aside, to reports of odd happenings by my friends. In short, over the years I gradually became an interested, involved observer rather than a library dilettante whose only knowledge came from books.

Looking back, I believe it was this change from passive reader to active observer that *finally* made me able to approach unhesitatingly more of the strange and still unknown forces that are said to affect our lives and our world. That change also, I am sure, conditioned me for a particular experience I will relate later, one that convinced me I was absolutely on the right track and should stay with it.

But long before that incident happened, I began trying not to ignore anything, not to discount instantly any feelings or hunches I might have, and not to use the word "preposterous" so much. In short, I began to be more aware, and in that increasing awareness I saw my own eyes opening a bit. I began to put behind me that last obstacle to belief: the absence of personal experience. And thus did I make myself finally able to learn. I think I should trace a little of that process for you.

Chapter 10

Dowsing, for Instance

Let me give you an example or two of how one thing can lead to another when the mental impediments are eased. I live in New England, and one cannot live there for long and be unaware of the phenomenon called dowsing, or divining—finding water or mineral deposits by traversing the ground holding a forked stick or some other implement. The stick is supposed to bend down when positioned over an underground stream.

Kenneth Roberts was hooked on dowsing and wrote excitingly about it. The local newspapers can be counted on to have some report or article about it at least once a year in these parts. Friends who live in the country near Boston tell convincing stories about it. But most of us around here, in spite of these frequent reminders, still believe there must be a more plausible explanation for dowsing than the presence of unknown psychic forces. Most people either don't believe the reports, or if they do accept the fact that a stick seems to wiggle in a dowser's hands, chalk it up to his subconscious mind (obviously, he's hypnotized himself). The water he finds is ascribed either to luck or to foreknowledge of the underground stream patterns. Those were exactly my views for years.

But I have this friend Bill who some years ago—somewhere midstream in my own God-search—bought himself a summer place in the hills of New Hampshire. He needed a well, and planned to do most of the work himself. (He's an engineer, and just as querulous and stubborn as I used to be about super-natural phenomena.) He bought the gear he needed for the well at a village store, and as he was leaving, the storekeeper asked him who was going to dowse the site. Bill knew enough about New Hampshire types to recognize that the question was not a wisecrack, but a genuine effort to be helpful. Not wanting to start off on the wrong foot with the locals, he asked the man to suggest one.

A day later a dowser showed up. Bill padded along as the dowser walked the property, stick in hand, and watched with a knowing grin when the end of the stick would dip down as they criss-crossed the hills. Finally the dowser said, "Dig here—about eight feet," and marked the spot. Bill paid him the ten-dollar fee, viewing the investment as quite reasonable purely from the public relations standpoint. But he also thought he might have some fun with the dowser by removing the marker and repeat-ing the trip. Bill expected to show in a friendly way that all this hocus-pocus was just that, when a drilling spot different from the first one was specified, as Bill was sure it would be. The dowser had obviously met types like Bill before. He surprised Bill by not only readily agreeing to repeat the exercise but by inviting Bill to hold the stick and see for himself.

Bill did just that, and wound up shaking his head in disbelief. Not only did he feel strange tuggings from time to time, but he felt a most pronounced tug at precisely the spot the dowser had earlier marked. Bill surmised, as do most people who experience this for the first time, that the dowser was probably exerting some hypnotic effect and was causing Bill's muscles to react without Bill's conscious control. He dismissed the dowser, chuckled nervously over the episode with his wife, and prepared to start digging—at the dowser's spot, of course.

An hour or so later, Bill's brother showed up. He is an accountant, blessed with the same skeptical genes as Bill, and the two of them decided to repeat the experiment without the dowser present. They cut a forked stick, just as the dowser had and from the same tree, and proceeded to walk the property. You can guess what happened. The results were the same. They even played a game of it—one of them walking the terrain by himself and marking the tug points with concealed stones, the other following in a separate trip, marking the sites of his own tugs. They then compared the markers and found rather good coincidence of the two separately marked paths. In this way they charted an entire hillside, and could see, when they were finished, what would appear to be the courses of underground streams.

Bill did find his water, right where the dowser said. Bill and his brother are not hypnotists, and they are now believers—in dowsing. Beyond that they seemed not to care to go. For me, though, coming as it did after I had done some studies on the mind and had learned of the ESP experiments, this experience of Bill's was every bit as good as if it had been a personal one of my own. I knew Bill so well and was so like him in my engineer's view of the world that I could accept without question his strange account. And I could then read with more understanding the numerous accounts of this phenomenon scattered throughout the books on the supernatural.

Dowsing, divining, radiesthesia (the terms all describe the same thing) is as old as mankind. References to it appear in the most ancient literature. The strange power has been used for much more than just the discovery of water, though this is what we hear most about today. Radiesthesia has been widely used for mineral detection—the tin mines of Cornwall are said to be an example. It is used for sexing eggs, and by some for sexing unborn children. Many practitioners claim to have solved crimes by locating bodies, weapons, and even hidden murderers.

Some diviners claim that they can work from maps or drawings and dowse for water, minerals, or objects great distances away. There are medical practitioners who use it to diagnose disease. Indeed, there is scarcely an area of the supernatural (or the superstitious) that has not been explored with the forked stick, or the gold ring on a string, or with keys, or knitting needles, or whatever other implement can be dangled or suspended by human hands. And because of its long history and wide application, dowsing, like tealeaf reading and crystal-ball gazing has always been open to charges of fraud, deception, and wild exaggeration.

Dowsing is like everything else in these weird fields. You have to learn to suspect fraud at all times, but not to throw out all of the really credible reports just because widespread deception is known to take place. There are two good reasons why all supernatural phenomena have been marked by fraud since the beginning of time.

One is the inherent greed and gullibility of man. As long as some of us are willing to pay money for mystical readings and supernatural experiences, there will be those who will oblige us, using clever illusions and trickery if they have to. Some of the deception is so ingeniously executed that even expert investigators who have spent their lives in the field are taken in. We've already noted how dedicated Houdini was to the job of unmasking fraud and how well he duplicated supernatural happenings using only his bag of tricks.

But there's another reason why fraud exists and why it is sometimes so hard to detect. The ESP experiments proved time and again that telepathic powers are not dependably present in those that seem to have them. Dr. Rhine noticed not only a wide variation in test results with "gifted" subjects, but a frequent decline in powers over a period of months or years. The effect on a person of discovering that he possesses unusual psychic powers is sometimes a very heady one. People who find these powers within them not infrequently begin to exploit them, either for personal gain or simply to feed their egos. When the powers diminish, as they seem to so often, the possessor is apt to be tempted to make up for them in other ways, and the only other way is by deception.

When the fraud is discovered, we invariably choose to discredit *all* of the demonstrations ever made by that subject, thereby not only losing the valid content of his psychic powers, but driving another nail into the already well-sealed psychic coffin. It's no wonder that most of us are either out-and-out disbelievers or, at best, ambivalent skeptics about things supernatural.

As yet, no Dr. Rhine has emerged on the American science scene to make the study of dowsing his lifework and to provide the stamp of scientific approval to this phenomenon. (If he has, the work is recent enough to have escaped me.)

There have, though, been some highly respected and competent engineers and technical people who have accepted the reality of dowsing simply from their own observations and experience. William Greenawalt, one of America's leading mining and metallurgical engineers in the twenties, published his own assessment of the phenomenon in *Engineering and Mining Journal* in 1928. After relating some of his own experiences with dowsing, he terms it "purely a psychical phenomenon," and likens it to table-tipping and automatic writing. "Few people who have scientifically investigated these common phenomena doubt their reality. . . . Sometimes results are obtained bordering on the miraculous, then again, at other times, the results are entirely negative, apparently without cause."

I've read reports that engineers from our First and Third Marine Divisions did use dowsing rods to detect booby traps and tunnels in Vietnam, but the military people have been as uncommunicative about this as they have about UFO's.

The Russians, though, look on things paranormal as legitimate fields of scientific inquiry, and have for some time. Whereas most of American science, when it has paid any attention at all to the supernatural, has spent its time simply trying to prove or disprove that these things exist, the Russians for years seem to have accepted their reality and pressed ahead with research aimed at explaining them and utilizing them.

Thus, as long ago as 1944, in the prestigious *Soviet Journal of Electricity,* an article was published detailing many years of investigation into radiesthesia and suggesting strongly that the phenomenon did indeed exist. The article caused considerable debate in Russian scientific circles and led to the creation of several government-sponsored commissions to investigate further. The commissions' findings were apparently convincing. They were able to establish the conditions under which the response was most pronounced—the types of woods best used for the sticks, the effect of age on the wood, the effect of screening the dowser with rubber or steel or lead plates (no effect whatsoever), the differences between men and women in their dowsing performance. Today dowsing research is carried on under a new name calculated to sanitize its spooky past—"Biophysical Effects Method." In Russia, dowsing is for real.

It is so real, in fact, that the Russians claim to have been actively using the phenomenon to map mineral deposits throughout the Soviet Union. They say they have long since progressed from the wooden stick and the ambling operator, and now use a special instrument that not only gives the location of the deposit but provides a measure of its size, quality, and depth. The instrument's behavior is automatically recorded in order to make analysis simpler, and it is mounted in a vehicle that can cover terrain at speeds up to forty or fifty miles an hour.

Yet, in spite of this increased sophistication, the Russians apparently still must rely on human operators to produce the effect, and they find wide variability in operator sensitivity. Apparently, almost anyone can at some time and under some conditions produce results, but some operators have been found to have sensitivity many times that of the average. The least sensitive are those who are strongly skeptical about the phenomenon, and in one Russian test it was shown that a sufficiently large group of highly skeptical people surrounding a sensitive dowser could almost extinguish the forces he felt. They also discovered that, though metallic or plastic shielding has no effect, the wearing of leather gloves by the operator seems to stop the effect completely.

What kind of energy is this that can penetrate rock, earth, lead, and steel but can't get through a piece of leather? American and Soviet scientists have established that it is not an energy of any kind we have identified before and know how to measure. There are theories and speculations as to what it is, but that's all they are for now. There is sure knowledge that whatever the force is, it is affected by large electromagnetic fields, by the position of the sun in the sky, by lightning storms, by other natural phenomena, *and* by our mental and emotional states, as well.

It is a force which some investigators say can now be sensed by highly specialized equipment developed to measure weak force-fields. But it does not appear to behave in accordance with the laws we know govern electromagnetic radiation. It is *not* radio energy, or magnetic energy, or atomic energy, or any other sort of energy that we know and use. But is energy, nevertheless. We'll take another look at it a little further on.

Before we do, though, this seems like a good time to deal with one of the puzzling aspects of psychic phenomena—the wide variation among human beings in the extent to which they possess psychic powers, and the unpredictability of psychic manifestations even in those who have clearly demonstrated them.

Chapter 11

Why We Don't All Have ESP

How come I don't seem to have telepathic and other psychic powers? Why do most of the people I know seem not to have them? For a long time, I was hung up on this question. I know it interfered with my intentions to study the field open-mindedly. But I eventually learned enough and was able to surmise enough about the nature of psychic phenomena to satisfy myself that there are good reasons why we are not all psychic.

For me, the most important clue as to ESP variability is found in observing animal and insect behavior. I had been fascinated, for instance, by the behavior of ants, and I'd spent too much idle time watching these tiny, almost brainless creatures work together in ways that defy explanation. They build, they transport, they march in file, they fight—all with an ant-to-ant coordination that is unbelievably precise and controlled. A single ant, removed from the colony, seems purposeless and indeed brainless. But put him with his brothers and it almost seems as though his brain becomes useful as soon as it is part of a collective "brain" made up of all of the members of the colony.

Together, the ants in a colony seem able to *plan* what they are going to do, even to "think" about how to build tunnels or other structures, store food, move from place to place en masse, feed the queen, store the eggs and so on. Entomologists ascribe these things to "instinct," but that's merely a label that doesn't explain anything. There could be a much simpler explanation: The ants are in communication with each other.

There's no energy transfer taking place that we can detect—no sound waves, no measurable electromagnetic radiation. We're left with only two ways to explain "instinct." Either there is some kind of telecommunication taking place, or what the ants do has been preprogrammed into their DNA (yes, they have it too), and this preprogrammed ant-DNA shows each of the ants how to work together to build today's tunnel and fight tomorrow's war. The DNA explanation has got to look pretty far-fetched these days, when we've established beyond doubt that man himself possesses ESP. The easiest and I think the only convincing explanation of ant behavior is *ant*-ESP.

The animal world is so full of clear instances of ESP communication that we have only to look around us to see it at work. Go snorkeling in Caribbean waters and watch huge schools of tiny, shimmering fish swim toward you—and then suddenly dart away, each fish turning sharply at precisely the same instant and in exactly the same direction. It's not a matter of the lead fish executing a slow turn to carry his followers away from danger. *The whole school turns instantly,* following no single leader—just the fish who now happens to be on the edge of the school. Preprogrammed "instinct"? Or ESP?

Have you ever had a dog that occasionally amazed you by seeming to anticipate what you were about to do? I had one that used to start quivering a full day before we planned to drop her at the kennel before going on a trip. Either she understood our mumbled English pretty well, or she was picking up vibes she didn't like the sound of.

Dogs are well known to be capable of doing strange things—like tracking their masters over hundreds of miles of unfamiliar terrain when they become separated. Birds do the same kind of thing in their migrations, and science has spent enormous amounts of research time trying to arrive at a non-ESP explanation of how birds accomplish their navigation and homing. Undoubtedly, birds use the sun, the stars, and possibly the earth's magnetic fields to guide them over long distances. But how do we explain the fact that certain kinds of birds are known to return to the very same *nest* after their yearly migration? And the further fact that offspring of such birds, born during the winter migration period, will fly in the spring to the distant nest of their parents even though the parents have been restrained and do not accompany them? I can find only one answer—ESP.

I could go on for many pages describing instances of what surely must be ESP in animals, but I hope I've made the point. If I haven't, I invite you to think of your own collection of instances of mysterious animal behavior and to try to explain them without using the word "instinct." Our Russian friends, by the way, have accepted animal ESP long since, and have already successfully demonstrated telepathic communication, not just between animals but between the mind of a man and the mind of a dog.

What does animal ESP have to do with man's ESP, and how does it explain the rarity and undependability of ESP in human beings? I think it is largely a matter of man having developed another—and *perhaps* better—way to communicate. Man left his telepathy behind him when he climbed down from the trees. The ESP we see today, I believe, is but the vestigial trace of that earlier, standard form of communication.

If Darwin was right, at some far distant time in the past, man *was* an animal, and as an animal he communicated just as animals do today—telepathically. And if Darwin was right, somewhere along the way, for reasons we may never know, man learned how to arrange his grunts and snorts in a fashion that conveyed meaning to others, and found the new faculty useful enough to continue to perfect it over the millions of years that followed.

Just what the faculty of speech provided to man that was

superior to ESP is a matter of conjecture. According to evolu-
tionary theory, any special trait or characteristic, such as
speech, must provide enhanced survival power to the species if it
is to persist. An obvious connection suggests itself: Man is the
only creature possessing speech, as far as we know. Man is also
the only creature we believe to be capable of abstract thought,
though this may turn out to be only another example of man's
enormous vanity. Those ants seem to get things together pretty
well from time to time, and there's some feeling around that
whales know a lot more than they're telling us.

But let's admit that man seems to be the most outstanding of
all the earth's creatures in his ability to think. Is the power of
speech the *cause* of that ability, or merely one result of it? Is
speech really better than ESP when it comes to abstract
thinking, and is that why speech evolved eons ago?

Those questions have been argued both ways. But I'm inclined to feel that, for pure *thinking,* speech is more of a
hindrance than a help. True, when we engage in some kinds of
conscious, abstract thinking, such as with problems in logic and
mathematics, we cannot avoid thinking through our solutions in
words. There's no other way our minds can keep track of the
flow of logic or ideas. After all, many inputs to the memory
bank we draw on are in word form, and that's the way they
come out.

But some of our most insightful thinking, some of our real
leaps forward in understanding, seem to come in a "flash" of
ideation, in a problem-solution that is presented *whole,* in
complete, satisfying form. First comes the flash, and then we
struggle to put that flash into words, words that we pour out as
fast as we can while the "whole" idea is still fresh in our minds.
Many of the giant steps of human intellect have come in just
this way. Though you and I may never make a contribution on
the scale of a Copernicus or an Einstein, we have all had our
moments of flash lucidity. Speech does not beget them. Indeed,
it slows them down, and sometimes we lose them in our rush to
translate. So I do not attribute to speech the fact that man
seems higher than the animals in abstract cerebration.

What *does* speech do for us, then, that made it evolve as a distinctly human faculty? I'm sure the linguists can cite advantages that man derives from speech. But I can identify only one that I would deem of sufficient import to have altered the course of evolution. I can think of only one thing of which speech makes man capable that ESP does not. And that one thing is *deceit*.

Now, that may seem like a strange "power" to ascribe to man because of his faculty of speech. But if we stop to think about it, man's ability to shield his thoughts from others, to communicate in words something other than what his true thoughts and feelings are, accounts for a good part of man's mastery over his fellow man and all that stems from that. His leaders are selected not because of their physical strength, as with animal packs, but because of their powers to persuade, to cajole people to accept untruths as true—as we keep being reminded by our governments and other forms of human organization.

I find it quite possible to believe that man's evolution as a superior being on earth can be traced in important measure to his ability to organize himself into groups and societies of great combined powers. The source of this ability lies, very importantly, in the power to convey *not* the complete, candid, honest thoughts that are in our minds, but something that will serve our interests better at the moment.

Darwin could have been wrong, of course. We still haven't found that "missing link" between man and ape that titillated our imaginations in the twenties and thirties as people sought to grasp the implications of what the evolutionists were trying to tell us. We still cannot rule out the possibility that man's origins came not wholly from his anthropoid animal cousins but from an entirely different, mystical, unimaginable source. But, for examining this particular problem, it makes little difference how man came here. The fact is that he either came with or developed for himself the power of speech, and once he had learned how to speak and was determined to depend on speech for his communication, there was no room for ESP.

Think, for a minute, what it would be like to live in a world in which every thought we held could be immediately and readily read by others. By our spouses, for instance. Or our bosses and business associates. Or the pretty girl I admire on the beach. Or her strapping boy friend. There is no relationship we can think of that would not be instantly destroyed or totally altered if each of us could read the other's mind at will.

Since we could not live under conditions that made our every thought open to anyone who would read it, the telepathic faculties that undoubtedly reside in each of us have been submerged, repressed. Our conscious minds do this to us, just as they do with a vast variety of stimuli that reach us during our waking hours. Thus these powers lie dormant and largely unused in all but a few of us.

Studies have shown that ESP faculties tend to be more evident in younger people and in women than in older people and in men. Some of the most gifted psychics have been children and young women. Research has also shown that the least likely people to exhibit ESP are those with quite orderly, rational (left-brain) minds, particularly minds that have been highly educated. Mental attitudes have been shown to play a large part in submerging ESP—the skeptic seems to shut down his ESP faculties merely by being skeptical, as the Russian experiments in dowsing revealed. Now that we have learned how to demonstrate ESP and observe it under various conditions, investigators have been able to show that it is affected by a host of external factors—sunspots and their accompanying magnetic storms, planetary positions, phases of the moon, magnetic aberrations in the earth, and even atmospheric changes.

I think we have to accept without question now the theory that ESP (and undoubtedly other psychic powers) is a latent, usually submerged faculty that is in all of us, one which is awesomely strange in itself and which is affected in ways we don't understand by other forces and factors which are equally strange. ESP can be *expected* to be an elusive, unpredictable phenomenon, because if it were anything else, man could not function in the society he has built for himself over the millions of years of his existence.

But whether we choose to call ourselves psychic or not, there isn't a one of us who has not had a number of experiences which, when reviewed carefully, can best be explained in paranormal terms. The trouble is that they happen so sporadically and are usually of such triviality that we tend to call them mere coincidences and promptly proceed to forget them.

One of the most common is a vague sense of having previously experienced an event or conversation or scene one is presently involved in, a fleeting knowledge of what will happen next.

This strange feeling is called *déjà vu* (seen before) and it's a well documented phenomenon that is exceedingly commonplace. I've had it happen to me several times, and I would guess you have experienced it too. Unfortunately, when it happens, we never seem to take the opportunity to solidify the experience by stating aloud what we are sure will happen next or be said next. We never write our impressions down or invite others to hear us make our little predictions. If we did, we would quite possibly be surprised at how accurately we can describe what is about to happen in the next moment. Indeed, the scene unfolds uncannily just as we felt it would. But it all happens so fast that we can't sort out the premonition from the fact. We wind up saying, "I had this funny feeling . . ." and let it go at that.

However, there have been instances in which *déjà vu* has indeed been confirmed in the presence of credible witnesses. Most of them involve accurate prior descriptions of scenes being visited for the first time—strange houses, unexplored rooms, old buildings new to the observer. In this regard, *déjà vu* resembles somewhat the precognitive card-guessing experiments performed by Dr. Soal. Neither phenomenon clearly demonstrates an ability to predict all future events, but they both show a paranormal capacity for obtaining a mental image that anticipates an existing fact.

Psychology has offered all sorts of explanations for *déjà vu,* including dream recollection, time-sense aberration and other mechanisms which are equally unsatisfying in view of the work in precognition. My own *déjà vu* incidents are becoming few and far between lately (I am indeed getting older) and I've found no recent opportunity to press the experience and document it more fully. Perhaps you're younger and will want to try when next this strange feeling comes over you.

I'm going to skip past a number of similar "coincidences" that happen to all of us, not that they are not of significance (they are) but because they're much more interesting when they happen to you, not to me. Things like a wife and husband uttering the same words at the same instant, or having a pretty good hunch when the phone rings just who will be on the other end, or dreaming a dream that seems later on to have pictured a real happening. We usually brush these off without a second thought, but I can assure you that in some cases they are valid instances of ESP at work.

Keep in mind what the psychologists tell us about our "filtering" processes. There is very good indication that our receptivity to thoughts, ideas, and other stimuli is increased or reduced by our conscious desires to be affected or not by them. Most of us don't believe in the existence of the baffling psychic, supernatural world I have been poking at. We filter out experiences which might bring us closer to it, for any number of reasons. Thus is the circle completed: we're not psychic because we are sure we are not psychic.

Right now, I'm going to identify a few other kinds of strange psychic powers, including a couple that held particular interest and significance for me because of close association with the people or the events involved—and because my eyes were opening.

Chapter 12

Pictures and the Mind

During the late fifties, when I was working at Polaroid, there was brought to my attention a man who was using one of our cameras to produce what he called "thought" photographs. The man's name was Ted Serios, a forty-year-old former bellhop who had discovered this strange power sometime back while amusing himself with hypnotism at a party. What Serios did was remarkable indeed. He would stare into the lens of a Polaroid camera held a few inches away, his face contorted and flushed, breathing heavily and obviously under great strain. Then at an instant of his choosing, he would click the shutter. Ten seconds later, when the picture had been developed, there would usually be an image on it, sometimes so indistinct that the picture had no meaning, but frequently clear enough to show what were without question buildings, landscapes, statues or other scenes.

My company got into the act because investigators who were studying Serios needed film and cameras which could be guaranteed fresh and unaltered, and Polaroid supplied them. The results were the same. Somehow this man was using a strange energy to expose a photographic emulsion through a lens that was not in any way in focus for the distances involved and the scenes produced. Yet he was producing pictures that at times were quite sharp and of perfectly adequate contrast and clarity. We knew that this was scientifically impossible, that it defied all known laws of optics and light-energy. But the pictures were there nevertheless.

Over a period of time, Ted Serios was put through as complete a battery of tests as some good physicists and optical scientists could devise. He was stripped naked and examined carefully over each inch of his body. He was placed in completely light-tight rooms, and even in rooms with electrical and magnetic shielding. He was separated from the camera by leaded glass. He was moved over 60 feet away from the camera. He was even blindfolded and made to perform in a completely darkened room.

The results were pretty much the same: pictures that were unmistakably pictures, along with a number of all-blacks, all-whites, and some fuzzy-gray in-betweens. Some of the pictures were of places Serios had never been and could not identify, but which were later shown to be actual places somewhere in the world. One picture was a view of the U. S. Capitol building which could only have been taken from a plane flying at a slight elevation above the building. But it obviously hadn't come from an airborne camera. It seems to have come from Ted Serios' mind. So had pictures of Lincoln and King Tut's burial mask and the Taj Mahal.

Though Serios is perhaps the most recent and certainly the most dramatic demonstrator of this power, he is not the only person ever known to possess it. I learned of instances of thought photography reported years ago in England, in France, and in Japan. One experiment of note was performed in 1932 in the photographic laboratories of the *Los Angeles Times*. Three respected scientists from the area witnessed the experiment, in which nine people were placed in a darkened room and given a strip of photographic paper cut from a sheet taken out of a fresh package. The rest of the sheets were placed about the room to serve as controls. Each participant was asked to hold the strip to his forehead for three minutes while concentrating on some object of his selection. The strips were then collected and developed in freshly mixed solutions, and while they were being developed along with the control sheets, each of those present described the object he had concentrated on. When development was complete, there were images of recognizable objects on seven of the strips—statues, dogs, crosses, etc.—all corresponding to the descriptions given. Two were blank, as were all the control sheets.

There is no explanation for this phenomenon; it employs an energy form we know nothing about. Photographic emulsions work because the energy of a *single* photon of light—the smallest unit of energy known to science—strikes a grain of silver halide compound, gives up its tiny bit of energy when it hits, and thereby makes that particular grain of compound react differently to the developing agent than its neighbor that wasn't hit by a photon. Silver compounds can also be rendered developable by the application of much larger forces, such as high heat or physical impact, but for photographic purposes only the extremely weak forces of the photons that comprise light energy are used.

The energy that Serios and others employed can't be light, can't be heat, and can't be mechanical—these have all been ruled out. It is an energy of the *precise* amount necessary to produce an image without overexposing the film, and it is aimed sharply enough to avoid blurring the result beyond recognition. That's a pretty precise kind of energy, and we have no real idea what it is.

This is a good place to mention one of the continual problems one meets in poking around in the world of the supernormal. There is no demonstration of psychic powers I have ever heard of that doesn't eventually provoke a very convincing put-down from some impressive source or other. Just when the would-be believer has finally turned the corner and is becoming comfortable about the reality of what he has heard and read, some expert deftly pricks the balloon and the old skepticism flows back in as the air rushes out. Most of the balloon busters are traditional scientists, and they're fairly easy to cope with after you've been into these things a little while. But occasionally the questioners come from the ranks of the very investigators who are spending their lives trying to prove that some of these things are for real. These can be harder to deal with.

In the Ted Serios case, one of the most devastating doubters is none other than Louisa Rhine, wife of the good professor from Duke and for many years his close collaborator in the laboratory. At the tail end of a book in which she describes some of the Duke experiments in great detail, she moves into other realms allied to that work, and gives her opinion as to their possible validity. She doesn't think much of Serios, and she bases her doubts almost wholly on one book that was written about him by a Denver psychiatrist. She makes it quite clear that she doesn't like the "popular" style in which the book was written. She has no explanation for Serios' feats other than the suggestion of fraud, and she bases this innuendo on the fact that Serios at times (not always) used a little cardboard cylinder—a "gizmo" he called it—between his face and the camera lens when he made his pictures. He said it helped him focus his mind better, but as time went on he used it less and less. Obviously, the gizmo was inspected closely by the investigators who studied Serios and nothing was found amiss.

But Mrs. Rhine, having apparently read but one book plus an article by two suspicious news photographers, stomped on Serios for using the cardboard tube. She doesn't seem to have probed any further as to what had been learned about it. She even endorsed the theory that the little tube might have had a preprinted slide transparency, a lens, and a light squirreled away in it, and that's where the pictures came from. She may be a good psychologist, but she gets a D-minus in optics and photography if she really believes that.

Yet this is *the* Mrs. Rhine, and her words carry a lot of weight, even when she is just as guilty of unscientific thinking and investigation as were the traditional scientists against whom she rails in parts of her book. The difference is that the traditional scientists were picking on the work that she and her husband had done, and she knew that work was sound. When somebody else pulled something off in a field close to her own, she did just what she criticized them for doing. She viewed the matter unscientifically.

All this only proves once again that scientists are very much like people and that they sometimes abuse the privileges that their stature gives them. As for Ted Serios, you can believe that his pictures were for real if you want to. I do.

Thought photography raised my curiosity about what looked like a "reverse" form of this image-producing energy, one that has for many years been receiving careful scientific attention in Russia. It is eyeless sight—"dermo-optic vision" is the fancier term—and it has been noted many times in many parts of the world. In Russia, serious inquiry was triggered in 1962 by the case of a twenty-two-year-old peasant girl named Rosa Kuleshova who lived a simple life in a small city in the Ural mountains. Some of the members of Rosa's family were blind, and Rosa had learned Braille in order to be able to teach them and other blind persons in the area to use books in Braille. One day she discovered that she could tell colors and read regular printing with her eyes *closed,* merely by moving the second and third fingers of her right hand over the page.

She told her doctor of this strange faculty. He blindfolded her carefully and was amazed as she showed that she could read with her fingers just as fast as she could with her eyes. Her doctor was a neuropathologist and knew enough about neurological processes to recognize that this was a strange capacity indeed. He promptly demonstrated her powers at a regional meeting of psychologists, and it was not long before Rosa had received national notice and attention, including a demonstration made at the Soviet Academy of Science.

The facts about Rosa were simple and indisputable. She could read with her fingers while blindfolded, or while the reading material was enclosed in a thick paper envelope. She could distinguish colors accurately; she could "see" pictures and describe them in detail. Soviet scientists took all of the precautions they could think of to rule out trickery or telepathy and became convinced of the reality of the girl's powers. So convinced, in fact, that large-scale programs followed in Russia to try to determine how widespread this faculty might be, and particularly to see whether it existed in blind persons.

They reported encouraging indications on both scores. In one experiment with eighty graphic arts students, it was reported that about one in six could learn, after only a couple of hours of practice, to sense a color difference just from sensations in their fingertips. Other investigators claimed that certain of their subjects had been able to progress all the way to sightless reading, just as Rosa did. It was shown that the strange faculty persisted even with the material placed under glass or wrapped in foil. It is claimed that eyeless sight has been accomplished with the full palm, not just the fingertips, and at a distance of several inches from the text. The Russians say it has been demonstrated to occur through the skin of almost any part of the body—shoulders, bellies, noses, elbows, toes, and tongues.

The Russian interest stemmed not alone from curiosity about the paranormal, but because the Russians seriously hoped to be able to aid blind people. They have already published descriptions of successful dermo-optical training in blind children. They report something of the same variability in sensitivity that has been noted in ESP testing, leading to the surmise that the two are somehow akin. They have also found that eyeless sight can be taught only when the cause of blindness is in the eyes or optic nerves, not in the optic centers of the brain itself.

In trying to pin down the nature of the energy that accounts for eyeless sight, the Russians have learned that, whatever it is, it is affected by the electrical environment in which the experiment takes place. A charged conductor placed beneath the text improves the perception; electrical "grounding" of the percipient's arm inhibits the effect. In this respect, eyeless sight seems a little different from other paranormal phenomena such as dowsing and ESP. With those, a little fiddling with electricity near the percipient is not reported to produce such a noticeable effect, though we have seen that there are other conditions, such as the presence of strong electromagnetic fields, that do seem to alter ESP and dowsing sensitivity.

However, when I added up everything I had learned of the

Russian experiments, I didn't get that really "convinced" feeling that eyeless sight is a distinct and separate paranormal phenomenon. Though I prefer neat solutions to things, (and it would indeed be very neat to say that eyeless sight is simply the obverse of thought photography), there just may be explanations for it which are closer to the world of known phenomena.

For one thing, much of the Russian work that has been reported was based on perception of masses of color, not of text material. The Soviet subjects "feel" different sensations in their fingers and palms when they hold them over areas of different color. And the "feelings" exist only when the colors are illuminated, not when the room is dark. (ESP works fine in the dark.) It *may* be that some human skin has photoreceptors in it akin to those in the retina and that the energy that is being picked up is that of light photons. There are forms of animal life—certain worms, in particular—that do indeed have photoreceptors in their skins, and maybe some of us human beings have hung on to a few of our own. That possibility does not explain the ability to read text as Rosa did, but I think another explanation may be found—in clairvoyance, which we'll look at shortly.

Maybe we will find in time that eyeless sight is indeed a separate kind of paranormal phenomenon, and if we do, I'll be glad to add it to the others. There's certainly something going on there, and at the very least it adds more evidence to the fact that we don't know nearly all we'd like to about our minds and bodies.

And on that note I think it's time to tell you about my one dramatic experience with an other-world manifestation. It happened in the early sixties, and that's about where the casual chronology of this journey has brought us.

Chapter 13

Someone Was Telling Me Something

In my whole life I have had but one experience that I can certify beyond any doubt to have been a communication with another world, and this came not through my own mind but by relay through another.

It came at a time, some fifteen years ago, when I was beginning to arrive at the inevitable conclusions of my search, and it unquestionably helped those conclusions to solidify into a comfortable and deep-seated belief. But let me tell you what happened.

There lives in a distant city a lady whom I have known for many years through a family connection and for whom I have great affection and respect. She is a psychologist, an educator, a clinical hypnotist, a mother—and, in the confines of her own family, a medium. I had been told of that last fact by her husband, but was asked by him not to discuss it with her because of her desire to keep that power a very subdued part of her life.

I was surprised therefore to receive a phone call from him late one fall, telling me that she had received a message for me: Get your eyes checked. That was all. My eyes weren't bothering me, and I had had a checkup and new eyeglass prescription not too long before, so I did nothing about it and forgot the message completely.

Early the following spring the same message was relayed, with perhaps a little more urgency, and this time I promised myself that I would indeed have my eyes checked. But still I did nothing—things were just too busy. Late that June my wife was hospitalized for a disc operation and I was sitting at home, lonely and distressed, the first night after her surgery. There was another call. Same message, but this time truly urgent. The message, as it was received through the lady's trance, went something like this: "Tell Bob Casselman to get his eyes checked immediately or he will be in serious trouble."

I had read enough and thought enough about the supernatural and the afterlife by that time not to let any doubts or personal or business problems get in my way. The following morning I was in the office of my ophthalmologist. An old friend, he was greatly puzzled by my insistence that he see me then and there. I told him what had happened, and he proceeded without comment to begin to test my eyes—but not with just the usual instruments. He applied an anesthetic to my eyeballs and then placed on each of them in turn a device which measures the internal pressure of the fluid circulating within. As he went back and forth, checking and rechecking, changing the instrument to verify its readings with another, I sensed that something was wrong. Finally he told me that dangerous pressures had built up in both eyeballs, pressures so high that they would cause early blindness if not relieved. Here was a raging case of glaucoma, the silent, painless vision killer that causes most blindness today.

Fortunately, my vision had not yet been appreciably affected and the pressure was readily brought under control with drugs. Much later (and still unexplainedly) the entire problem virtually disappeared. Had the high pressure persisted for a few more months, I would have sustained steadily increasing loss of vision before any symptoms would have been apparent. It would have been too late to preserve normal sight.

I have told you exactly what happened, and all that happened. No one on this earth had the slightest idea that I could be in danger of going blind. Previous routine checkups had shown nothing amiss, and by the time I would finally have gotten around to my next regular exam it would have been too late. But someone out there knew of the problem and was able to get through in probably the only way I could have been contacted—through a medium who really wasn't a practicing medium and who just happened to be a close friend. She's the only medium I have ever known, and the only one who would know how to reach me.

I know where that experience left me, but I can't know where it leaves you. It reads very much like the countless recitals of other-world communication that cram the literature of the spook world. It is possibly just as easy for you to brush this one off as it used to be for me to discount all the others I read in my long journey. I can only assure you that this communication happened, just as I have described it. But it happened to me, not to you, and it can't possibly affect you as it did me.

But there is one thing I do invite you to ponder. One thing I'm pretty sure of is that I would have ignored the communications had I not been pretty far into these things at the time. Indeed, I did dismiss the messages twice over a period of many months. Was it my heightened awareness that had finally made me heed something I would otherwise have paid no attention to? I think so.

More interestingly, is it possible that the message would not have been aimed my way at all if I had been wholly unprepared to receive it or accept it? My bones tell me now that this may be the case. I find inescapable the conclusion that some part of our psychic connecting ability is tied to our mental attitudes, to our state of awareness. Even the mind-scientists hint at that, though they confine their observations to more worldly matters.

So don't be distressed if my tale doesn't remove your own misgivings in a lightning flash. It isn't supposed to. All it may do is tell you what is apt to happen if we make our minds ready.

Chapter 14

Seeing Beyond the Senses

You can't have lived in Boston for the past few years and not know of Peter Hurkos. He was the Dutch psychic that the state's attorney general's office (then under Edward Brooke) finally employed after all efforts to find the Boston Strangler had failed. In the nine months from June, 1962 to March, 1963 thirteen women had been murdered, all of them strangled after being sexually assaulted. The police were baffled, ready to try anything—even a psychic, as long as it was kept out of the papers. It's very hard for policemen and attorneys general to admit publicly to a reliance on spooky practices to solve crimes.

Peter Hurkos went to work on the case and quite promptly identified the slayer, purely through psychic means. The only trouble was that the man he fingered proved to be innocent. In fairness to Hurkos, it should be noted that the real killer, when eventually found, did bear some resemblance to Hurkos' man, and there are some who claim that Hurkos had identified the right man but had been made to look bad by the cops.

Whatever the story, public believability in psychic phenomena was shaken severely in these parts when the story finally came out.

Hurkos brushes off failures simply by observing that he has never claimed 100 percent accuracy was possible; in his experience, 80 percent was all that could be hoped for. In that, he may have been on the mark, judging from reports I came across about similar missions he performed for other police departments in the country. These are matters of public record. Hurkos has indeed solved a number of crimes by psychic means, and has given many other indications of an ability to see what the rest of us cannot see. Peter Hurkos is a clairvoyant.

Clairvoyance: "seeing" events or objects or scenes extrasensorily; a form of ESP, like telepathy, except that what is perceived does not appear to come from another mind. The clairvoyant "sees" a happening that exists in real time, but the information reaches him directly from the happening—not by transference from another human mind.

I should guess that all of us have been made aware of clairvoyance in one form or another, whether it be from stories of the use of psychics by police, or reports of dreams that revealed a distant death or disaster at the very time it took place, or by watching a mind reader tell us what the dates are on the pennies in our pockets. As you might expect, though there have been some well-authenticated instances of clairvoyance, there are many, many more cases in which deception or foreknowledge were shown to have accounted for these "visions." We're all allowed to have our doubts about clairvoyance.

Nevertheless, as with telepathy, laboratory proof of the existence of clairvoyance has been obtained. The earliest convincing experiments were performed by Dr. J. B. Rhine, using techniques almost identical to those used in his original telepathic ESP experiments. To demonstrate clairvoyance, Rhine simply removed the "sender" from the circuit and required his card guessers to concentrate on cards that were placed in sealed envelopes, shuffled, and then turned one by one. Nobody saw the cards. But the test scores he obtained showed the same pattern of occasional astronomically high odds for correct guesses versus chance, and something of the same variability among subjects. Some of his subjects, apparently, could *really* "see" the cards. Thus, once I'd reached the point of acceptance of ESP as a telepathic phenomenon, I was obliged to accept it in its clairvoyant form as well—the demonstration is the same, the statistical proof is of the same order, and the distribution of the faculty among human beings follows the same pattern.

I had a lot of trouble with this one, though. One of the things an engineer's mind does almost automatically as he studies any process at work is to fish around for plausible explanations for what he sees. That's a little hard to do in matters supernatural, but the reflexes are there nevertheless. In the case of mind-to-mind telepathy, though nobody really knows how it works, I had arrived at a vaguely satisfying (and pretty obvious) hypothesis that goes like this: There is an energy, as yet unknown, that can flow between two minds. The sender's act of "willing" an image in his mind involves use of energy. The receiver's mind picks up that energy, as though it were a mental phone call. Telepathy is thus an energy transfer, and the only thing we don't know is what kind of energy it is.

That's not all that dumb a hypothesis, inasmuch as we know that mental processes are always accompanied by measurable electrical forces—that's how we detect brain waves with electroencephalographic (EEG) equipment. And it's not all that implausible to postulate an unknown kind of energy, either. After all, many kinds of electromagnetic energy forms we now use were unknown not too many years ago, radio and radar being the most well-known.

But that explanation sags badly when we look at clairvoyance. There's no way you or I can imagine an inert layer of printing ink on a cardboard card sending out an energy message that says, "Here I am and this is what I look like." Not only is there no appreciable electrical or other field emission from a piece of inked cardboard, there's not even an *implausible* way of postulating an energy release that can travel thousands of miles from an inert body like a piece of cardboard, or a piece of glass, or metal, or concrete, or any of the other thousands of objects which have been "seen" in authentic clairvoyant demonstrations.

Clairvoyance thus takes us one step deeper into the mysteries of the mind, because it shows clearly that psychic "seeing"—telepathic or clairvoyant—*must be accounted for within the mind of a single human being. No other agent or external force is needed.* Now we're having to get closer to the kind of tidy explanation which nature seems to prefer—not separate and differing assumptions to account for each one of the phenomena we don't understand, but one sweeping theory that can unite all of these matters in some common basis of understanding. We go back to the *mind* again, and look for anything that might give us a lead.

I found it helped to begin with something as mundane as how we see with our eyes. We know a great deal about the optical system of the eye—the light-sensitive cells in the retina, the energy exchange from the light photons that strike these photocells, the resulting electric signals that travel the neuron fibers of the optic nerve. We can trace the electrochemically produced signals right into the visual centers of the brain. Using brainwave detectors we can even watch flashes of light entering the eyes transform themselves into exactly corresponding pulses of electrical energy deep in the brain.

But right about here science has to sit back and begin scratching its head. It simply does not know *how* the brain assembles those billions of bits of photon energy that reach the retina into an image we can recognize instantly as a rose, or a map of Massachusetts, or the face of someone we once dated in high school. We can't even explain far simpler things, such as how we can see a straight line and know that it is straight, without a trace of a curve. The *mental* part of seeing is just as much a mystery as thought and memory—indeed, all three are intertwined, and they look very much as though they are all one and the same.

When we read a gripping novel or listen to radio drama, we "see" images. We call that *imagination*, and the word connotes unreality. But the images are every bit as real as the ones we see with our eyes. A good book, a convincing radio drama, a bad dream—all create powerful images in our minds. We constantly construct such pictures, examine them, watch them move and change just as does an image received through our eyes. As far as our minds are concerned, an imagined picture *is* a complete, satisfying picture, just as real as any other kind. It would seem obvious that it is formed by our minds in just the way visual images are formed, since it's unlikely nature would have seen fit to concoct two separate systems for forming images in the mind. Any system that can handle the complex imagery of the real world so well would seem to be more than adequate for our "mental" pictures. I'm satisfied that the mechanism is the same.

We may have trouble equating *mental* images with *visual* images, until we think what happens when we dream. The dream world is a *real* world while we're in it—real enough to cause our hearts to skip beats and our bodies to perspire in the excitement and drama of a gripping dream. The dreams themselves are not real happenings (usually, that is) but the imagery is every bit as real as we ever experience when we're awake. We can't readily control our dreams, much as we'd like to sometimes. We can't have only nice happenings and lovely pictures in our dreams. Our subconscious minds are in charge of our dreaming, and sometimes they afflict us in most unkindly fashion.

The dream phenomenon shows us that images are created in the *mind*, not in the optic nerve or in the visual centers of the brain. We don't know that there is one center for mental images—Wilder Penfield coaxed them up into consciousness by electrically stimulating quite different areas of the brain. Patients who have suffered damage to large portions of their brains still dream and can still "imagine" as well as before. The closest we can come is to say that the *brain* appears to contain the mechanism for processing visual stimuli, but the *mind* accounts for the imagery itself—for the "pictures" we perceive, whether our eyes are open or closed.

There's some interesting work that has been done on dreams that helps tie together some of these loose ends of ESP, imagery, visual perception, and dreams. In 1962 a Dream Laboratory was established at Maimonides Hospital in Brooklyn to investigate dream states and the possibility of telepathic communication during dreams. The experiments, reported on four years later, were basically rather simple, though they were by no means easy to carry out. Recall of dreams, as we all know, can be a rather unsure thing, and in these experiments it was important to know as accurately as possible just what the dreamer had been dreaming when he awoke. Fortunately, it is known that brain-wave patterns vary markedly in different stages of sleep, and the dreaming stage can be rather accurately identified by watching brain-wave recording instruments.

The experiment was this: An "agent" in a separate room (over forty feet away) from the sleeping subject selects at random one of twelve pictures of well-known paintings containing strong visual images. He concentrates on the picture while the sleeper sleeps—nothing more. Shortly after the recording machines begin to indicate a dream state, the sleeper is awakened by a third person and asked to describe his dream. (The third person has simply been monitoring the instruments and has no way of knowing which picture had been selected by the "sending" agent.) The patient then goes back to sleep, and in the morning is shown the entire set of twelve pictures and asked to identify and rank any of them that remind him of any dreams he had during the night.

The results—both the immediate accounts on forced awakening and the next morning's picture ranking—showed that telepathic transmission had occurred in a number of cases. Here again, the elusive, undependable nature of ESP shows up. Some agents scored far higher than others with their sleepers, and some sleepers reported much more accurate dream images than others. But the statistics are convincing. "Chance" cannot explain the close correspondence between picture and dreamed image. Telepathy to the unconscious mind had taken place.

Some of the dreamers' recorded comments are interesting to note. Here are two dream descriptions evoked by the sender's concentration on Cezanne's "Apples and Oranges," depicting a pitcher, a plate and bowl with some fruit in it: "It had something to do with earthenware ... something that we have at home—not the more primitive, but a more subtle type of finished pottery." "The Near East ... it could be ancient drawing, ancient pottery drawing."

Or these descriptions, from a transmission of Chagall's "The Yellow Rabbi," a picture of an elderly rabbi seated at a table with a book on it, both hands strongly visible. " ... it has to do with, well a feeling of older people. The name of St. Paul came into my mind." "The doctor ... was sitting and he was reading a book." "Something about a helping hand ... It appeared that someone was about to make a talk."

Let's see what we have here. We start with a real picture, viewed with the eyes of the sender and constituted in his conscious mind as a distinct image, visually received. And next we have a real picture—very real to the dreamer—that corresponds remarkably with the first—not in every detail, certainly, but in the *impression* the picture conveys. A *visual* image becomes a *mental* image becomes another *mental* image in an unconscious mind forty feet away. And if we stretch matters a bit, the final mental image may just possibly be closer to the idea the original imager—the painter—had than it is to that of the middleman, the agent-sender.

This is telepathy, all right, but of a different sort than we've encountered before. In ordinary telepathy, *both* sender and receiver are consciously trying to communicate. In clairvoyance, only the *receiver* is trying to communicate. In the dream tests only the *sender* is trying. But in all three cases, the results are the same: information—an image—is communicated. It's reasonable to suppose that, since the results are the same, the mechanism is the same. Thus do the dream tests suggest that clairvoyance is simply another manifestation of the basic, innate ability of the mind to receive information—vivid, richly detailed, lifelike, accurate information—without the use of the normal senses.

Where does that bring us out? We are obviously dealing with the subconscious mind when we look at dream-telepathy, and we can be pretty sure that it is the subconscious as well that enables the clairvoyant to see as he does. The images he describes have entered his conscious mind, of course—otherwise he couldn't talk about them—but they were called up from his subconscious. How did they get there?

There aren't any good theories as yet. What little investigation has been done has been directed at simply proving or disproving that clairvoyance exists, not trying to identify its mechanisms. But that is true of just about everything else in the paranormal world, which leaves the matter wide open for individual surmise. In this book I'll be building up to an explanation, but it's best done after we have been through some additional bits of evidence of the supernatural and the kinds of energies they suggest.

Chapter 15

The Mystery Force in the Laboratory

I promised you this book would not become an endless itemization of all of the weird things that seem to happen at times in this world, and it won't. But as you can see, we're on the trail of what may be some sort of energy form, one that science as yet doesn't quite know how to deal with. It's useful to look at another manifestation of what could be the same or a related energy. Once again, we start with some work that Rhine did many years ago. Maybe you're getting tired of hearing about that man, but the fact is that he was the first American scientist to tackle these things systematically, and once he got started, he never stopped.

In the course of his ESP work Rhine became curious about psychokinesis (PK), the ability of the mind to exert a force on material objects, causing them to behave in ways other than would be expected from natural forces alone. To investigate PK, he chose dice as his test objects and began a series of experiments modeled closely after his ESP work. He sought to find out whether the fall of the dice could be influenced in any way just by "willing" a certain result—snake-eyes, box-cars, what have you.

The laws of probability are nicely suited to dice games, as casino owners throughout the world have long ago discovered. Also, it's quite easy to rule out odd dice and anomalous behavior by precise construction, automatic rollers and the like. Rhine boiled things down to the point where there were just honest dice, honest machines to throw them, honest people to "will" the results, and statistics to measure their significance.

You can probably guess what his results were. Rhine's statistics showed that PK was just as real as ESP. He found something of the same variation in sensitivity that he had with ESP, and he demonstrated scores that had the same extraordinary statistics associated with them that he had shown with ESP. Dice turned up with the "willed" numbers with a frequency that was so much greater than chance would explain that the odds against chance were in a few cases as high as several billion to one. If you find this hard to believe, I don't blame you. So did all the scientists who reviewed his work. So did I, even after I had become thoroughly convinced about ESP.

But, in this line of work, you can't buy an experimental method which clearly demonstrates one phenomenon and then reject the same experimental method when it demonstrates another phenomenon simply because the second seems spookier than the first. Either both sets of experiments are valid, or neither is.

Reports of PK abound in the literature, describing things that are much more exciting than rolling dice against chance. Young Matthew Manning, the English lad with the poltergeist problems and the automatic writing that we described earlier, did some experimenting of his own with PK and obtained startling results. He was persuaded by his parents to try some metal-bending of the kind that Uri Geller, the controversial Israeli psychic, had demonstrated on TV in America and England. (*Time* magazine came pretty close to calling Geller a fraud, but most of what he did has yet to be successfully duplicated by the talents of magicians who shared *Time*'s view.) Matthew's own account of his first attempt at PK makes good reading:

"My parents had watched this (Geller's TV) program with me, and when it ended, my mother asked me to try to bend metal objects. I told her that I would not succeed, but I took a stainless steel spoon on which to experiment, more to please her than for any other reason.

"I sat rubbing it gently and urging it mentally to bend. After ten minutes the spoon was still in its original shape and was evidently not being affected by my invocations. After another ten minutes, when my father entered the room, I showed him the spoon and explained that nothing was happening.

"His entry into the room had distracted my concentration, and my concentration was diverted from the spoon as soon as I began talking to him. At that moment I felt something happening to the handle of the spoon. Somehow the handle was no longer rigid. On closer inspection we could see an obvious bend in its handle. Following this it continued to droop quite rapidly until it resembled the shape of a hairpin.

"Even then I was dubious about the bent spoon. I really thought that inadvertently I must have bent it physically. My parents, who strangely enough were not surprised at this achievement, thought later that night of a simple method of proving whether or not I had bent the spoon and a fork by force. My father produced a six-inch nail of a quarter-inch diameter made of galvanized steel. We thought that if I managed to bend this, I must be using a paranormal source of energy. Not believing that the nail would actually bend unless I physically applied pressure to it, I took it in my hands and found that I was quite incapable of bending it with my fingers, nor could I bend it by placing it in a vise and exerting manual pressure on it.

"I tried in vain for fifteen minutes to bend the nail by paranormal means. When I realized that I was getting very tired, I gave up. I decided to go to bed and, looking at the pendant watch that I wear around my neck, I saw to my surprise that the large minute hand was twisted toward the glass of the watch. This convinced me that I had used a psychokinetic force earlier. The watch had not been opened for some time and the hands had always been quite straight. As I lifted the watch on its chain over my head, the chain appeared to break. I always remove my watch by this method when I take it off, rather than undo the clasp. The break in the chain may be merely a coincidence.

"As an interesting experiment, I decided to sleep with the six-inch nail under my pillow, merely to see if anything would happen to it during the night. At eight o'clock the next morning there was a bend of about thirty degrees in the steel nail."

Matthew continued his experiments and succeeded in bending a number of other objects. Strangely, he discovered that silver spoons were much more difficult to bend psychically than steel ones. All we can do with that fact at the moment is add it to the long list of the unexplained. Careful metallurgical examination was given to at least one object (a pair of specially toughened handcuffs) that Matthew bent psychically, and the laboratory report carefully states that no physical force had been applied to the bent part. The crystal structure and strain patterns were entirely normal, showing no stretching or compression such as would accompany a cold bending.

Matthew's experience does not by itself establish incontrovertibly the existence of powerful PK forces, but taken with the Rhine experiments and with hundreds of other authenticated demonstrations of material objects made to move without application of known physical force, Matthew's ingenuous account is pretty impressive stuff. For a more complete look at the PK phenomenon, I turned to some laboratory work done here and in Canada and looked again at the Russians, who have been investigating PK for a long time.

Back in the mid thirties some work at Yale University established the fact that all living matter, including the human body, is surrounded by a very weak electric field that is constantly changing. It appeared as though the field was a sort of energy "envelope" which sheathed the body externally and whose characteristics changed in some relationship to the life processes going on within the organism. Following up on this discovery, Dr. Leonard Ravitz, a neuropsychiatrist at Yale, demonstrated that the strength of this energy field, measured by electromagnetic detectors placed near the skin, could be altered by the state of mind of the subject, or by the depth of the hypnotic trance under which the subject was placed. Here was a clear indication that there was an unknown kind of electrical field energy involved in organic functioning, and that it could be controlled in some way by the mind.

More recent work at the University of Saskatchewan in Canada has led to the development of a "force-field detector" that can pick up these weak emanations from a human body, amplify and display them, and use them for correlation with observed mental states. The equipment is sensitive enough to be used at a distance of several feet, and reports on the work by Saskatchewan's Dr. Abram Hoffer claim that the equipment has reliably indicated anxiety states of patients as they enter a psychiatric examining room.

The Russians have demonstrated equipment ostensibly of the same type (they have not disclosed the details) to Western observers as part of their research work on psychokinetic forces. As they did with dowsing and ESP, Russian science long ago seems to have accepted the reality of PK.

They use their "Who's Who" of science in these investigations, men like Nobel physicist Nikolai Semyonov, Dr. Gleb Frank, Director of the famed "Science City," and Dr. Victor Adamenko, a young physicist with some reputation in world scientific circles. (Adamenko has spent some of his time helping to develop equipment to be used for, of all things, improving the reliability and availability of acupuncture.)

In 1967 the Soviets hosted a conference on paranormal phenomena in Moscow, inviting a number of Western participants to observe a full-dress demonstration of some of the Russian work and techniques. There have since been other glimpses of Russian work afforded to Western investigators, and the reports all seem to add up to the same thing: the Russians seem to be on the track of identifying and harnessing some of the strange forces that are at work in the realm of the paranormal.

In the 1967 convocation a film was shown of a Russian woman, one Nelya Mikhailova, then in her forties, who displayed quite extraordinary PK powers—making compass needles spin, moving wooden matches housed in a plastic cube, causing nonmagnetic metal cylinders to slide about on a table top. In another film she was seen to separate a raw egg placed in saline solution under a bell jar, completely removing the yolk from the white and then neatly reassembling the egg as it was—all without any physical force applied.

During these experiments Nelya was wired up like a space-man, with electrodes running from several parts of her body to a variety of recording machines. Great changes in pulse rate, respiration rate, blood sugar, and brain-wave activity were recorded as Nelya "revved up" for her psychic performance. Most significantly, the force-field detectors placed several feet away showed strong increases in the electrical field surrounding Nelya and indicated that there was a low-frequency (5 cycles/sec.) pulsing, vibrating characteristic to the field which was mirrored in the other recording instruments. The field was strongest not at the head, but a few feet from the head, suggesting some form of focused concentration of the vibrating field energy. And the site of greatest activity in the brain seemed to be in the *back* of the head, well removed from the cortical tissues involved in human sense and thought processing.

The Russians are not the only ones trying to track down the nature of the mysterious PK force by these techniques. For example, at the Canadian seminar that I mentioned when I described Matthew Manning's automatic writing a while back, Matthew's PK powers were studied intensively in much the same manner that the Russians studied Nelya's. The brain-wave patterns recorded as Matthew sought to bend metal were termed "extraordinary"—not just because of the appearance of great "power" in the traces, but also because they emanated from the oldest part of the brain, a portion believed by some neurologists to be the vestigial and nearly degenerate remains of man's old "animal" brain. The psychic energy level, measured in fashion similar to the Russian methods, was exceptionally high—far higher than in any similar Canadian tests on other psychics. This was July, 1974, and this was an eighteen-year-old school-boy.

That same schoolboy is the one apparently responsible, though unwillingly, for the multitude of objects that flew around his house when he was younger. Not only Matthew and his family observed this; numerous other apparently detached and well-respected observers witnessed the same things. The objects moved in complete disregard for the laws of gravity and even the confines of space: An eraser lifts from the floor and settles gently beside Matthew's sister just after she complains about not being able to find it. A large table in a second-floor bedroom suddenly turns up in the cellar, three flights of stairs and 105 feet away. Along the way there were five doorways, some less than thirty inches wide, and ten right-angle turns. All of the books, papers, pencils, and ornaments that were on it were still in their customary places, undisturbed by their trip through the "space" of Matthew's house.

I cite Matthew's experiences because his accounts are well documented and because we have met him before, not because they are so unusual. There are as many accounts as one cares to read describing happenings just like this, some reported here in the United States. Many have been attested to by thoroughly responsible, credible people. I find I have no choice but to accept the fact that objects do fly around from time to time, even though nobody seems to know why.

What is this force that makes objects move in defiance of gravity, magnetism, and inertia, and atoms in metal rearrange themselves without disrupting the original crystal structure? No one knows yet, but the evidence says that, whatever the force is, it is the human mind that either generates it directly or provides the access to it. The amount of power involved in some of the manifestations of this energy is so large that it seems improbable that it could all be internally generated, as is human muscle power. It seems plausible to link it to the energy field that surrounds us, but that does not explain it, nor does it explain how a few human beings seem to have learned how to tap and utilize it. We simply don't know enough yet, but at least man is beginning to try to find out.

Is this also the energy that accounts for dowsing? It's hard to find a reason to believe otherwise. What about Ted Serios' thought photography? Surely an energy that can bend nails, roll snake-eyes, and delicately separate eggs could be tuned to just the level needed to expose a photographic film correctly. I suspect that Serios taps the same strange energy.

I had some trouble imagining such a precise handling of energy until I found something with which to compare it. I reflected on the fantastic range of control our eye/brain system gives to our sense of sight. We can see perfectly well at the top of the snow-covered Alps, where the photon stream reaching us from the sun is almost painfully overpowering. That same system will record a *single* photon reaching us out of pitch blackness. That's a sensitivity ratio that numbers in the billions to one, and we handle it in stride.

Can we concentrate energy the way the nail benders and egg separators do? Well, pole vaulters do it all the time when they "will" the rush of oxygen and resultant electrochemical energy to trained muscles that will propel them over the bar. Singers do it when they produce enormous "audio" power from their tiny, straining vocal chords. All of us do it every day of our lives as we consciously or unconsciously make our bodies do the things we need to have done. We're all masters of concentrating and focusing energy, and we think nothing of it. It's only when the energy is of a sort we're not familiar with, and manifests itself outside of our bodies, that we begin to have problems of belief.

H. G. Wells gave us a hand in reckoning with unknown energies in his enchanting novel *Country of the Blind*. The citizens of the sightless world that Wells described hooted at a visitor's claims of being able to "see" things with his eyes, at a distance, out of reach of his fingertips and out of his ears' hearing. There was no way a blind world could grasp what he was trying to tell it, and its worthy people accused him of heresy.

If you and I lived in the country of the blind, we *might* be brave enough to try to understand this strange gift described to us and might even secretly ask our visitor to help guide us in ways we could not guide ourselves. But most likely, we would be like everyone else and denounce the stranger. The leaders and wise men of the country would have made it most unpopular to believe the nonsense we were hearing.

We would hear the scientists of that world using the same words that some of our own very eminent ones have thrown at us in dealing with ESP:

Professor D. O. Hebb, psychologist, McGill University says: "...the idea (telepathy) does not make sense." But he admits this opinion is "in the literal sense, just prejudice."

Dr. Warren Weaver, a famed mathematician and one of the originators of modern communications theory, relates: "I find this (ESP) a subject that is so intellectually uncomfortable as to be almost painful. I end by concluding that I cannot explain away Professor Rhine's evidence and that I also cannot accept his interpretation."

So would it also go in the country of the blind, a country each of us finds himself in when he ponders the paranormal.

And there we are. We have proof of telepathy, clairvoyance, precognition, and psychokinesis, proof that no man who calls himself reasonable can cast aside. The simple fact is that they exist—fleeting, tenuous, unpredictable as they are. They exist, at least in a latent sense, in all of us, though most of us are rarely if ever aware of having used them. A very few human beings seem to possess these psychic powers to a remarkable degree—so remarkable and so different from our own experience that we tend to disbelieve them, usually because we are afraid we will look foolish to ourselves or to others.

We're pretty sure that normal people like us don't have these powers, and we're not always all that kind to those who do appear to have them. And besides, of what use would they be, anyway? Even if they do exist, so what? What would we do with these powers if we did have them? How would our lives be different if we believed in these things?

They would be different only if these paranormal phenomena told us something about even larger mysteries and guided us to a better understanding of what our lives and our universe mean. At the very least, acceptance of the reality of these things right around us should prepare us to think about things beyond.

I should now have been ready, having dealt positively with a number of authentic mysteries surrounding this life on earth, to take on what should be the related mysteries of the life hereafter, if such there be. I should have been able to go from telepathy between two living minds to telepathy between a mind alive here and one alive in the hereafter. I should have been ready to move from mind-controlled dice and mind-bent nails and the flying china of the poltergeist to the pencil guided by an unseen hand. I should have been ready for an easy belief in survival after death, and some kind of God would assuredly fit in there somewhere.

But that next step into the hereafter was not to be. Not quite yet, anyway. There were two pieces that just did not fit together, and until they did, I could not find a way to complete a picture I could live easily with and trust completely. I had skipped over a couple of things too lightly in my excitement over the discovery of authentic new powers.

Chapter 16

The Problem with a Future That Already Exists

Everything I have thus far described comes under one of four headings of paranormal phenomena: telepathy, clairvoyance, precognition and psychokinesis. The first two are not too disturbing to our sense of reality. Though telepathy and clairvoyance are assuredly odd powers for human beings to possess, they don't in themselves make everything else in our lives unreal. After all, animals seem to have them and use them, and they get along fine. And I've already cited some reasons why these faculties may have been supressed in the minds of most of us ordinary examples of the higher species.

But *precognition* is something else again. I tended to skip past it with a wave of the hand once I had accepted the reality of telepathy and clairvoyance. I heard myself saying, "Oh-ho! *That's* how the fortune-tellers and prophets do their thing," as I turned the page to the next item of other-world wonders.

But not so fast there. If precognition is a fact—and it assuredly is—that means *the future must already exist!* That . . . is unnerving. It is just too much to grasp.

Yet we have seen that man's mind, under very carefully controlled laboratory conditions, can predict with accuracy what the future will hold—at least that slice of it between the time a man's mind guesses which light will flash a minute or two hence, and the time it flashes, triggered by a completely random decay of an atom of radioactive strontium. That can happen *only* if that particular bit of future is already formed, waiting to be revealed.

Now, I don't like the sound of that, when I think about it, and I don't imagine you do either. It is simply inconceivable to me to believe that the future is already laid out, already existing. How can I make myself believe that everything I shall read in tomorrow's newspaper, or next year's, is already cast in some form of celestial concrete? Was it preordained that my car wouldn't run this morning? I know it would have started had I not put off the tune-up it has so sorely needed for a month. Was my laziness in getting the tune-up also chiseled into that same concrete? Were all the little distractions that kept me from getting the car fixed all preprogrammed for me in a way I was powerless to offset? Is *everything* that has ever happened and will ever happen to me completely outside of my own control? *I can't believe it!*

Right here I faced defeat. Everything within me told me to deny precognition and all that it implies. Yet one of the ground rules I had set for myself, as I have noted before, is that I cannot allow myself to disbelieve incontrovertible proof of a phenomenon simply because the phenomenon is impossible for me to believe. I vowed when I began that I would follow the evidence wherever it led, and I encourage you to do the same if this book is to be of any use to you. How on earth was I going to handle *this* one?

Let's look first at the "scale" of precognition we must deal with. The laboratory work you read about simply showed that man's mind could anticipate accurately events that were to happen in completely random fashion a minute or two into the future. The test conditions had ruled out, insofar as man's mind knows what to rule out, everything that could possibly have accounted for the results except an ability to see into the future—*precognition*. But the time scale is short—the best scores seem to be obtained a couple of minutes before the event happens. That's the nature of the scientific evidence we have to date; it's all pretty near-term stuff.

But at the other end of the precognition scale we have the Jeane Dixons and other well-known psychics and seers who claim to be able to see events months or years ahead. One has to admit after reading accounts of the Dixon variety of prophesying that some of the predictions have turned out to be uncannily accurate. Jeane Dixon accurately predicted Kennedy's election and his assassination, and much more besides. Those predictions are a matter of record (in the *Wall Street Journal*, among other unlikely publications). One also recognizes, though, if he reads enough accounts of this sort, that many of the predictions, including those by people like Dixon, have turned out to be dead wrong. Skeptics that we are, we prefer to think that the false predictions prove that prophesying is hokum and that the instances of accurate prediction are just random lucky shots.

I'm not sure we can get away with that anymore. One thing we do know for sure is the undependable, uncertain nature of things paranormal. No laboratory investigations, no longtime accounts of any psychic's powers have ever shown an *assured* repeatability of any psychic phenomena. Psychic manifestations can't be turned on and off with the certainty of an electric light. They are capricious, unpredictable, and eminently fallible, as we've seen with each of them in turn.

That accounts, in part, for the fact that even the unusually gifted seers frequently make predictions which don't turn out to be true. Though they say they are reading the same kind of signs, making the same interpretations they make on the correct occasions, either the visions they received or the interpretations they made of them frequently prove undependable.

The other cause of shaky prophesy is undoubtedly the fact, I trust, that the future the seers see in their visions is one that can be affected by the exercise of human free will. We shall be looking at the phenomenon of free will while we try to deal with a future that sometimes seems to be uncannily predictable, one that must exist in its entirety, not just in the few minutes measured by a laboratory flasher.

One of the things which helped me to take the leap from the flasher-laboratory to the likes of Jeane Dixon was the extraordinary number of individual, one-time accounts of premonitions reported by very ordinary people. I have known myself to have vague "hunches" of what lies ahead, never so powerful as to leave me quaking, but occasionally strong enough to cause me to reconsider whether I really wanted to go ahead with something I had planned. As I say, these were quite fuzzy, and notably unremarkable. I always passed them off without pondering whether I was receiving a supernatural message. They were rather like my *déjà vu* experiences—neither disturbing nor convincing at the time, and now that I am getting along in years, increasingly rare.

But other ordinary people—thousands and thousands of them —have had future-vision experiences that were so graphic that they were deeply impressed by them and recounted them in detail before the events transpired. These individual reports occur in writings throughout history and are so numerous that taken altogether they become hard to deny. It's easy to reject as hallucination, or fancy, or fraud, a few scattered reports of divination on the part of persons who call themselves prophets. They could be sick, or vain, or dishonest, or all three. But when thousands and thousands of reports accumulate for hundreds of years, all coming from apparently decent people who have nothing to gain but derision for admitting to such implausible experiences, then the sum total, taken with all the other evidence, has got to add up to a little truth.

Most of the premonitions that get reported occur in dreams, and most of them involve highly charged, life-threatening situations. There is, for example, a welter of apparently well-authenticated reports from people involved in the Titanic disaster, some of them from scheduled passengers who canceled the trip as a result of a dream or conscious "feeling" of dread. Other premonitions were reported by friends or relatives who "saw" the deaths of their loved ones days or hours before the sinking and mentioned their visions to others before the tragedy was reported.

Another example. After the mine disaster of 1966 in Aberfan, Wales, in which 144 miners died, many people of the town reported having had premonitions of the disaster. All of these reports were carefully checked out by a sober and serious investigative team, and twenty-four of them were verified to the extent of establishing that the persons involved had talked to others about the premonitions well before the catastrophe— more than two weeks beforehand, in almost half of the cases.

The great suffragette leader Susan B. Anthony, had a precognitive experience, reported in the diary of her close friend and coworker Elizabeth Cady Stanton. Miss Anthony was sleeping in an Atlantic City hotel, under doctor's orders to get some rest, when she was awakened by a vivid dream of being burned alive. In the morning she told her niece, "We must pack at once and go back to Philadelphia." They did, and the next day that hotel, ten others, and miles of boardwalk were destroyed by fire.

And so the cases go, as many as you care to read, all told by people who had no doubts about the fact that messages warning of future events were being sent them.

Here we are, hard up against two realities which are in stark contradiction to each other. We have, on the one hand, the *fact* of predictability of future events, and that fact says that certain future events already exist and are inevitably going to take place. But, on the other hand, we have our own undeniable knowledge of individual free will. We know that we have many times made conscious decisions which unquestionably affected future events exactly as we had planned. I *know* I could have fixed my car yesterday so that it would have started today. I *know* I can decide this instant to fly to New York in an hour or not to fly there, and the future will be quite different for me in the next few hours depending on that decision. I *know* I could even arrange my own death, or that of another, if I were so inclined, and death is probably the most momentous event that awaits any of us. So I *know* I have free will in matters small and large, and nothing I can ever read or think can change that conviction.

There's the dilemma. If the future already exists, there can be no free will, at least to the extent that the future is drawn in detail. Free will could then operate only as to events *not* drawn on the big blueprint in the sky. Are only the *big* events already drawn? No, there seem to be plenty of instances of perfectly minor events being predicted accurately, like the flashing light. The big event of death itself—at least the causing of it, if not the deferral of it—can be, as I've just noted, an act of conscious will. So *all* deaths and *all* events need not be preordained.

Our choices in meeting this dilemma appear meager. We could become out-and-out fatalists, like some of our Eastern cousins, and live our lives out in the conviction that everything that is going to happen to us is predestined. We then turn into mindless passengers on a trip we know not where.

Or we could go back to where we were before we began thinking about all these things, if we don't like the sound of fatalism or determinism. Just chuck the whole thing and muddle through. Forget about precognition and the problem it presents, and forget about telepathy and all the rest. I confess to having been sorely tempted to do just that. But I could not. I had come too far.

As I'd learned to do before, I looked first at what my own senses told me about the nature of the future, and of time. And then I turned to science to learn how modern scientific intellect currently views the future and time. Finally I checked everything out with reports that describe (so the psychics who bring them to us say) how time appears on the other side of the veil.

Chapter 17

Understanding Time

Time. We all know what it is: the relentless ticking of the clock that converts future into present and present into past. We can slice it into years, centuries, millennia—or minutes, seconds, billionths of a second—or anything in between. The essence of time is that it can be *measured*—by a clock, or the sun, or the opening of oyster shells on the seacoast—it makes no difference how. Time flows unrelentingly, and in one direction only. We know *absolutely* that all of this is true. Every moment of our life we are reminded of it. Time is moving, not to be stopped.

But time *is* a little rubbery, even to us human beings who have been run by the sun's clock for millions of years. Not all time goes by at the same speed. The big hand climbs with agonizing slowness when we are children in school on a sunny spring day, waiting for the recess bell to ring. The same hand races many times faster as the recess draws to a close. Three minutes of annoying TV commercials seem like a half hour, yet twenty minutes of packed action speed by in what seems like seconds. Freed of the clock, we all experience time as *variable*, depending on what is going on around us at the moment.

Clock time loses all meaning when we dream. Dream events happen at their own speeds, sometimes very rapidly by clock time but unhurriedly in our dream. A phone ringing us awake will be neatly—and obviously almost instantaneously—written into the dream we were dreaming when the ringing started, without the dream action so much as skipping a beat. Our subconscious minds can evidently ignore clock time; so can our conscious minds, unless we request them to pay attention in order to get us somewhere punctually.

Yet our subconscious minds can, if we train them, keep almost as good time as the electric clock at our bedside. Not a few of us have learned the knack of setting a mental alarm clock to wake us at a selected time, and have frequently been amazed at how well the trick works. What does that tell us? It tells us, at the very least, that we are creatures of the particular time-environment of the little planet on which we've lived these millions of years. That environment is regulated in important ways by the rotation of the earth and the consequent endless succession of nights and days. This ceaseless rhythm has become part of us. We have, we say, become conditioned to it. Our subconscious minds can somehow retain the drumbeat of unremitting time in the same way that Pavlov's dogs were trained to drool without fail at the sound of a bell.

It looks as though there is a paradox here.

It is true that we perceive time as passing at different rates. Without clocks to guide us, we're not very accurate when it comes to guessing the passage of exactly one hour. Our guesses will vary depending on what we are doing and thinking at the time. There is obviously no metronome ticking away inside our conscious brains.

But it is also true that our subconscious minds can wake us up at a precise clock time. Oyster shells will indeed open at just the time of high tide, even if they are transported a thousand miles inland from their seacoast home. And they'll open there at exactly the time the tide would have reached them in their new location had the tide traveled the extra thousand miles, too. The oysters' behavior is just one of hundreds of instances demonstrating the existence of an internal rhythm, a biological clock that controls the basic functions of every organism. Most of the rhythms are geared closely to the day-night cycle of the sun, though some seem tied closer to the moon, and some not to anything anybody has yet pinned down.

Much study has been given to these bio-rhythms. Some of it is aimed at learning enough about them to allow us human beings to live a little more happily by paying attention to the up-and-down cycles our bodies demonstrate. We're learning that we can't expect to be at our best at 4:00 in the morning, even though the clock at Heathrow says 9:00 A.M. as we taxi up through the English fog. The bio-rhythms are there, and they affect us importantly.

But the clock that runs them is *not* there. At least it hasn't been found yet, and I'm pretty sure it won't be. Much scientific study has gone into the search for the bio-clock, to no avail as I write this. A Harvard biologist has gone so far as to remove the tiny brain from the heads of moth larvae and then artificially alter the day-night interval to see if the larvae will squirm out of their pupae on schedule. He has proved that it is the moth's brain that senses the changing length of the day and tells the moth that spring has come. He has also proved that, for this purpose, the moth's brain works just as well when he inserts it in the creature's tail. No brain, no clock. Brain present, the clock ticks. But where is it?

We noted sometime back that the pineal gland in lower vertebrates has light-sensitive cells in it, and that the pineal is definitely involved in certain reproductive bio-rhythms. That's possibly what the moths have going for them, too. But that still doesn't say what the *clock* is, what the mechanism is that takes these photo signals and translates them into the chimes the body obeys.

The paradox of our sometimes flexible conscious time sense versus the apparent internal clock resolves itself, for me, this way: The "clock" is in the *mind*, not in the brain and not in the cells and molecules that make it up. The source of all of our

time sense is the *subconscious* mind of man—and, yes, of the
oyster and the moth and all the other living things that amaze
us with the way they behave. There is a part of man's *mind*, not
his brain, that keeps track of time—sun-time, moon-time, spring-
time—just as it constantly monitors our environment while we
sleep and wakes us abruptly when danger nears. And that same
mind determines the flexible, variable time sense of our dreams
and our waking hours. It is our *minds* that control time, not our
clocks.

Our mental "clock" time is only a trained faculty, derived
from man's coaching by the sun for millions of years. What we
call "real" time, the time we run our waking hours by, is indeed
as rubbery and flexible as we have all sensed it to be. Albert
Einstein seemed to agree, once remarking jokingly, "When you
sit with a nice girl for two hours, it seems like two minutes;
when you sit on a hot stove for two minutes, it seems like two
hours. That's relativity."

Einstein appears to be referring to what psychologists call
"duration"—our perception of the speed with which time goes
by. Studies have shown that our sense of time's passing seems to
speed up with the number of events that are "memorable"
during that time. They have also shown that "successful" events
appear to fill a shorter time span than failures; pleasurable
moments pass faster than unpleasant ones. Time speeds when
we're happy, drags when we're bored. What, then, is *real* time?

Is *real* time the time our electric clocks keep? No, our clocks
are simply mechanisms which divide the earth's day into bits
that let us measure how fast one event follows another here on
earth. Our clocks would have no meaning to inhabitants of
Mercury, whose day is as long as our year, or to the inhabitants
of any other planet anywhere else in the universe.

Our human concept of time, and indeed of reality, holds that
events happen in succession, with a space of *time* between them.
We build clocks to measure the time, and deduce much from
that measurement. We conclude, for example, that a particular
event can have "caused" a *later* event to happen. But if two
events happen at exactly the same instant, then we assume that
neither could have influenced the other. We view them as

completely separate happenings, unrelated to each other because no "time" has intervened. Thus have we arrived at our
convictions of "cause and effect," which are the backbone of
scientific investigations and thus have we accepted the idea of
"simultaneity," one of whose offspring we call "coincidence."
Time—measurable, ticking, relentless clock time—is the human
concept that underlies all of this. In one tick, future becomes
present becomes past, says the clock.

But our subconscious minds aren't so sure, and—it turns out—
neither is science. "Cause and effect" and "simultaneity" are
receiving skeptical looks these days. Albert Einstein wasn't
really talking about duration in his little joke about the girl and
the hot stove. He was really telling us that our subconscious
minds may be more right than our clocks are, that there is no
such thing as "absolute" time.

I am not going to try to unravel for you his special theory of
relativity. But the essence of his pronouncement, for the
purpose of getting a handle on time and the concept of future, is
pretty straighforward: There is no such thing as "a" time, or "a"
speed at which some universal clock moves that ties the universe together. Two observers stationed far apart in space will
not be able to agree on the exact time of an event they both see,
such as a star exploding. They won't agree on where the star
was, either. This is because the observers as well as the stars are
all moving through space. *Everything* in space is moving. There
is no handy fixed reference point from which all else can be
measured. There's no center, no surveyor's "stone bound" in the
sky, from which we can set our transits. One observer's "twelve
o'clock" has no meaning to his distant colleague. "Twelve
o'clock relative to *what?*" he asks.

Let's step out into space to see what this means. Pick a star in
our own galaxy, the Milky Way. Pick one that's fairly close to
us, as space goes—say only fifty light-years away. (That's still a
long way from just the center of our own galaxy, which is some
30,000 light-years away from us. A light-year is the distance that
light travels in one of our earth years, and measures some six
trillion earth miles. So this near-neighbor star is 30 trillion miles
from us.)

The light we see from that star, the light that reaches our eyes at what we call the "instant" of the present, actually left that star fifty years ago. We are seeing that star's *past,* not its present. (We can't even be sure it's still there until another fifty years go by.) When that light left the star, it left at a time *we* call the future, fifty years ahead of earth time. Now, if that star happens to have a planet like ours spinning around it, the inhabitants of that planet are existing—at the moment the star's light left on its journey to our eyes—in *our future.* Fifty years into our future!

What does that say? It can only say that our concept of past, present, and future has no meaning *except for those things that happen on our own earth. Our* time of the future already exists for our cousins circling the neighbor star; *their* past is our present.

Think for a moment about the fact that everything I have just said about our neighbor star's planet people applies equally well when *they* look at *us.* The light reaching them from our sun spent fifty years on the journey. To our neighbors, *our* present instant of time is fifty years into *their* future, and they are reading our past from the light of our sun.

And there we do indeed have a paradox. Each of us is existing in the other's future at the same time each of us is existing in the other's past. It would be easier if we could say we are both living in the same present and that we really have only the problem of a slow messenger to thank for this confusion. It would be very convenient to say that we are really both on the same time—both existing *now.* If light were instantaneous (as our ancestors thought it was) we wouldn't have this problem of trying to conceive of living in our neighbor's future and they in ours. The whole universe would exist in the same time, and we could all continue to think of past, present, and future just as we do here on earth.

But Einstein won't let us get away with that. Not only is the speed of light immutable, probably the most basic constant the universe knows. The very concept of "speed" to describe light is only an earthling's convenience to help him define his universe. Light is pure energy, perhaps but one form of the fundamental energy system on which every atom and all existence is based. Using our earth-concept of time, we ascribe a "speed" to it in earth-time terms. One hundred eighty-six thousand miles per *second* is how we describe this unchanging constant. But that doesn't mean that the constant describes the energy. Our faraway neighbors will have their own constants, and they won't describe the energy either. The *energy* is the fact, and the *energy* is what makes each of us live in the other's future.

Einstein also shows us that every body in space affects every other body in space by its gravitational field. He showed, for instance, that light is *bent* by bodies in space, as are all other forms of electromagnetic radiation. That means that the radiation we receive is continually being altered before we receive it. The very course our little planet will follow in space has already been determined by all the other bodies in space, and our planet has affected them as well in a tiny way. Though we can't sense it, our earth is moving in many directions at the same time. Not only does it spin with a speed of about 1,000 miles per hour at its surface, and not only does it circle the sun annually at some 70,000 miles per hour. The solar system of which we are a part is moving within a "local" star system about 25,000 miles per hour. The local star system is traveling within the Milky Way at over 700,000 miles per hour. And the Milky Way itself is rocketing along at over 350,000 miles per hour with respect to the outer galaxies. Each one of these velocities and courses is determined by the combination of forces acting on us from everywhere else in the universe, and that determination came from bodies that are operating in our future.

Narrowed down to our problem of the moment, this all says that the *future* exists, the *present* exists, the *past* exists, all as one, in the reaches of the universe. There is only a vast *now,* comprising all of time past and all of time to come. On the stage of the universe, it's as though everything that has ever existed still exists, and everything that will ever exist already exists. What we human beings perceive to be the present is simply that slice which our own kind of human senses and consciousness permits us to perceive. That's part of what relativity theory is about.

Scientists are better able to understand this sort of thing than the rest of us. They reach the universal "now" by the compelling logic of mathematics, and trust this view of time because there is no other that satisfies their probings. When they put their conclusions into words we can understand, the picture doesn't clarify instantly, but its believability improves:

J. G. Whitrow says that in the world described by relativity theory, "external events permanently exist, and we merely come across them." Louis de Broglie says that "each observer, as his time passes, discovers, so to speak, new slices of space-time which appear to him as successive aspects of the material world, though in reality the ensemble of events constituting space-time exists prior to his knowledge of them."

Such an idea of time is simply too much for us to grasp, because we have no tools, no senses, no words with which to grasp it. Yet, look for a moment on what we call "past." We use that word to describe what we hold in our memories. Have we invented the word "memory" to account for our sense of the past? Could it be that the past *is* as real as the present, and that we have chosen to think about it as "past" simply because we have no way of affecting it?

We like to think that we can affect our present by our conscious acts of will. We like to think that we can affect our futures also, by planning and acting in ways that will bring about certain things we hope for. Thus we look on present and future both as "times" we can do something about, while past is behind us, unchangeable, immutable.

On the face of it, such a view of "present" and "future" has got to seem a little parochial when we think of what Einstein is telling us. Future, present, *and past* exist as one in the universe, and there is no getting around it. Einstein doesn't exclude *past;* it is the same as, and as real as, the other two.

If this be true, and I see no way to believe it is not true, then "memory" may not be something that is tucked away in our DNA or some other arcane mechanism in our brains. It may be purely and simply another one of the perceptive faculties of our minds, one that enables us to read what we call the past in just the way our five other senses let us read what we call the present. If this is so, Wilder Penfield, when he pokes around in our skulls with his electric needles, is not triggering a chemical outpouring from a particular arrangement of atoms we contrived to arrange forty years ago in one corner of our brain. He is simply heightening by electrical stimulation our faculty of perceiving the real *and existing* past.

I find this to be a most intriguing idea. Viewed this way, is our memory-sense all that different from the way our eyes perceive what we call the present? I mentioned a while back that our knowledge of the physiology of vision explains everything that happens to the photons of light that reach our eyes, *right up to a certain point.* Beyond that point, we have no explanation. That is the point at which the mind puts together these billions of bits of information and tells us that the thing that we are looking at is a rose. Seeing the roses of the past in our minds can be every bit as real as seeing the rose of the present. The *mind* is what does both, and maybe both in exactly the same way. Only the receptors need be different.

We human beings are built with sense receptors that respond only to the physical, material world of what we call the present. We can't feel last week's fire anymore, or smell last month's rose. But both the fire and the rose happened. We say they existed only during the time our senses told us they existed, and they ceased to exist when our senses said they ceased. But our memories say they both still exist, and so does Professor Einstein. The fire is a constant succession of "presents," starting with logs and ending with ashes; so with the rose, from bursting bud to withered stem. Each "present" existed, and still exists, in time—the time we call the past.

It was extremely hard for me to draw back from what we call "reality" and speculate that there may be another kind of reality that is just as real as that which we understand from our human senses. But that is the only conclusion I could reach, unless I were prepared to toss all modern thought out the window. I couldn't do that and get anywhere at all. I had to force myself to accept the concept of a universal "now" that includes past, present, and future, even though I could only dimly understand it. I liked the way it may explain memory, but I was still uneasy about the reinforcement it provided for precognition.

My head told me Einstein must be right about our concepts of time, and it therefore followed that the future could be predicted, since it exists already. My head told me that, if *memory* (which we all have) is simply our faculty of perceiving the past, then precognition (which only a few of us seem to have in solid measure) is the same kind of perceptive faculty as memory, but tuned to the future instead of the past. My head kept telling me these things.

Little by little, I managed to accept them more deeply. That beginning, wholly forced and "rational" acceptance of the universal, all-inclusive "now" was another turning point in the rest of my search for meaning. Without that turning point, I should have had to abandon the effort and retire in complete bewilderment. But once I had reached that point, even though the recognition was initially tenuous and ill understood, other realizations began building on that awareness. Things began to fall into place.

Everything, finally. Even the fact that the future already exists, and that my future is already in some ways determined. That was a thought that I simply could not accept when I first reflected on precognition. But I still had to deal with my free will. I had to reconcile a future that exists with the fact that I *know* I can make choices that affect that future.

Chapter 18

Free Will and the Future

I approached the "free will" problem by reminding myself that nothing in life seems to be truly either-or, black or white, true or false, right or wrong. Everything, I've learned, is just a "little" gray, or has "more" truth, or is "less" wrong, when we examine almost any issue or theory or pronouncement thoroughly and with real objectivity. There just don't seem to be any absolutes that can be latched onto forever, as a lot of very good scientists freely admit. Ambiguity, paradox, contradiction— these are the names of some of the principal chessmen on the great board that human intellect seeks to master.

So it is with free will—a fact we know to be true in our lives— when it confronts a future that we know already exists. The two facts seem to exclude each other. If one is true, how can the other possibly be?

Both have to be true.

How can I say that, and how can I understand what I'm saying? Once again, I look to see how other intellects have handled ambiguous situations like this.

The physicist, in dealing with ambiguity, frequently abandons language and uses instead the notations and logic of mathematics to carry him past the chasms of paradox which human language cannot bridge. The faultless logic of mathematics will bring him an answer he knows is correct, but then he has to find a way to describe in words what the answer means. Sometimes he can't find one set of words—one theory—that covers the ground. I'm not a mathematician, but I've lived with examples of how the logic and mathematics of science can lead to two different *right* answers.

Let me give you one. It turns out that two quite different theories, each mutually exclusive, are required to explain the behavior of light. I learned that when I first went to work for Polaroid, whose principal product at that time was an optical polarizer. It was used in sunglasses and optical instruments because of its odd properties.

A sheet of polarizing material placed in a beam of light will let through all of the light vibrating in one direction, and will stop all of the light vibrating in another.

The phenomenon is easily understood if you visualize a picket fence, with a rope passing through it and tied to a post a few feet beyond. If you wiggle the rope up and down—make waves in it—the waves in the rope will pass right through the space between the pickets. But if you wiggle the rope sideways, the waves will stop at the pickets. The pickets absorb all the energy, and the rope beyond them stays at rest. Light behaves just like the rope. It will get through the fence of the polarizer if its waves are in one direction, but it won't get through if its waves go the other way.

The picket fence analogy is a perfectly sound way of explaining the behavior of light. Most of optical science is based on the "wave" theory of light. Light *does* behave in a picket-fence way, under most circumstances. That behavior is an observable fact, and the wave theory is a good theory because it works—it explains why things happen as they do with light.

Or most things, anyway. One problem wave theory doesn't handle is how the light gets through the absolute vacuum of space. Waves require that something be waved in order to transmit energy—one particle nudges its neighbor, and that neighbor its neighbor, and so on. What nudges what in the emptiness of space?

Nothing does, it turns out. The wave theory simply can't account for the transmission of light, or for a few other things that light is known to do. There is, therefore, a separate and equally sound theory which says that light is really made up of discrete energy bits called photons, and these travel not in waves but in straight lines, like birdshot leaving a gun. This "particle" theory stands side by side with wave theory in modern physics, both in mutual opposition, obviously contradictory—but together they explain the behavior of light.

Physicists accept both equally and use each where it is most helpful. Intellectually, they may be privately uneasy about what appears to be a theoretical cop-out, an admission that they have failed to find a unifying explanation. But mathematically, they are happy as can be. Their special language lets them handle this kind of ambiguity without distress.

Modern physics has a word for this disturbing situation. The word is "complementarity" and the noted physicist J. Robert Oppenheimer explained it to us: ". . . . the notion of complementarity . . . recognizes that various ways of talking about experience may each have validity, and may each be necessary for the adequate description of the physical world, and yet may stand in mutual exclusive relationship to each other, so that to a situation to which one applies, there may be no consistent possibility of applying the other." His message is pretty clear. As you get closer and closer to dealing with the basic realities of the world in which we live, you had better be prepared for contradictions and paradoxes that the mind of man cannot resolve. You will reach the point where no fact is immutable, where no one explanation is all-inclusive. But you will still be able to explain the world well enough to live comfortably and productively within it.

All that the physicist's notion of complementarity does for me is to allow me to live comfortably with paradox. I know I'm in good company when I say I'm sure that free will and a determined future are *both* valid ideas. There *are* matters about

which I can exercise my own will, my own choice, and life will
be different because I do. That is *one* reality. There are other
things that are probably going to happen regardless of what I
choose to do, because the future already exists. That is *another*
reality. *I will never be sure which reality will govern, or
whether either will, entirely, and it really doesn't make any
difference.* As long as I continue to act, and plan, and think
about what I want to do or become, some part of that will
probably happen. I *can* influence my own future and that of
others, and I need never stop trying just because some other
parts of my future may already be set for me. I'll never know
the things I can influence from the things I can't, and for that I
am exceedingly grateful.

Strangely, I no longer find upsetting the notion that there are
limits on what I can cause to happen in the future by my acts
of free will. For one thing, free will is not all that free, when you
stop to think about it.

Any choice I might wish to exercise right now is seriously
constrained by what I did in the moments or years previous to
right now. I can choose which tie I shall wear, but my immediate choices are limited to the ties I own, and they were the
result of earlier choices. If we think about this long enough, we
realize that everything we are, everything we have, every choice
we have ever made or will ever make, stems from earlier choices
made by us or by someone or by some happening that affected
us.

Why do I live in Boston? I can't answer that without
unraveling a chain of events which is literally unending: I went
to school here, and liked it. Why did I go to school here?
Because my stepfather went here. Why is he my stepfather?
Because my own father died and my mother married again. And
so on for the history of my life. The chain and the why's are
endless. Event added to earlier event to affect the next event—
all the way back to the moment of my conception, which
involved one sperm cell and one egg out of the millions that
might have merged, to form *me* instead of a brother or sister.
And behind those two cells ...

Many of the events that brought me where I am today were

completely out of my hands. If I wish, I can call them "chance" happenings and conclude that the course of my life is basically controlled by "chance." The control I exert by my own conscious choices and decisions affects things, too, probably importantly. But "chance" is certainly as dominant a factor in life as our own choices.

My own view of chance has radically changed. I don't use the word "chance" anymore in thinking about the factors that affect my life. I no longer think there *is* such a thing as chance operating in our lives, or maybe anywhere else, for that matter. I believe that *what we call "chance" is really the future rolling into the present.* Chance is only the presentation to us *now* of an event that pre-existed in what we term the future. *Now* that event is in the present, and in a moment it will be in what we call the past.

That's what we've been talking about for these many pages. Dr. Einstein helped me to conclude that the future is real and exists, waiting to slide into what our limited perceptions call the present. I shouldn't be surprised if that future holds things that I hadn't planned or expected—things I used to write off as "chance" happenings. Quite obviously, if *everything* in the future were exactly known to us at all times, we wouldn't have invented the term "future." We wouldn't need it. The future would be now.

Back to free will and fatalism. If we call "chance" by its real name—the pre-existing future—where does free will come in? *It comes in every time we are given a choice to make.* Hundreds of times a day, thousands of times a year, we use our free wills to exercise those choices. Sometimes those choices lead us where we wish, sometimes they don't. But every time we make a choice, we affect our future.

And just as one star in the universe affects all other stars, we affect the futures of others as well—our children, our friends, our societies, our very civilizations. *We are constantly shaping our futures, and our futures are constantly shaping us.* Mortal man can never know which is determinative, which prevails in any given instance.

We can accept the notion of complementarity—just as the

physicists have—if we want to feel more scientifically supported in all this. Neither the reality of an existing future nor the reality of free will explains everything adequately by itself. We must use both, and trust both.

How does this view of the future and of the nature of time square with what the seers and psychics tell us? Do we find support in those quarters for Einstein's view of time—and conversely, do we add credence to the psychic world when we compare its views with those of our physicists?

The seer says that he receives "visions"—fleeting pictures of events that already exist in the future and will come to pass when the future rolls into our present. Prophets like Jeane Dixon and hosts of others, to say nothing of the parade of astrologers throughout history, use these quick glimpses as the basis for their predictions. They do not usually claim that they see the vastness of the future spread before them like some unbounded and unending theatre in which all of mankind are the actors and all of creation the set. They do not say they do their thing by surveying the total scene and then zooming in for selected close-ups. Only a fragment here, an event there, seems to penetrate the screen of their human consciousness that separates today from tomorrow. Those fragments are what appear to constitute the visions of the seers.

Some of them describe the future-seeing experience as being like climbing to the top of a high mountain range and seeing all of the universe and all of time spread out below—the future, the present, the past—all one continuous "now," unmarked by the arbitrary divisions we employ to keep time.

Here is where human language lets us down. There are no words to describe what cannot be described, and we can't really understand what the mediums are trying to tell us. Those of us who have not been transported to that world of higher consciousness cannot really imagine the scene these people are talking about.

Perhaps the physicists are better able to, because they reach the same conclusion by a different route. Their mathematics tells them that there is only a "now"—past, present, future, all existing as one. In their professional lives they believe and trust that implicitly. They have to. In their private lives, dealing with the world their senses tell them we live in, who knows? A few are avid students of the mystical world. Einstein, called an atheist by some, said: "My religion consists of a humble admiration of the illimitable spirit who reveals himself in the slight details we are able to perceive with our frail and feeble minds." He acquired his own faith, one that included the reality, perplexing even to him, of a limitless "now."

And there we see two entirely different worlds touching. The world of the scientist and the world of the psychic, agreeing on a reality that the rest of us non-psychic mortals cannot truly grasp, no matter what kind of imagery we attempt. The rest of us have been trained to believe that we can truly know only what our senses tell us. We were taught to accept what they reveal as our *only* reality.

It does you and me very little good to probe deeper and deeper, as the physicists are doing, only to discover that everything we call "real" in the world is illusion. We *have* to believe that a table is a table, separate from the floor on which it stands, even though theoretical physics can show beyond question that the atoms that form the table are only empty space, only a complex of energy existing in a continuous field of energy, without substance or identity apart from the entirety of the field.

It does us little good to wrestle with that mystery, because, real or not, that table supports the pile of bills to be paid and the pictures of our loved ones that help to lift our days.

Just so with the future. It gets us nowhere to sit and worry over the fact that our futures are in some sense laid out for us. It wastes our time to try to sort out the part that may be immutable from the part we can control by our thoughts and actions. All we can do is accept the fact that the future already exists, that it sometimes can be foretold, and that it can be affected by our acts of choice.

You are probably familiar with a prayer that Reinhold Niebuhr wrote sometime ago, one that has caught the public fancy so well we can buy it embroidered on wall hangings and carved into snack trays in almost any souvenir shop:

> God, give us grace to accept with serenity
> The things that cannot be changed,
> Courage to change the things that should be changed,
> And the wisdom to distinguish the one from the other.

I always rather liked that prayer, because it allows for the futility we all feel from time to time, and offers a way to deal with it. It says: Keep me from beating my head against things which are just going to bloody it, and let me use myself productively. And by the way, tell me, God, in advance, just which those things are that will confound me, so I won't waste my time and energies on them.

For many years, that prayer made as much sense to me as any I had ever heard. It seemed so *practical,* so intelligent. If prayer does any good, if prayers are ever answered, this would seem to be the kind that has a chance. It's unselfish. It doesn't really ask God for a whole lot.

Yet a few pages back I found myself saying something exactly opposite to the hope expressed in Niebuhr's prayer. I said: "I'll never know the things I can influence from the things I can't, and for that I'm exceedingly grateful." Do I really not want the wisdom to know the difference? No, I really don't. And I'll tell you why.

If I were to know in advance what are the particular matters I cannot change, what future events or outcomes I cannot alter no matter what I do, I would be most uncomfortable. *Everything* else I might plan, every accomplishment I might seek, would inevitably be tailored to the knowledge of these unchangeable events the future has in store for me. I would have to know the *entire* future, else I wouldn't know which way to turn.

If the future were as simple as a game of Uncle Wiggly, and if the God of Niebuhr's prayer could tell me *all* the moves that were to come, I could probably figure a way out of the briar patch. Games are like life, but with many fewer variables. As in life, each move affects the next move, and the game unfolds as past choices limit present choices and affect future possibilities. In real life, God would have to tell me not only which moves have been preordained, but guide every move I make if the game is to come out the way it is supposed to. In that kind of game, there *is* no choice, and that's not the game I want to believe I'm in. So spare me, God, from knowing in advance what I can change and what I can't. And thank you, Dr. Niebuhr, for a prayer that made a lot of comfortable good sense until I tracked it all the way through.

Chapter 19

Clues from the Saucers

I guess I would have preferred to write this book without mention of flying saucers, because that subject seems to type books pretty narrowly. But I should include them. They were indeed part of my discovery process, and they provided some important clues that tied things together downstream aways.

Flying saucers are in here because, as I said a couple of chapters back, there were two pieces of the paranormal puzzle that gave me trouble as I tried to put the whole thing together. Precognition was one of them, and you saw what it took to unravel that one. The other was psychokinesis.

I have told you that material objects can be made to move without the application of any known physical force. Many are not able to accept that easily, but I believe the facts are indisputable. Objects *move,* and there are no fine wires, magnets, secret air currents or other tricks used to fool us into believing in PK. Whatever the failings of our good scientists may be, they usually get high marks as observers and mechanics. They have not been fooled.

The question, then, is not whether PK exists, but what kind of force it is. Is it purely and only a psychic force, one that resides in the realm of the mind and can be tapped only by the mind? Or is it possibly a *natural* force, one that we just haven't got around to discovering?

I looked at flying saucers to see whether they had anything to tell us about such a force. I also looked at them to learn what I could about the possibility that they—and PK—might have had something to do with the beliefs of some of the very ancient religions, beliefs that have filtered down over the ages right into our own faiths.

I sound as though I am convinced of the reality of flying saucers, and I am. I have been for many years, almost since the big commotion about them began after World War II. That was about the time I was beginning to become deeply involved in this quest. But there was not even a faint suggestion in my mind then that the two might be connected in any way. When our government, through the pronouncements of its Air Force, kept decreeing that flying saucers were a myth and an illusion, I became more curious than I would otherwise have been. I have not always believed everything government tells us, and when it tells us it is absolutely positive of something, I tend to be particularly querulous. The position our government .took on UFO's forced me to learn all I could about these mysterious objects just to satisfy myself that the government might be wrong. I did, and it was.

You probably deserve more than just my own assertion, though, if I'm not going to risk losing you in what follows. Perhaps the best hint of the reality of flying saucers comes in the Air Force reports themselves. If you read them carefully, you will find that though they claim to have accounted for over 96 percent of all sightings as being merely cloud formations, marsh gas, weather balloons, jet contrails, auroras, other air-craft or what-have-you, they admit that there is a remaining small percentage that cannot be accounted for. The Air Force ignores this remainder and tells us that the evidence is over-whelmingly against UFO's, just because their statistics seem to say so.

They are not being very good scientists or investigators when they do that. Probability theory doesn't let one ignore that last 4 percent. After all, Alexander Fleming discovered penicillin by observing the *one* petri dish out of hundreds that was not behaving the way all the rest were.

If we accept everything government reports tell us as being true, and forgive the Air Force hierarchy when they contrive occasionally ridiculous explanations for sightings which many of their own trained, intelligent pilots have made, the government is really admitting that flying saucers *do* exist. Their own statistics show it. They just would rather not have us think about them, because it might panic us the way Orson Welles' radio show about the Martians did.

So much for the official position, and the fumbled opportunity it represents to have made a constructive, dispassionate, and ultimately necessary investigation of these vessels from outer space. What basis beyond the government reports do we have for believing these objects exist and do indeed come from beyond our world?

Ask any modern astronomer what he thinks is the likelihood of intelligent life existing elsewhere in the universe. He will say it is no longer possible to believe that intelligent life does *not* exist somewhere. Our Milky Way galaxy alone numbers over 100 billion stars, and astronomers believe possibly half of these have planetary systems associated with them. If even as few as one tenth of one percent of these planets are orbiting within the ecospheres of their stars and are thus capable of supporting some form of life, there is life potential on some 50 million planets in our galaxy alone. Is it inconceivable that one or two of these might have developed life-forms similar to ours? No, it would be inconceivable to believe that *none* has, say these observers. I think we should accept that.

Think now about the age of the universe, and the age of our earth. Assuming that "age" has meaning in the cosmos, there are guesses that the universe is some eight billion years old, and our earth perhaps half that. Man's entire existence of a million or two years is but a tiny fraction of a second on the (nonexistent) clock of the universe. And, more to the point when we

examine the technology that would be required to build and fly
interstellar spaceships, our time of high technology isn't even a
measurable tick on that celestial clock. We went from Kitty
Hawk to the moon in less than one lifetime. Is it so hard to
imagine that other intelligent beings might have been a bit
ahead of us? A few thousand years, maybe? A million years,
perhaps?

Can any of us believe we ourselves shall forever remain tied to
the controlled explosion of chemical rocket fuels to accomplish
our weak forays into neighboring space? No, I think we can be
assured that some of us alive today will see man using other
forms of energy to cover greater space distances at enormously
greater speeds. We could almost do it now, using nuclear fission
reactors. We can assuredly do it tomorrow, when we master
controlled nuclear fusion. We may ultimately expect to learn
how to develop photon engines, or how to tap the energies of
cosmic ray particles. Those energies are so enormous that the
energy contained in a single atomic particle, a single hydrogen
nucleus flying through space, is sufficient to drive a baseball a
yard in the air.

The energy is there. But the problem most of us have when
we begin to think about interstellar travel is that of the
enormous distances, and the resulting interminable times we
think are required to get from place to place. Science is pretty
sure (though not absolutely positive) that nothing can travel
faster than light, a mere 186,000 miles per second. With unlimited energy we could power spaceships to reach speeds
nearing that of light, but even so it would still appear to take
many years to travel to nearby stars. If *we* can't imagine
hundred-year space trips, what kind of life-form would we have
to postulate on other planets that would be able to exist
throughout these long voyages?

Well, we could speculate about that ad infinitum, the way the
science fiction writers do. But we don't need to in order to
account for the time of space travel. All we need do is reflect on
what Einstein and other relativity theorists have been telling us
for over half a century about the nature of time.

When Einstein published his *Special Theory of Relativity* in
1905, one of the most controversial postulates of the theory was

that clocks must slow down as their velocity increases. In the years since then, Einstein's assertion has been confirmed as a fact by laboratory experiment. Timing mechanisms actually *do* slow down as they move faster in space. Any instrument or organism that measures time as we conceive of time slows in proportion to its speed relative to light, and would stop completely if it were to reach the speed of light.

Our human hearts are clocks of a special sort, clocks that regulate all of our other life processes, including aging. *They* will slow down, too, as they are made to move faster. So will the hearts, or their equivalent mechanisms, of the flying-saucer people. Those folks can age, say, less than one tenth as fast as we do, so long as they keep moving fast enough. A journey to us from the nearest stars could take them only a few years, earth-time.

Relativity theory, confirmed in the laboratory, thus handles nicely the problem of how our visitors can manage their long journeys. Today's knowledge of energy and power sources says the journeys are practical possibilities. And astronomical science tells us we can expect neighbors to exist, some of them millions of years ahead of us in their evolution. There, in a nutshell, is why we would all take flying saucers seriously if our governments and our human vanity would permit us to do so.

For the purposes of this book, there are two important aspects of flying saucers that I want to note. One is the way they maneuver in defiance of our natural laws, and the other is the possibility of visits having been made eons ago, and the import of such visits, if made.

First, the maneuvering phenomenon. If we confine ourselves to those UFO sighting reports made only by our most competent and credible observers—our airplane crews—we read in almost every report descriptions of abrupt course changes at high speeds, and of accelerations far faster than anything our modern aircraft can match. These course alterations seem to happen almost instantaneously. Nowhere are there descriptions of huge tongues of flame spurting out, or of the slow, stately ascents that we have become used to seeing from Cape Kennedy as our own spaceships fight earth's gravity. The propelling force that the saucers use must be of an entirely different sort than we have ever seen.

The really baffling thing about the flying saucers is not just how they overcome gravitational forces with such apparent ease, but how they overcome *inertial* effects. The course changes and accelerations described should not only wreak havoc on the craft itself and everything bolted to it, but would assuredly flatten the riders to a jelly on the inside walls of the ship or strain them through their seat harnesses. No life-form that we know of would be able to withstand the enormous "G" forces that are entailed, if the observations are even close to being accurate.

We can probably accept the observers' reports as at least being in the ball park. We do have radar observations of UFO's, and our airmen have been trained through long hours of experience to estimate relative speeds and closing distances accurately. The accelerations recorded and reported are many times higher than anything we have ever encountered, and this puts the G forces well outside the range that beings like us or machines like ours could safely withstand.

That leaves me with only one possible explanation: our visitors have learned how to counter inertial forces. They have discovered some way to get around Newton's laws of inertia, which for 200 years have explained why we get thrown off-balance when the subway train starts or stops or takes corners at high speed, and why it's harder to heave a shot put fifty feet than a grapefruit. Newton's laws seemed so reasonable that they were unquestioned until Einstein amended them early in the twentieth century. He showed that what we had been taught to believe was the "force" of gravity was really not a force at all. It was simply another manifestation of *inertia*. That fact makes a big difference if you're visiting us from outer space.

We are so used to "feeling" gravity as a force that pulls us toward the earth that it is hard for us to believe that it is not a natural force in its own right, as Newton thought it was. But Einstein showed that gravity is really a "field" that surrounds the earth, analogous to the magnetic field that surrounds a magnet. What we call the force of gravity is an *inertial* force that results from the mass of objects—our bodies, shot-put balls, and grapefruit—moving in space and responding to the gravitational field of the earth.

I've used that term "field" before, and maybe I should try to explain it, because we're going to see it again. If you have ever fiddled with iron filings scattered around a magnet, you've watched them arrange themselves along definite curved lines circling the magnet in an unusual pattern. These are the "lines of force" of the energy field that the magnet produces in the space around it. But no "force" as such manifests itself until materials with the right characteristics are placed in the field. Iron, because of its particular internal energy state, will respond to the region of energy that the magnet creates. Bits of paper or glass will not respond at all. A "field" is this kind of an energy state, one that is at rest, not pushing or pulling anything all by itself but capable of interacting with other energy patterns to produce a push or a pull under the right circumstances. And that's just what gravity is—a *field,* not a force, even though we feel its effect as a force pushing us into the ground.

Back to the spaceship. Its main problem, correctly stated, is that of overcoming *inertial* forces, including what we call gravity.

How does it do it?

Some of our imaginative scientists have suggested a number of ways by which our UFO visitors might accomplish their maneuvers. They all sound pretty far-out, yet each has some plausibility. I had to keep reminding myself that when I was a freshman in college, there was still a vigorous debate going on in engineering circles as to whether a rocket engine would deliver any thrust once it left the earth's atmosphere. There were some who held that a rocket had to have something to push against, like air, to move itself forward. Robert Goddard, the father of rocketry, refused to believe that, and that's why we finally got to the moon. And that's why I don't reject any theory out of hand if it's made by a responsible investigator.

The mass-energy equation is one of the possibilities that invites speculation. Mass is what gets slammed around by inertial forces, and mass and energy are in a sense interchangeable. Perhaps we shall one day discover magnetic means to effect controlled transmutation of mass to energy, and energy to mass, to counter inertial forces.

Or we may someday learn that the tachyon, an imagined particle that always travels faster than light, does indeed exist. If it does (and no logic today rules out its existence), the tachyon could hold startling answers to puzzling questions about interstellar travel, including the behavior of mass when it moves at high speeds.

There is yet another concept worth touching on, particularly because it relates to the phenomenon of time. One obvious way to reduce inertial effects is simply to reduce the rate of change of speed and direction—in effect, take the sharp curves at 30 miles an hour instead of 500. The flying saucers don't do that, of course. They maneuver at speeds well in excess of 500 miles per hour. But note that "per hour." Speed and acceleration are time-dependent. They have "time" as one of the bits of the equation. If time *itself* could be stretched, if an earth-second could be lengthened to ten seconds, or a hundred seconds, then the inertial forces resulting from a given rate of change of speed or direction would be reduced by the *square* of the change in time. A space technology that learned how to alter the flow of *time* would have its travel problems solved.

That sounds like a real wild one. But, as our little session with Dr. Einstein revealed, there is much we have yet to learn about time. A few years ago I came across one scientist who is not content with our present concept of time and who thinks it is something far more significant than just the ticking of a clock.

Dr. Nikolai Kozyrev, a Russian astrophysicist, believes that time is another form of *energy,* one that flows continuously and which in flowing, is the underlying source of much of the energy that exists in nature. He has described experiments which he says show that time has "density," just as material objects and other forms of energy have density. He claims to have measured slight changes in time-density at particular points where mechanical or chemical action is taking place. He theorizes that time flows, ceaselessly, throughout all matter and all living things, and *changes its density* as it flows. The change in time's density, he says, is what imparts additional energy of a special and powerful kind to the other energies with which we're familiar—mechanical, electromagnetic, chemical or any other kind.

Kozyrev observes that time, as a form of energy, exhibits a *rate* of flow through various substances, and that as the rate of flow changes, *weight* is lost. Weight, as we have just seen, stems from the inertial effects on a body moving in the earth's gravitational field. Since "time" is part of the inertial equation, a change in time flow would indeed be observed as a change in weight.

Kozyrev is not a man to be taken lightly. He is a distinguished scientist with world-respected credentials in astronomy and physics. Whether more conventional explanations will be found for the strange effects he observes remains to be seen. If not, we have to allow room for the possibility that time is indeed an *energy* form, one that could explain a great deal not only about our visitors from space but some of the other phenomena we have been talking about as well.

A logic suggests itself that goes something like this:

...PK exists, and demonstrates a force that confounds our inertial (gravitational) laws.

...Flying saucers exist, and they too demonstrate a force that confounds our inertial laws.

...Time is not just a ticking clock except here on earth, where our limited human senses compel us to view it that way.

...Time *may* be a basic and alterable *force* that binds the universe and powers all life.

...If time *is* an alterable force, its alteration would confound our inertial laws, affecting relationships of mass, energy, and rate as we know them (acceleration, gravity, and all the rest).

This logic implies, of course, that flying saucer behavior, Nelya's egg-separating, and Matthew's flying table are all based on the same energy form, one that stems from *time* itself.

I *have* to accept the reality of flying saucers, and I think Kozyrev's theories are probably as good as any other current explanation for them. Sure, his theories may not hold up, but if they don't it should be because something better takes their place. Whatever that better theory may be, I have a hunch it will reinforce, rather than diminish, the evidence for an unknown kind of energy that accounts for the mysteries of PK.

And I don't think we'll find that those mysteries are confined solely to forces originating in the mind. I suspect that the energy—whether it be "time" or not—that causes PK in all its many forms is just an energy in nature that we don't yet know enough about, but ultimately will. Impossible? Well, if we trace man's discovery process over millennia, all the way through chemical energy, kinetic energy, electrical energy, magnetic energy, atomic energy, and all the hybrids in between, we find this invariable assumption: we have *at last* discovered the *final* form of energy.

Man always seems to think that there can be nothing left, no energy he doesn't already know about. I believe there will indeed be discovery of other energy forms—maybe not too far in the future. The next one, my bones tell me, will be the energy that powers PK.

Chapter 20

Some Speculations on Pre-History

Once one accepts flying saucers, there is some rather far-out speculation that goes along with it, and I am going to indulge in a little of that right now. Though it doesn't prove anything incontrovertibly, it does help lead into the final task of putting all the pieces together. It's a way of shedding light on a few of the ideas our ancestors held and on why they may have held them.

If our little planet has, in fact, been visited recently by beings from outer space, as I believe it has, then—given the time scale of the universe—there follows the inescapable surmise that such visits could have been made many times, over many thousands of years. Now, we can't prove that, any more than we can prove absolutely that the visits we've observed over the past two decades actually took place. For many folks, that proof won't come until we capture a spaceship and display it on the White House lawn. But we can make reasonable inferences from the data at hand.

If you are one who still has to accept the Air Force denials of its own pilots' observations, I'm not going to be the one to try to tell you that Ezekiel *did* see the wheel—that little wheel run by faith and the big wheel, etc. I'm just going to suggest some ways to reflect on the possibility of earlier visitations without having to take the word of ancient sky watchers like Ezekiel.

There has been a spate of books lately that try to connect old mysteries with visits from outer space—Von Däniken's *Chariots of the Gods?*, Berlitz's *The Bermuda Triangle,* Toth and Nielsen's *Pyramid Power,* to name a few. They make interesting reading, up to a point, as they speculate on the likelihood of advanced civilizations having existed tens of thousands or hundreds of thousands of years ago, and on possible prehistoric visits from outer space. Some of the evidence they cite for believing there are uncovered ages in man's history is impressive. I'll give you a few samples which appear to be factual and undisputed, in case you haven't read any books like this. Then we'll try to see if they hold any meaning.

In the early 1700's there were discovered in the Turkish Palace of Topkapi some maps which had belonged to an admiral in the Turkish Navy named Piri Reis. At the time they were found and identified they were considered primitive even for those days, in that the distorted land masses they depicted were quite unlike the more accurate world maps in use in the eighteenth century for worldwide navigation. It was only on reexamination of the maps in more recent time that it was realized they were rather accurate *in one sense:* the distortion of the continents drawn on the maps was of exactly the same kind we have become used to seeing in our satellite pictures of earth.

In 1957 at Weston Observatory, just outside Boston, the Reis maps were examined in careful detail. The director of the observatory, one Father Linehan, observed that the maps were surprisingly accurate, particularly in their detail of Antarctic regions not discovered by modern man until the early 1950's.

The simplest explanation for the accuracy of the maps is that they were drawn from pictures made from a great height—say four or five thousand miles up. That would account nicely for the correctly distorted views of the major continents shown in the maps. The pictures would also have to have been made at least twenty thousand years ago, at a time when the Antarctic region was different than it appears today, because some of the formations shown are now deeply encased in ice. We have only recently been able to identify their contours with echo sounding devices. No one knows, by the way, how old the Reis maps really are. They are believed to be copies of much older documents, which may have been copies themselves.

High-altitude observation, as I say, is the simplest explanation for the accuracy of the Reis maps. The only other one is that some ancient cartographer created the maps purely out of his imagination. He *might* have consciously tried to display the kind of spherical distortion that matches modern satellite observations so closely. But only by the oddest chance could he have drawn in the contours of Antarctic land masses unknown until recent times.

Off the coast of an island in the Bahamas, scuba divers a few years ago discovered a peculiar underwater arrangement of rock slabs that are evenly and smoothly laid on the ocean floor in what seem to be the pattern of a paved street. Lining the "street" on both sides are larger rocks, weathered by time but looking for all the world like the remains of ancient walls. All of this is several fathoms underwater, becoming visible only recently as shifting sands uncovered them in the wake of storms. Similar remains have since been found in several other places in the Caribbean.

The last time this area could have been above water was some 12,000 years ago, when much of the ocean's water was captured in the ice of the last glacial age. Yet there are the streets and walls, and no one who has seen them, or even pictures of them, can conclude that they are anything but what they appear to be—the remains of a civilization that once existed where now there is only water. All *that* fact says is that our history is by no means as complete as we have been taught it is.

In a remote region of Bolivia, surrounded by mountains and inaccessible by other than air or pack train, lies a plateau 13,000 feet above sea level, the site of the ancient city of Tiahuanaco. No one knows how the city got there, or what happened to its inhabitants. It was obviously a city of some size, judging by the widely scattered remains of its buildings. Huge flagstones, worn by time and by the travel of ancient feet, help describe the plan of the city. Stone water conduits lie tossed about like so many match sticks, evidence of an advanced civilization and of powerful forces that wiped it out. As puzzling as anything else is the size of some of the stone blocks used in the construction and in the monuments that lie about—sandstone bases weighing one hundred tons, topped by single-block stone walls weighing sixty tons. How were they cut and transported in the thin air of the high Andes?

One of the archeological marvels of the world is found here: The Gate of the Sun. This large gateway was hewn from a single stone weighing many tons. Carved on the monument are forty-eight figures flanking a central figure, a being who very much looks to be flying. Other carvings in stone show quite lifelike heads of human beings, with a wide variety of shapes of noses, ears, lips. Some of the heads wear what look to be helmets.

There have been some intriguing artifacts found in widely scattered places in the world. In Peru, ancient ornaments made of platinum have been unearthed. Platinum requires temperatures in excess of $1,800°F$. before it becomes workable, temperatures we always thought only relatively recent man has been able to create and maintain. In China, excavation of an early grave yielded part of a belt made of aluminum. Aluminum metal is not found in nature. It must be refined from ore and requires some highly sophisticated processing techniques.

Thousands of miles from China, in Lebanon, there has been found radioactive aluminum in "naturally" occurring bits of aged, glasslike rock called tektites.

In Guatemala the burial pyramid of Tikal yielded a handsome necklace of green jade. The pyramid suggests a connection of some sort with old Egypt, thousands of miles away. The jade suggests a connection with China, more thousands of miles away; it is believed to have come from China.

There are other links that tie ancient civilizations together. In the old alphabets of Egypt, China, and Italy there are quite similar symbols used in similar ways to convey similar meaning. Some of these still survive: the Hebrew word for ox is "aleph"; the Semitic letter "aleph," the Greek "alpha," and the Roman letter "A" all probably derive from the sign of the bull's horns, a common Egyptian hieroglyph.

And now we read of studies made by two American prehistory scholars which trace the origins of the bull's horns and other symbols clear back to the paleolithic age, perhaps as long as 30,000 years ago. Allen Forbes and Thomas Crowder suggest that the cave drawings left by Ice Age man in France and the Ukraine actually contain written inscriptions, using symbols and letters that long pre-date the time that we call the beginning of history.

Certain Russian archeologists assert that an advanced prehistory society lived in Indonesia more than ten thousand years ago, citing as evidence the discovery of some accurate astronomical maps, and of optical lenses of a type that would today require an electrical process to produce the needed materials.

One of the problems Egyptologists have not been able to solve is the identification of primitive cultures that preceded the civilization that seems to have appeared almost full-blown on the Nile. It is from Russia that a theory issues which holds that this Indonesian civilization was the precursor one to ancient Egypt, bringing to that desert land the remarkable engineering wisdom that still astounds us as we view the marvels of stone that survive today.

This same problem of accounting for heroic stone work exists in many other places besides those I've mentioned. Stonehenge in England poses identical questions. So do some 200-ton blocks found in Peru, cut and faced in a distant quarry and somehow transported over mountainous terrain to their final sites atop cliffs 1,500 feet high. Perhaps the most massive stone of all lies in the foundation of the Temple of Jupiter at Baalbek, Lebanon. It is estimated to weigh more than 2,000 tons. We could not move it today.

Enough of these curiosities. There are as many more as you

care to read about, and they all add up to the same thing; bewilderment at the very least. There simply are no "accepted" explanations for them, and because there aren't, they make boundless speculation fair game for anyone. That's why some of the books about them become a little tiresome, once they have conveyed the message that there are plenty of strange things around. When the "gee whiz" succumbs to the "so what," endless recitations of oddities like these begin to lose some of their interest.

For me, though, they helped to put in place a few pieces of the puzzle that would otherwise have continued to baffle me. They pushed me toward a conclusion that I find hard to escape, on the evidence: the technological competence revealed in these glimpses of pre-history, and the apparently communicating cultures, quite possibly were aided by visits to earth in remote times by intelligences far advanced from our own. Knowing how short our period of recorded history is in terms of the age of this earth, there is simply no other explanation I can find that can account as well as this one for all that we have noted.

Admittedly, we have only a few scraps of evidence of earlier civilizations of high technology. But, like the small percentage of unexplained UFO sightings, the scraps won't go away. They are real, and they have to be accounted for. In the time scale of the cosmos, celestial visits many thousands of years apart, and whole civilizations living and dying many thousands of years apart, should not be at all inconceivable.

Our human views of time are narrow and distorted. We forget that our ancestors a mere *hundred* generations back lived 1,000 years before Christ; two hundred generations take us back beyond the oldest writings we can translate. On a four-billion-year-old earth, is it so impossible to think that a hundred thousand or a million years ago man made something like the same kind of progress we see today—and lost his civilizations when powerful forces wiped him out? We know that prehistoric ruins exist in the the ocean depths, covered for ages by glacial forces that have changed the face of the earth many times. We pump out of the Arctic today energy the sun stored in tropical plant life millions of years ago. The depths at which we find oil, coal, and diamonds all over the earth should remind us how deeply the earth buries her ancient past. Natural forces—flood, ice, earthquake, meteorites—can change anything, erase everything, and have assuredly done so over the past four billion years.

And man-made forces might just possibly have done the same. We cannot prove that man—or man aided by visitors from space—did not long, long ago reach a high technology close to what we have achieved in the past few decades—and blew himself up because he didn't know how to master it.

Fantastic? Yes. Plausible? Well, yes—to me, at least.

The notion of prehistoric eras of high technology explains things I find no other way to explain, including some of the foundations on which our religions rest.

It would explain how our ancient forebears could have acquired knowledge about forces we know nothing of. Forces that can lift massive weight against gravity, just as flying saucers move in defiance of inertial laws, and just as objects transport themselves through space in response to psychic commands. It would explain why most of the ancient religious legends describe visitations from huge ships in the sky, and why pictures skillfully drawn in ancient caves depict vehicles that look like our own spaceships and beings clothed like our spacemen.

It would explain the descriptions in the writings of many old religions of fiery destructions that were visited on man in times long preceding the writings themselves, and it would explain predictions like those of the apostle Peter of future destruction to come.* The ancients, we are told, knew nothing of nuclear energy, or even of gun-powder. Yet they describe past and coming days of judgment that read like a thousand Hiroshimas.

In 1884 the first English translation was made of the Ma-

---

* Second Peter 3:10: "But the day of the Lord will come like a thief, and then the heavens will pass away with a loud noise, and the elements will be dissolved with fire, and the earth and the works that are upon it will be burned up."

habharata, an Indian religious epic thought to date back, at least in part, to about 3,000 B.C. In it are found descriptions carried down from much earlier history, descriptions of weapons and destruction that appeared so fanciful to the translators in the 1880's that they felt obliged to caution the reader about some of the "ridiculous" content. Here are some excerpts:

"An incandescent column of smoke and flame, as bright as ten thousand suns, rose in all its splendor.... It was an unknown weapon, an iron thunderbolt, a gigantic messenger of death which reduced to ashes the entire race of the Vrishnis and the Andhakas.... The corpses were so burned as to be unrecognizable. Their hair and nails fell out.... To escape from this fire, the soldiers threw themselves in streams to wash themselves and all their equipment."

At another point the ancient writer describes the scene (in translation) as one of "great clouds opening one over the other like a series of several gigantic parasols."

All of this might be written off as pure fancy if it were confined to a single writing from ancient India. But we come across stories of metal flying machines, of gods that came from the stars, of heavenly fireships and boats, in many other religious legends and inscriptions from all parts of the world. American Indian legend has its thunderbird. Mayans believed their gods visited earth from the region of the star group Pleiades and told the Mayans that our earth was round. Eskimo legend holds that the first tribes were brought to the North by gods with metal wings. Egyptian and Babylonian inscriptions depict the same thing—flying gods coming from the heavens and returning to them after visiting earth.

And, in Pakistan, in the ruins of cities destroyed millennia ago, there have been found human skeletons that are radioactive.

I mentioned earlier some of the ideas of old Eastern religions that are being looked at today with renewed interest. The mind-over-matter demonstrations of ancient Yoga are being rediscovered by the Western world, for the simple reason that much of what Yoga teaches seems to work, at least for those who take it seriously and stay with it. Whether we call the strange powers of Yoga and other mystical cults a form of self-hypnosis or a true religion makes little difference. The mind *does* exert a mysterious control over the body under some circumstances, and the ancients have known that for a very long time. Did they discover this purely by chance many thousands of years ago? Why does it now appear to be so new to us, in our modern age of rushing technology and exploding knowledge? Could it be the old mystics retained knowledge from some earlier clues whose origins have been erased by time?

A suggestion of this earlier wisdom popped out at me while I was reviewing what science knows about that mysterious gland I spoke of earlier, the pineal body that lies buried deep in the oldest part of man's brain. You will recall that Eastern mystics have called this the "third eye" for thousands of years, and believed it to be the source of the psychic "sixth sense" of telepathy and clairvoyance. Why an eye?

Modern science has learned that in lower mammals, the pineal gland *is* in fact light-sensitive—a third eye of sorts. It has cells in it that give a photoelectric response to the animal's brain just as our eyes do.

In man's pineal such cells have disappeared, but we have recently discovered that the nerve pathways connecting with the pineal also connect with the eyes' optic nerves within the sympathetic nervous system. That means that pineal and eye functions are inter-related. *We* were able to discover that, because we have become quite skilled in neurology and physiology. Were the ancients similarly skilled? Or did they start with some knowledge which we have yet to acquire?

Very recent reports on pineal research describe a couple of other oddities that made me wonder how much the old mystics knew. Two of the chemicals manufactured in the brain—serotonin and melatonin—are synthesized with enzymes produced by the pineal gland. Though much work has been done to try to understand the roles of these compounds in human functioning, we are far from sure today just what those roles are. But we do have some clues, and they tie very closely to man's psychic makeup.

LSD and psilocybin, two of the most powerful psychedelic

drugs, have a chemical structure that is very similar to serotonin. It has been shown that one of the chemical effects produced by these drugs is a lowering of serotonin levels in the brain. Recovery from a mind-bending LSD "trip" does not take place until the normal serotonin level has been restored. And, as you have undoubtedly been made aware, a psychedelic trip produces many of the changes in time-sense and many of the visual and auditory images psychics report when they go into trance and commune with the other world.

Melatonin, the other pineal chemical, causes marked psychic effects when administered in fairly large doses to human subjects. (The melatonin used for this kind of experiment is extracted from the pineal glands of cows). When administered to human beings, the chemical causes a marked increase in the "alpha" activity of the brain, the kind of brain-wave pattern that appears when the eyes are closed or when decreased attention is paid to the environment and subconscious thought dominates the mind. Melatonin makes sleep come readily and causes vivid dreams to occur. In the awake individual, melatonin leads to feelings of elation and unusual visual imagery, not unlike that experienced with LSD.

All of these near-psychic responses, I remind you, are caused by natural chemicals secreted in the human body and secreted in lessening amounts as we age. (Psychic powers also appear to diminish with age, as I've noted.) Were our ancient mystics that far from the truth when they called the pineal the third eye and credited it with playing a role in our psychic consciousness? No, it is becoming apparent that they were pretty close to the mark. Your guess is as good as mine as to how they came by that knowledge, and you already know what my guess is.

How much of all this—the natural disasters, the space visits, the holocausts, the knowledge of some of the secrets of the mind—formed the foundation of the religions of the day? Do the old Egyptian and Mayan and Indian beliefs trace their origins further back into pre-history, tens of thousands of years ago? For me, there is no better conclusion that can be reached. We read earlier of the unmistakable antecedents of the Christian faith. We know the founders of that faith borrowed liberally from religions that preceded Christianity by thousands of years. It is not only likely but probable that those older religions from which we borrowed much of our own legend likewise borrowed— or inherited—much of theirs. Why should it be otherwise? All of human knowledge and belief rests on earlier knowledge and belief. I think it's safe to say that man's religion is a continuum, an evolution, going back as far as the mind of man reaches. We don't know how far back that is, but man's brain has been as competent as it is today for at least 100,000 years and probably much more.

What kind of ideas about God, and life, and afterlife might have filtered down through these untold ages, these cycles of great achievement followed by disaster and slow reconstruction? Almost certainly, the ancients would have looked to the heavens, and the stars, and the space beyond the stars as the home of their gods. That's where all of their even more ancient legend pointed. That's where all the powers they could no longer understand came from, powers their own legends taught them were real. Our own "heaven," the heaven modern theologists have such trouble dealing with, traces all the way back to pre-history.

So, probably, does the idea of God as a being that looks and acts and talks like man. The Bible says God created man in his image. Atheists reply man created God in man's image, because man couldn't picture anything else. Maybe both are wrong. We are certainly permitted the conjecture that man became man not through evolution alone, but with a boost from early visitors from outer space, beings who knew (and know) some things we don't yet know, perhaps about hybridization or mutation of the human species. If true, the "gods" of antiquity did indeed create man in their image, and endowed him with gifts of intellect his primitive anthropoid cousins have not acquired in all the millions of years of their existence.

If one wishes to do so, one can extend this kind of speculation into every corner of religious belief and account for some of the mysteries that have come down to us. The idea of virgin birth, as old as our records of man himself, can look very much like artificial insemination. Or like "cloning," a phenomenon we have only recently become aware of, one that reproduces organisms asexually from a single common ancestor. The "faith that moved mountains" may have been a manifestation of psycho-kinetic power, the power that may be part of the explanation for the giant works in stone that lie scattered throughout the world. The speaking in tongues, the visions of biblical prophets, even the power of prayer itself, may all have their origins in the psychic facts of history, in powers of the mind which were once clearly demonstrated and once clearly understood.

I'm not musing on all this in hopes that you will accept such explanations as true. I don't know whether they are true or not, and I don't expect we'll find the answer for a long time—maybe never. I cite them, first, because, on the evidence, they have some plausibility, and second, because they impart a dignity and at least a suspicion of truth to ancient beliefs which we have always been taught were mere superstition based on ignorance. I'm not so sure anymore that our forebears of one hundred or two hundred generations ago were as ignorant in all things as we make them out to be. I think they may have known some things we don't give them credit for.

My mind returns once more to the spectacular achievements of the one early civilization time and catastrophe have not let us forget—the old Egyptians. Their life for thousands of years was powered by their religious beliefs. Those beliefs had a hold on ruler and ruled alike that was so commanding that their age prospered for millennia, and their culture reached unbelievable heights. Their conviction in their gods and in the certainty of an afterlife was so compelling that they created an age the likes of which modern man has not seen. Their minds were just like ours, their passions the same as ours, their innate lusts for power and wealth no different from ours. Yet, somehow, they melded their humanness into a society that still amazes the world, one that survived for thousands of years because its people tried to live as they thought their gods wanted them to.

True, they *may* not have known anything we don't know. But at the very least they appear to have led their lives in accordance with what they knew and believed. And *that* says that their religious beliefs held a power for them that makes our Western religions seem pallid. You will have your own ideas about the source of that power. I have mine, and it's time for this book to look at them.

Chapter 21

Science and the Life Force

All of the modern knowledge about our minds and bodies, all of the psychic manifestations of unknown powers, all of that strange collection of ancient beliefs and unexplained artifacts—all of these had to be stitched together. They had to fit consistently in a final picture, and there could be no picking and choosing, no casual discard of the pieces that didn't fit.

How to stitch them together? How to go from the established fact of psychic powers in mortal man ... to the existence for all eternity of each human personality? How to believe in the release at death of an imperishable mind from brain tissue that ceases functioning at the last heartbeat? How to tie this world with the next and become totally convinced the tie is real, as real as life itself, as real as anything we have ever known? How to find out whether there is a God involved in this, and if there is, how to understand what he is like and how he works?

Well, I reasoned, if I'm to remain *me* as I step to the other side of the veil, something has to be retained that distinguishes

me from the billions and billions who have made the same trip
before. What will remain? What will it be that is *me?* What
clues do we have other than those coming from mediums
purporting to communicate with the next world?

We have several clues right in this world.

One that I found hard to put aside comes from some obscure
work done quite a while ago by the Medical Director of
Massachusetts General Hospital. In 1906, Dr. Duncan Mc-
Dougall performed some experiments which I doubt could be
repeated today. McDougall was curious about what happens at
the instant of death, most particularly about the possibility of
something escaping the body at that moment causing a change
in weight.

Somehow, he was able to obtain the permission of the families
of terminally ill patients to suspend the dying patients, bed and
all, in sensitive scales that could measure and record the
slightest change in wieght. The scales were kept constantly in
delicate balance as the patients gained and lost moisture
through respiration and perspiration, as medicines were administered and life processes continued.

Because of the complication of the procedure and the somewhat grisly nature of the undertaking, McDougall was able to
carry out the experiment with only a handful of patients. But in
every case, the scales recorded a measurable loss of weight when
the patient stopped breathing and was declared dead. The loss
varied from as little as a quarter of an ounce to as much as an
ounce.

That seems like rather a wide variation if all the weighings
are presumed to be measuring the same thing. We don't really
know how accurate the scales were, (McDougall said they
measured accurately within one tenth of an ounce). We don't
know how much of the variation can be attributed to other
experimental error. We don't even know whether McDougall
was as objective as he should have been in making his observations.

But we do know that this was a well-respected physician,
heading one of the world's most prestigious medical institutions.
We know that he was able to persuade some of his peers of the
importance and validity of his work, and was willing to face

some predictable ridicule following the publication of his observations. He obviously risked his professional career to do all
this. He must have believed the results were convincing and
worth reporting.

Did McDougall's scales weigh anything? Did he record something inside us that stays with us throughout our lives and then
leaves us when our physical bodies can't function anymore? Is it
something tangible enough to have weight, to have substance
that even fairly crude equipment could detect? There is other
evidence that seems to say yes, there is something else inside us,
other than the flesh and bones that make up our bodies.

I reported earlier on a number of laboratory experiments
made in America and elsewhere that demonstrated the presence
of an electromagnetic field surrounding every living organism.
The field can be readily measured today by sophisticated field
detectors, and has been many times. It is widely acknowledged
that the energy field is there, though nobody seems yet to have
explained convincingly just what it is.

We do not ordinarily consider energy to have weight—certainly not the kind of weight that could be measured on 1906
scales. Electrons, of course, do have mass—not very much, but
nevertheless definable.

We've also seen that mass and energy are the same thing,
though in different forms. A little mass can become a lot of
energy, as the atomic bomb taught us. And huge amounts of
energy can become mass, as we are reminded every spring when
plants convert the energy of light into leafy green through the
magic chemistry of chlorophyll. If you doubt that energy forms
mass, ask yourself next fall what it is you are raking up and
why your back gets tired. And as you burn those leaves, remind
yourself that the warmth you feel is that same energy from the
sun being released as heat to warm your hands and feet on a
cold November day.

What McDougall was measuring could have been small
amounts of mass transmuted to the body's energy field at the
moment of death. Or he could have been measuring the field
effects themselves.

An energy field doesn't weigh anything, as far as I know. But as gravitation teaches us, it can produce the *effect* of weight on bodies moving in it; motion of the field itself will also produce effects on bodies at rest within the field. And one field will affect another field, producing forces between the two. Because we don't know enough about the energy field surrounding our bodies, we have no good way of determining its interfield effects with gravity. We have no way yet of measuring the forces produced when the field moves, or when it alters in strength. We do know that the body's field strength varies widely, depending on a number of factors. Perhaps some of that variation is reflected in McDougall's measurements.

What all this boils down to is that McDougall's findings are not inconsistent with what we know about energy and about field behavior, assuming it was some change in the body's energy field that he was recording. We probably won't know the answer for quite a while, at the rate we seem to be going in America with investigation of this energy field that envelops each of us. But the little we do know about that energy adds some credence to what McDougall discovered.

We know some other things, too. We know that there is a strange and separate energy "state" existing within every living thing—quite possibly the very same energy that accounts for the body's force-field just described. We *know* this special energy state exists, because today there are ways by which we can see it with our own eyes and record its presence on photographic film.

An early hint of this energy was given in a paper published in 1920 by Dr. W. J. Kilner of St. Thomas Hospital in London. Kilner discovered that when the human body is viewed through a filter darkened with dicyanine dye there can be seen a distinct cloud of radiation extending for some eight inches around the entire body. Kilner was a medical man, in no way a mystic. He found that the appearance of this "aura" seemed to change in some relationship to the state of physical health of the body, and that it disappeared completely at death. He pursued the phenomenon as far as he could, in hopes it might aid the diagnosis and treatment of disease. But the mysteries of the aura did not yield to his labors. The work was finally abandoned and the hope forgotten. But the aura itself was not to be forgotten.

We are indebted to a Russian electrician, one Semyon Kirlian, for picking up the thread of this discovery, though he didn't know he was doing so at the time. Kirlian was handy at many things, including photography. In the early forties he happened to notice a subtle luminosity on the skin of patients at the point where electrotherapy electrodes were being applied for treatment of bone and joint maladies. Kirlian was curious to know what caused this luminosity and whether it could be photographed.

Working alone, with some help from his wife, he managed after nearly ten years of experiment to develop equipment that could photograph the faintly luminous emissions that other eyes had either missed or ignored. His equipment utilized a high-voltage, high-frequency "Tesla" coil of the kind used in X-ray and spark generators. When a Tesla coil is energized and connected across two metal plates, it creates an intense electric field between the plates. Kirlian found that if living tissue is placed between the plates and a piece of photographic film is inserted under the tissue, a strange image is recorded—not an image of the electrical energy (which does not affect the film) but an image of a completely different kind of radiation appearing to emanate from the tissue itself.

Kirlian kept plugging away at his work, which for many years did not seem to get the attention today's knowledge about the phenomenon shows it deserves. He was finally able to devise equipment that made it possible to examine the changing behavior of living (and dying) tissue under high-frequency radiation. The results were so impressive that Kirlian's tinkering could not be ignored. Russian scientists began to study it in earnest in the early sixties.

What the Kirlian technique reveals is a multi-colored luminescence streaming from the surfaces and edges of all living matter. At times the luminescence spurts out like a solar flare; at times twinkles like stars on a clear night. There are spots that glow brightly and then subside, and others that flare up in vivid greens, reds, violets—and then die away. At times the image, under suitable magnification, looks like nothing so much as a giant fireworks display.

During the last ten years investigators in many parts of the world have sought to discover the cause and meaning of these strange emissions. Using plants and animals for their experiments, some have concluded that what the Kirlian technique reveals is a "life" energy that exists in all living tissue, *an energy whose pattern mirrors the physical shape of the tissue structure* and whose pulsing, glowing, and flaring characteristics seem to reflect the state of health of the tissue.

Leaves attached to a living plant all show the same general Kirlian flare pattern. If a leaf is severed from the stem, the pattern it emits persists for some little time and then begins to diminish slowly in intensity as the leaf dies. In the finally withered leaf, all of the emissions are extinguished. At the point on the stem where the leaf is cut, a powerful flare erupts, as though the very life of the plant were streaming through the wound. This, too, subsides as the plant heals itself. The normal patterns from the healthy leaves remain undisturbed.

Some of the most revealing experiments are those in which only a portion of an organism—perhaps a quarter of a healthy leaf—is removed, and the remainder is examined. The Kirlian photograph will continue to show the pattern of the *whole leaf,* undisturbed by the surgery.

This finding has led to a description of the energy pattern as an "energy body"—an *exact double* of the physical organism in which the energy exists. The persistence of the energy structure has been noted so many times in animal and plant experiments that many investigators in this field now seem to take for granted the reality of an energy body—one that is organized spatially just like the host tissue, but separate from it and existing independent of the physical organism.

The Russians call it the "biological plasma body," or bi-oplasma, for short. They use the word "plasma" because it is an accepted word that describes a state of matter that is not a solid or a liquid or a vapor. To the physicist, "plasma" is a highly ionized "gas" consisting of electrons, charged atoms, and neutral particles. Whether what the Kirlian photographs show is really a plasma in the sense the physicists use the word remains to be seen. Obviously there is something there that high-frequency radiation at high voltage causes to luminesce. And maybe "plasma" is the only word around that sounds close enough and scientific enough to make people pay attention. So plasma it is.

I've not read of instances of the entire human body being observed or photographed using the Kirlian technique—it's apparently dangerous to subject the whole body at once to this kind of high-voltage, high-frequency energy. But the bits and pieces appear to have been studied—hands, feet, joints, other sections of the body—and they show the same energy-body characteristics that the plant and animal pictures reveal.

They show other things as well. It has been observed many times that quite noticeable changes in the energy flares and patterns take place, seemingly corresponding to the state of mind and the state of health of the person being photographed. Fatigue is reported to increase the flare activity, as though more energy is being lost by a tired body than by a rested one. People who are ill show a disorganized flare activity. People who are angry or full of anxiety appear to emit increased energy patterns. Very recent research in the United States has also shown that the size of the flares can be importantly affected by the moisture content of the skin—moist skin, more pronounced flares, dry skin, subdued flares. This variation not only underscores the need for care in interpreting Kirlian photographs, but may further couple the flare phenomenon with emotional states.

The sites of the principal flare-points in human beings seem to be specific, unchanging, and well organized. This fact, added to the observed changes in flare activity that seem to correlate with the state of human health, prompted some Soviet investigators to try to tie the energy-flare sites to the acupuncture sites of ancient Chinese medicine.

For over 5,000 years the Chinese have used acupuncture, originally to detect disease and treat it *before* it manifested itself in physical illness, more recently to effect cures in diseased bodies and as an anesthetic in surgery. Western medicine has only recently discovered acupuncture, and it took a man of giant stature, Dr. Paul Dudley White, to make American doctors begin to pay attention. Not many of them have yet.

The Chinese ancients identified some seven hundred points on the surface of the human body at which the "Vital Energy" which flows through the body can be tapped. They held that the Vital Energy or "Life Force" flows along specific pathways that have nothing to do with the nervous system or the circulatory system—indeed, no such pathways have ever been discovered by dissection. Each of the several hundred points is said to be in communication with an organ deep inside the body. These pathways were all mapped thousands of years ago and have never changed. The master acupuncturist is one who knows exactly where the skin sites of these pathways are and exactly how to stimulate them to bring about change in the matching organ inside. The Chinese hold that the stimulation of a fine needle inserted at the correct point will correct the imbalances of the Vital Energy flow which are the real cause of illness.

I'm making no pitch for acupuncture, though it is well known that it does seem to work—at times, for some kinds of cases, and sometimes with startling results. No one really knows how or why it works, not even the practitioners who get good results. The origins are buried too far in the past. The Oriental acupuncturist today can tell you only that he believes completely in the presence of the Vital Energy, and that it does flow along pathways accessible through the seven hundred points on the skin. He will assure you that our mental states will affect the flow, and even that the mental states of others can have an impact on our own Vital Energy flow. So, too, will our environment—the quality of the air, the activity of solar flares, the positions of the moon and the planets. Far-out, to be sure. But acupuncture does seem to get results. Western science hasn't yet been able to shed further light on the phenomenon.

The Russians may be getting somewhere. They have used some of their heavy scientists in their efforts to couple Kirlian techniques with the ancient Chinese acupuncture sites. They are trying to make it easier to locate the sites with the precision that seems to be required, thus making acupuncture more reliable and more widely available. They claim they are succeeding, though our Soviet friends probably aren't telling us all they might about their work.

Once again, I find myself wishing that our own scientists, doctors, and government officials weren't quite so haughty and so hidebound about things like this. If we were ever to take these phenomena seriously, who knows what the outcome might be? At the very least, we might be able to slow the quackery that inevitably springs up around ideas like acupuncture. My guess is that we'd do a lot more than that.

So. I've described four clues—loss of weight at death, the existence of an electromagnetic field surrounding the body, Kirlian observation of an internal energy form, and acupuncture—all saying to me the same thing: There is more to our physical lives and bodies than just the chemicals that form our cells.

Back to the question of what part of us remains, if anything, when we die. Maybe you're way ahead of me as I near the conclusion that *what remains is this energy-body,* this bioplasma that pervades my body while I'm alive. That conclusion will be such a significant one that I think I should explore further some of the known characteristics of this energy-body.

Very importantly, for the purposes of this book, it appears to be "shaped," to be organized spatially, just as the human body is. As the picture of the partially removed leaf showed, the pattern of the energy substance remains as it was before the leaf was cut. The Kirlian picture looks as though the whole leaf were still there.

Some observers believe that this energy-duplicate of the physical body is what governs the intricate organization of our bodies from the moment of conception. They believe that it determines which cells and how many of them shall become skin, or bone, or muscle, or brain, or other organ tissue. In this view, our physical bodies mirror our energy bodies—not the other way around.

This question of the organizing principle of the body continues to baffle the biosciences. All of our highly differentiated cells bear exactly the same DNA structure, and all are daughters of the single cell that started us out in our mothers' wombs. What tells the cells to specialize? What tells them to stop when organ growth is completed? What sometimes fails to tell them to stop, or lets them grow in the wrong place, and leads to what we call cancer? We do not yet know the answer to these things, though we are working harder on them than on anything else that has ever fired imagination in the laboratory. It's just possible that some part of the answer—maybe almost all of it—will be found to lie in the mysterious energy body that American science is slowly getting around to looking at.

Note again what the Kirlian photos show about the energy flares that seem to spurt from the body. I mentioned that they are more vigorous in the fatigued body, and in the anxious or angry body. They appear to indicate energy *leaving* the body, becoming lost in the surround of space. We frequently hear a term—I know I've used it and perhaps you have, too—to describe a feeling we ordinary mortals experience in times of stress. We talk of spending "psychic energy" in wrestling with some of the stubborn problems that life deals us, usually in our relationships with other human beings. It's certainly not the physical, muscular kind of energy we use in walking or weight-lifting. It's not quite like the "mental" energy we expend and that can be so tiring when we do puzzles or add long columns of figures. It's an entirely different kind, and it's the kind that drains us, the kind that makes for a hard day at the office.

Why do we call it "psychic" energy? I don't know, since most of us are not demonstrably psychic and wouldn't have reason to use the term unless somebody invented it for us. But it's a term we know we need, because that kind of energy *is* different from the rest, and when we spend it, we're tired. I can't help but suspect that it is the same energy that the Kirlian pictures show, the kind that causes the increased flare activity when we're angry, or anxious, or tired out from an exhausting day. Is it really tied to things psychic? Is there anything that links the Kirlian energy pictures to our psychic selves?

There have been some laboratory experiments that lead to just that conclusion. Begin with the electromagnetic field I described, the one that surrounds each living thing. Remember, that discovery is now over thirty years old and is a fact accepted by scientists just about everywhere. This is the force-field that the Canadian and Russian scientists were measuring when they wired up Matthew Manning and Nelya Mikhailova. They watched the pointers swing while these two powerful psychics did their PK thing, and they demonstrated that the body's external field alters greatly in intensity and in spatial distribution when the psychic power is turned on.

Kirlian studies have been made of psychics as they produce powerful PK forces. The pictures tie the body's external electrical field and the internal energy patterns together convincingly. In Matthew's case, Kirlian pictures were made in Canada and later in Holland while Matthew was demonstrating his PK powers. The Canadian investigator called the pictures the most remarkable he had ever seen. The energy levels, as suggested by the size and prominence of the luminescent flares, were extraordinarily high.

In the Dutch experiment, three different machines had to be used to obtain good visualization of Matthew's bioplasmic energy. Matthew blew out the first two when the investigators told him to "put all the energy he had into the machine." The head of the research company (Aura Electronics) said of Matthew's encounter with these new, powerful 35,000 volt machines, "I am not quite sure about what really happened. At one moment he seemed to absorb the total energy of the machine, and at the next, he forced such an energy back into the machine that the machines just 'gave up the ghost.' "

These two differing experiments—the external force-field and the Kirlian bioplasma pictures—don't prove that the energy-body is the *sole* source of all the psychokinetic energy in all of the various PK phenomena we have noted. It may be, and then again it may not be. Perhaps the energy that can be summoned directly from the body's bioplasma is limitless enough to account for all of the extraordinary things we've seen. Or perhaps the bioplasma is merely a conduit, a connection to other energies in nature of which we know nothing yet. Just as the internal energy structure of a piece of iron responds to a surrounding magnetic field, so may our bioplasma tap other energies of the kind we speculated on earlier. To press the analogy, only a few of us have the "iron" structure; the rest of us behave as glass in a magnetic field.

For our purposes right now, it doesn't make much difference

what the mechanism is. I don't expect we'll understand it for a long time. What we understand now is enough for me: the psychic powers of human beings reside not in brain tissue, not in strange molecules as yet undiscovered in the cells of the brain, but in a wholly separate part of ourselves—the bioplasma, the energy-body, the substance that I believe is mind itself.

That's a pretty big leap, from bioplasma to mind itself. But there is some additional experimental evidence which forces me to make it: The Russians appear to have linked the energy-body to *telepathy*. Think back to the dream experiments made here in America some years ago, and recall the proof they offered that the *subconscious mind* can receive telepathic communications during sleep. The *mind,* not the eyes, not the brain, not the physical part of man, does this. If bioplasma can be tied to *telepathy* as well as PK, then it is assuredly tied to the *mind,* and to thought, to memory, to the personality that is uniquely "us."

The Russians claim to have made this connection of energy-body to telepathy, and they did it as an outgrowth of their efforts to develop improved acupuncture techniques. One of the products of that work is a piece of equipment that looks like a small flashlight. As it moves over the surface of the body, a small light glows on and off. The glows identify the points of greatest bio-luminosity on the skin, and their brightness indicates the relative bio-energy levels at those points. They built this equipment to make it easier to correlate bio-plasmic energy changes at various points of the skin with mental states, environmental changes, and the state of physical health of human subjects.

But here is the key discovery, for our purposes: They have experimented with this gear to see if they could detect changes in bioplasma energy levels in subjects receiving telepathic communication. They used hypnotized subjects to maximize the telepathic response and to minimize transmission error, and they describe test conditions that seem to have careful experimental controls built in. *They claim that very noticeable changes occur in the bioplasmic energy levels of subjects receiv-*

ing telepathic transmission. They report that the levels rise and fall markedly as the sender alternately turns on and turns off his thought messages.

I could wish that reports were available from other laboratories tying the energy-body to telepathy as tightly as the Russians claim to have done. Not that I distrust the Russians so much—their scientific publications have usually matched our own standards. It's just that this is a particularly critical connecting point, involving several of the phenomena we have been probing. At key points such as this, there can never be too much information at hand to support each observation.

The Russian use of bioplasma detectors to show changes in energy level corresponding with telepathy inputs links the physical known, the psychic unknown, and the mind. I accept their reports because they fit so well with other pieces of evidence which indicate the same kind of coupling, and because the Russians have not been known to deceive us in their scientific journals. But it would certainly be nice to see an American byline or two on such crucial scientific work, as there was when the irrepressible J. B. Rhine was in his prime.

But I think the day is coming when we in America will decide to catch up. Paul Dudley White almost succeeded in changing our traditional medical views about acupuncture. Perhaps some equally noted and courageous doctor or scientist will soon try again in the even wider field of the nonphysical mind.

When this happens—and I think the right word is "when," not "if"—I expect we shall see incontrovertible evidence of the reality of the chain that I have described, the chain that links together the mysteries of the human mind, the latent psychic powers that exist in all of us, and the intimate coupling of body and mind that we all sense intuitively and that Eastern mystics have shown us how to exploit. I think we'll see that chain tie all of these to our energy bodies. And then, when we ponder what it is that survives us when we die, we'll know.

We'll be encouraged to believe—all of us—everything I have told you. Today we have to string the bits and pieces together as best we can, and weigh each bit and each piece as we go along. I'm well satisfied that the weight of the evidence is there, that everything adds up without contradiction and without holes. I could use more volume of evidence, and I suspect we'll eventually begin to see that coming. For years, I haven't lost any sleep over it. I am as sure as I have to be that where all this is coming out is right, and that when we finally get around to examining that outcome seriously in America, I'll be OK. I think we'll all be OK.

Chapter 22

Confirmation from the Psychic and the Not-So-Psychic

It's time now to leave the laboratory again and see what the mystics have to say about all this. We did this once before when we were wrestling with the physicists' concept of time, and found some reinforcement. Some may find the idea of an energy-double, a second body that mirrors our physical selves, almost as hard to comprehend as the universal "now," but these things have to be dealt with. After all, if it were simple, somebody would have explained it to us long ago and we'd all be believers.

One of the writers in the psychic field whom I've come to respect very highly is Eileen Garrett. She is a medium, a woman with startling psychic powers. She is one who has used them not just as a communicator with the other world for the amazement of her sitters, but as an intelligent, objective investigator of psychic phenomena. In addition to the very informative books she has written about her personal experiences and her reflections on their meaning, Mrs. Garrett was for years the driving force of the Parapsychology Foundation. This New York-based organization has been doing a responsible job of publication and investigation of psychic phenomena for nearly three decades, and Mrs. Garrett was at the helm for most of that time. She is an investigator who has commanded respect from believer and nonbeliever alike. Her whole life has been spent searching for understanding, not for disciples.

Mrs. Garrett sees "auras" surrounding people and all other living things. She has always seen them, and not until mid-childhood did she discover that hardly anybody else did. She took them for granted the way we take sight for granted. Just as a child born blind has trouble imagining what we are describing as we look at the world, we have difficulty understanding what Mrs. Garrett and others like her are describing as they look at the world. They see something most of us can't see, something that is very much like the luminescence produced in Kirlian equipment.

They see it surrounding plants; they see it surrounding animals. They watch it change in color and intensity, and they sense intuitively that the changes are tied directly to emotional and physical states of well-being. Most books written by psychic people tell of this aura, this luminous surround that envelopes all living things. When Mrs. Garrett writes about it, she bridges the gap between the luminescences of the Kirlian laboratories and the nature of the human mind and life-force as the psychic sees it.

In her book *Awareness* she describes how we look to the psychic eye that sees beyond our own: "A person's *surround* encloses and encompasses him like a misty aura, changing in color and density as his moods and conditions change." She goes on: "To me, the only strange aspect of this capacity of perception is the fact that it is not common ... [yet] many people, without seeing any *surround,* develop this capacity of penetration in some measure, as the physician gathers an inner understanding of a 'case.' ... The expert in any line of work is one who ... comes very close, by 'intuition,' to the same sense of subtle state of being as I gather from the perception of the *surround.*"

Is Eileen Garrett describing the energy-body of the Kirlian

pictures, the vital energy of the ancient acupuncturists? I don't see how I can think otherwise. If I accept the one, I believe I must accept the other. I can't throw aside the laboratory evidence. It won't go away. And I can't ignore Mrs. Garrett, knowing her as I do through her books, and knowing that hundreds of other psychically gifted persons have said the same thing.

Further, I can see no reason to suspect that there are two entirely separate things going on here, one shown to exist by scientific equipment and the other an entirely different phenomenon observed by the psychics. What is "seen" by the two modes of perception is just too similar, too closely corresponding in detail after detail, to warrant such a conclusion. It would be too strained to think they are unrelated, too out of keeping with the basic tidiness of the universe. Nature keeps reminding us that the simplest explanation is usually the right one. I have to think that what the laboratory experimenter sees and what the psychic sees are one and the same.

This is one of the most important deductions this book will seek to make, which is why I examine it as carefully as I can. This is the point at which I had to leave the measurable, testable world of our human senses and make the rest of the journey relying heavily on what the special senses of a relatively small handful of psychics tell us. I hadn't had to place reliance on that source yet. So far, I had turned to that world beyond our ordinary perceptions only for clues to guide me, or for corroboration of some of the things that have come out of the laboratory. But Mrs. Garrett and others like her had helped to bridge, for me, the two worlds I had been seeking to connect.

Though from now on I would have to listen primarily to what the psychics had to say, I would still have to test what they told me against everything else I'd learned, and against my intuitions as well. I would have to sift through the mass of psychic accounts very carefully, and base further conclusions only on those that had a solid ring of authenticity to my by now fairly well trained ear.

Here, now, the first step. This second body that we've detected in the laboratory, and that Eileen Garrett and others describe in their extrasensory images, *seems to be able to leave the living physical body under certain circumstances, and then reenter it.* Long ago, when I first came across stories of this, I dismissed them as being absolutely incredible. I didn't care *who* claimed to have experienced or seen a "second" body leave the real one. There was just no way I was going to believe anything that sounded so close to the ghost stories we used to make up as kids. Psychology had the right word for this sort of thing— hallucination (though I'm no longer sure what that word means).

You've seen how often I have had to rethink this kind of reaction, yet how my skepticism tended to erode when I took the trouble to study the matter deeply and tried to relate it to other phenomena I had earlier learned to accept. That's what I had to do with the reports of this releasability, this detacha- bility of the energy body from the living human being. Is it something that can really happen, or is "hallucination" still the best word for it? Well, the dividing line would be pretty fine were it not for various clues that finally made me more able to accept the validity of this strange idea.

Let me give you one of the classic and best researched instances of "astral projection" (as it is sometimes called) which the literature holds:

Sylvan Muldoon, an English lad of twelve, one night sud- denly found himself being whirled about in a vast empty void. Moments later, when things subsided, he found himself looking down at his bed. There he was, *in his bed.* But he *knew* he was in the air, looking down at himself. The frightened child rushed to his mother for help, but she could not hear his cries, nor would she waken when he touched her. She could not feel him. He returned shortly to his sleeping body, never to forget the unnerving experience.

A dream? Dr. Hereward Carrington didn't seem to think so. Carrington was a well-known British psychic investigator, one who had long been curious about out-of-body experiences. He worked with Sylvan for a number of years, becoming convinced of the boy's ability to separate his second body and to act and observe through this body while it was many miles from its physical counterpart. In 1929, Carrington and Muldoon jointly published a book *(Techniques of Astral Projection)* about their investigations, including the methods they developed for causing the separation to take place almost at will. Carrington himself learned to do it, he claimed. The book describes instances in which the second body appeared in entirely human form and was recognized by others at some distance from where the physical body lay.

The credentials that surround the book are impressive, and it still stands as something of a classic, one of the most thorough examinations of this phenomenon that has been undertaken. But we have to remember that a book like this is only as convincing as our belief in the people who write it allows it to be. It's hard, when we don't know them, to be instantly persuaded.

Another report of out-of-body travel impressed our scientist-investigator J. B. Rhine sufficiently to cause him to publish a description of it in 1952: "... we have a visitor at our laboratory, Dr. John Bjorkhem, a Swedish psychiatrist who has done more experimenting to produce these apparitions (projections of the second body of a living person) than anyone else. This triple-trained minister-psychologist-physician has done a great deal with hypnosis.

"One day in Uppsala, Sweden, a 17-year-old girl was brought to Dr. Bjorkhem. In the course of an experiment, the psychiatrist put the girl into the hypnotic state (her first experience) and told her to go home and visit her family 250 miles away. Without moving from her chair the girl described her experience [presumably immediately after her return from her 'journey'] to the hypnotist.

"She said she was at home, in the kitchen, with one foot on a chair. Her mother was doing household tasks in the kitchen. Her father was reading the paper. She described the first item at the top of the page.

"A few hours later a friend in Uppsala received a long distance phone call from the girl's parents asking what was the matter with her. They had seen her in the kitchen with one foot on a chair. Then she disappeared without speaking."

Rhine makes no claim that this or other reports like it constitute proof of the existence or separability of the second body. He merely wanted us to know that there is still much to be explained in this vast world of the psychic unknown. This particular phenomenon doesn't readily yield to the mass experimental approaches that he used to confirm the existence of telepathy, clairvoyance and psychokinesis. Rhine had to leave it where it was, no matter how intrigued he may have been with reports like Bjorkhem's.

And reports similar to Bjorkhem's abound. In two books published a few years ago, an English investigator, Dr. Robert Crookall, provides nearly 400 descriptions of second-body projection and makes a serious attempt to characterize the phenomenon. By pointing out the comparable aspects of the cases, and particularly by citing so many of them, Crookall imparts a believability that the reading of a few isolated cases cannot. In this sense, his book did for me something of the same thing that the large number of UFO sightings did, and that the thousands of instances of precognition by ordinary people did. Though no one case, no one witness can convince me absolutely by what he says, when *all* of them coincide in their testimony, I have to view as very small the possibility they had all reached a prior agreement to perpetrate a hoax. It's another kind of twist to the law of large numbers, and I'm a believer in that law. That doesn't prove, of course, that they weren't all experiencing something else, though what that might be has never been described. So I call Crookall's massive account a good clue.

One of the interesting things Crookall's book brings out, as do other reports, is the frequency with which observers watching the energy-body leaving the physical one notice a fine, wispy connecting "cord" between the two bodies. Psychically gifted people report seeing this cord readily. But it is also reported to have been seen occasionally by perfectly ordinary people, usually those sitting by the bedsides of relatives or friends who are severely ill. Many of the cases of out-of-body experience seem to have occurred when illness or accident or some other life-threatening situation exists, just as we noted was true in most instances of precognition on the part of ordinary people. Mention of this apparently infinitely stretchable cord is frequent enough to give it some of the validity of the out-of-body experience itself. If you buy the idea of a separate second body, it probably doesn't hurt to buy the cord that goes with it.

This "silken cord" or "silver cord" is an idea as old as history itself. The psychics state perfectly matter-of-factly that it is there, that it is what permits the second body to return to the physical body when the journey is completed. Severance of the silver cord causes death, they tell us. They also tell us that the separated condition is in some ways a dangerous one, and that no one should mess around with the physical body while separation is underway. Rude awakenings, severe physical handling, and strong emotional shocks can lead to severance of the connecting cord, and to death, say some of the psychics.

Well, it's awfully hard to tell about that one. Nobody goes around snipping these cords deliberately just to see what happens. Most of us will probably never see one, and I'd guess the silver cord is way down on anyone's list of phenomena to be investigated scientifically. The idea itself doesn't bother me, nor does it strike me as illogical. But it isn't an important thing to get hung up on, because whether it exists or not doesn't change the outcome a bit. I mention it because it's widely written about and might well be a true phenomenon. I suspect that it is, but I don't think even the psychics know too much about it. So, if it makes you nervous, forget I mentioned it.

There's a psychologist at the University of California in Sacramento who has been fascinated with out-of-body experiences for some time. Dr. Charles Tart has done some historical investigation, among other things, and has identified out-of-body scenes in Egyptian tomb pictures and tracked down descriptions of such experiences in ancient Greek and other writings. He has been building his own collection of modern out-of-body accounts and has also been conducting laboratory experiments to try to produce and understand the phenomenon. He reported recently on an experiment with a college girl in her twenties who slept in Tart's lab for four nights, wired up with all the usual monitoring gear used for sleep experiments. She had claimed previous out-of-body experiences, and Tart decided to test her in a very simple way. As she slept, he placed on a shelf five and a half feet over her head a small piece of paper on which had been printed a random number unknown to anyone involved in the experiment. The idea was to see if the girl could read the number on one of her "travels." For three nights she reported having left her physical body, but made no mention of the piece of paper. On the fourth night she awoke at 6:04 A.M., reported another journey, and called out the correct number—25132.

Dr. Tart hasn't explained this, and doesn't claim that he has wholly ruled out clairvoyance. But he obviously thinks this is something other than clairvoyance. The encouraging thing is that a scientific professional these days can pursue matters like this without having his epaulets ripped off.

There are other professionals who are examining this whole area in quite a different way. One of the recent accomplishments of medicine is the ability in a growing number of cases to bring back to life persons who are "dead" in the conventional medical sense—no heartbeat, respiration, blood pressure, pupil contraction, etc. There have been instances recorded throughout history of people who claimed they had "died" and come back to life, but until recently they were so scattered and the medical information so sparse that nobody paid much attention to them.

Now, however, with new techniques to restore breathing and heart function, and even to provide them externally for considerable periods of time, the number of cases of recovery from what would formerly have been certain death is quite large. Not a few curious doctors and other investigators have begun to collect and examine reports of such instances. Some have started to report their findings, among them at least two American doctors, Elisabeth Kubler-Ross and Raymond A. Moody. Dr. Moody was a philosophy professor before he went to medical school, which perhaps accounts for some of his interest in this area.

In 1975 Moody published a book, *Life After Life,* based on ten years of tracking down reports of people who had had a "death experience"—in all, about 150 cases. Most of his book is devoted to instances in which he was able to interview men and women who had been pronounced dead by their doctors or who came very close to death through accident or injury. He obtained about fifty interviews personally, and these are used liberally in the book to enable the reader to judge for himself the significance of the experiences recorded.

Rather than select one or two to give you a feeling for what is being said, I think it's more useful to record Moody's own synthesis of all of the experiences. He has written the following "model" of the death experience, based on what this fairly large number of people have said it is like:

"A man is dying and, as he reaches the point of greatest physical distress, he hears himself pronounced dead by his doctor. He begins to hear an uncomfortable noise, a loud ringing or buzzing, and at the same time he feels himself moving very rapidly through a long dark tunnel. After this, he suddenly finds himself outside of his own physical body, but still in the immediate physical environment, and he sees his own body from a distance, as though he is a spectator. He watches the resuscitation attempt from this unusual vantage point and is in a state of emotional upheaval.

"After a while, he collects himself and becomes more accustomed to his odd condition. He notices that he still has a 'body,' but one of a very different nature and with very different powers from the physical body he has left behind. Soon other things begin to happen. Others come to meet and help him. He glimpses the spirits of relatives and friends who have already died, and a loving, warm spirit of a kind he has never encountered before—a being of light—appears before him. This being asks him a question, nonverbally, to make him evaluate his life and helps him along by showing him a panoramic, instantaneous playback of the major events of his life. At some point he finds himself approaching some sort of barrier, or border, apparently representing the limit between earthly life and the next life. Yet, he finds that he must go back to the earth, that the time for his death has not yet come. At this point he resists, for by now he is taken up with the experiences in the afterlife and does not want to return. He is overwhelmed by intense feelings of joy, love, and peace. Despite his attitude, though, he somehow reunites with his physical body and lives.

"Later he tries to tell others, but he has trouble doing so. In the first place, he can find no human words adequate to describe these unearthly episodes. He also finds that others scoff, so he stops telling other people. Still, the experience affects his life profoundly, especially his views about death and its relationship to life."

The verbatim accounts themselves are much more interesting to read than the synthesis Dr. Moody has prepared. They carry an earnestness and simplicity that adds appeal and credibility to the accounts. I suppose it could be held that all of these people are simply reciting a scenario that has been conditioned into their subconscious minds by religious training, novels, films and dreams, and that nothing mystical underlies their reports. That's something each of us has to judge for himself, because psychology can't prove anything here, one way or the other. For me, these reports have a certain ring of truth, and they fit remarkably with everything else I have learned.

I leave now the last of the eyewitness reports we shall have, at least from witnesses who are just everyday, ordinary non-psychic mortals like most of us. I turn to the world of the psychics one more time, to see what they can tell us about the second body and the death experience.

Of all of the psychics that I might cite I choose again Eileen Garrett—not just because of who she is and what she's done and the fact that I came to respect her. Eileen Garrett is an accomplished writer, and when we come close to the moment of death itself, there is much more room for poetry. Let her tell you of that moment:

"More than once I have seen this human life-essence release itself from the physical body, so that, without it, the body was dead. In each case I knew—I was *aware*—that it was the *synthetic essence* [Mrs. Garrett's term for the synthesizing force, the second body within, that organizes and directs the whole human being] that had withdrawn, leaving each cell in the corpus alive and active at its own level, but bereft of its universe, its god, shorn of the creative power that had controlled its destiny.

"The first time I saw the vital synthetic essence leave the body was at the death of a cousin, in Ireland, when I was a little girl. She was sleeping, and my aunt left me to watch, with instructions to call her if Ann waked or stirred. My aunt knew, though I did not, that her tubercular daughter was very near death.

"Ann finally stirred, in a kind of spasm, then lay quiet again, so I did not call. And I became aware of a dim mist that was exuding from her body, weaving intricately within itself in a rhythm that was without agitation, tension, strain or pressure. Fascinated, I watched the faint small cloud move off into space. Did it leave the room by a window, or by penetrating through the wall? I do not know. Yet it withdrew, into infinite space, weaving within itself, and in utter concentrated absorption I watched it, followed it, accompanied it, into nameless psychic distances, until I was roused from my absorption by the entrance of my aunt. She, finding that her daughter had died in her absence, berated and punished me for having failed to call her.

"Looking back at the incident, I have realized that in my childish ignorance I actually did not in any conscious way know that my cousin had died. But in my psychic perceptiveness—which was the level at which I most truly lived in those years—I had intimately attended at the final event.

"Later, when my two sons died within a few months of each other, I was again aware of the withdrawal of that essence which is the sum of the synthetic human individuation. The dim misty cloud spiraled out from those small bodies as I held them in my arms, and moved away; and with an intensity of desire that was made poignant by my emotional feeling of personal loss, I followed those dim vitalities out and out into endless distance, till the throbbing in my head broke in upon the focus of my concentration."

* * *

There ... is death, the death that awaits us all.

And there ... is life, the life that I now know, in the deepest reaches of my heart, will continue for time untold. There is no other thought I can think, no other ending I can find, no matter how or where I look. Nothing that I know points anywhere else. Nothing convinces me any longer that the death of our human bodies is the final death of ourselves. We know nothing that proves physical death is truly death, except that most of us cannot see or touch beyond what lies in the casket. But not being able to see, not being able to touch, is no proof nothing is there, as I have learned so many times in the course of this journey.

No, there are things we cannot see, and things we cannot touch, all around us, in the real world of earthly nature just as in the real world that lies beyond. If we have proof that anything at all exists beyond our senses, we have more than a suggestion of proof that our souls will never die.

Now, I haven't used that word "soul" before. I can use it now, because now I know what it is, and you know too. No longer is soul just another murky word I used to hear in church. It is *us*. It is our minds, our personalities, our memories, our thoughts and hopes and dreams. It is *all* we are, and it is *all* embraced in our inner energy-selves, in our second bodies that must someday leave our wearying forms and move through the veil, to eternity.

Chapter 23

Death and the Life Beyond

Heaven. That's where I find myself once again, long after I had earlier left it with the readings of Houdini, Jim Pike, and hundreds more like them. You now know exactly how I got back here, how everything I had learned pointed, step by step, more and more surely, to the fact of survival of personality after death.

I probably take some risk in using that word "heaven." I'm long past the point where it conjures images of white-robed angels floating in fleecy skies. But I'm not so sure about you, and I think I won't use the word again until I try to make you understand better the world I shall describe, the one I now *know*. I told you at the outset that you may not like that heaven, or the God I found there. But I must draw that other world which, for me, has become so real.

I will describe it just as I feel it, just as I know it to be. I won't cite references and weave the fabric thread by thread as I've done up to now. That would be tedious, because the threads are numberless. But, be assured, they are there, spun from hundreds of reports of the afterlife that reach us through mediums, mediums whose lives impress me and whose psychic practices seem to me ingenuous and convincingly above reproach. They are people who have questioned as deeply as I have every aspect of the supernatural world, and who have relayed to us without conscious embellishment or retouching the exact messages that have come through their bodies.

What follows derives not from the mediums alone nor from the glimpses of that other life we have been afforded by people who have almost, but not quite, died. Taken all together, these are still not enough, for there are many differences in the accounts that are puzzlingly inconsistent until they are examined with another kind of insight.

That insight must come from the mind, the only source we have left for answers to what may appear to be unanswerable. I learned to trust my mind. It brought me through mysteries I never thought I would fathom, and it helped me build the reality of the eternity that awaits us.

I describe it now, the ending to my search, the answer to my deepest problem, and the beginning of meaning.

THE MOMENT OF DEATH

The sensations we shall feel when death comes will be much the same for all of us. There will be no fear or pain whatsoever—nothing more ominous than perhaps a feeling of being drawn into an enclosed void, something like that tunnel, perhaps with a brilliance at the distant end. If death comes in its natural way, when a spent body refuses to go further, we shall have a total awareness of the moment, and we will sense a peace we have never known before. But we will still not be sure of what is happening. Our minds will be clear. We'll hear distinctly the voices of those who attend us in our last moments. We'll be unable to tell them of the peace we feel, and we may struggle to hold on to both that peace and to the life we are leaving. For a moment that seems without time, we'll watch from above our wasted bodies lying where we left them. We're puzzled by that, still unable to believe what is happening to us.

How should we know we are dead? We still feel, we still think, we still "are," just as we were. And then we know. We find we can move freely, unrestrained by walls and doors. We can touch those we left behind, and talk to them, but they can neither feel us nor hear us. We will finally know we are dead, some of us soon, some later. But we won't become used to the idea for a long time to come. Time has no meaning now. A "long" time will not be measured by any clock, but rather by the effort we must expend as we struggle to pick up in this new life where we left off in the previous one.

If we died violently, we will be more acutely puzzled and disturbed. There will be no pain, no piercing memory of a shattered body. Only peace, and deep bewilderment about what has happened. We'll still be there, where we died, knowing all that happened and all that is around us, but unable to comprehend our death. We won't know where to go, what to do, how to begin. We will feel we have suddenly been dropped into a foreign land, knowing nothing of the customs or language, knowing no one to turn to. And yet we will know we are *not* in a foreign land. We are right where we were when we died, and we see everything now which we saw then—the car or gun that killed us, the surroundings of the place in which death came. But it's different, and now foreign, and it takes us a while to realize that what is different is death.

We are not alone long—perhaps not even for an instant, though in our bewilderment we may not know that. There are others—one, a few, many—beside us, telling us what has happened. We see them as real, we touch them and feel them as real, just as we see and touch ourselves. They have bodies that we soon learn are real when we *think* of them as real, yet bodies whose substance vanishes when they are not in and of our minds. We speak with them not in words or language, but we speak nevertheless. Their *thoughts* are ours, and ours theirs— whole thoughts, not word-by-word verbalizations. They have neither age nor youth, they show no scars or disfigurements left from earlier struggles. Yet we *recognize* them as persons, as the faces and shapes of people we knew and whose lives we shared before they made their own journey ahead of us. They are people who, knowing us and knowing of our death to come, were close by to receive us, over there. We have passed over the threshold, through the tunnel, and there is light and life on the other side.

THE VIEW ON THE OTHER SIDE

One of the hardest things for us to comprehend about our new world beyond is that it looks, physically and materially, just like the world we knew here. We shall see land, and hills and streams, and flowers and trees and all of the other things that make for the beauty of this earth.

Let me pause now and resolve one of the difficulties I had to overcome in facing this other world. In every case in which departed souls have tried to describe the physical scene in this new world the message comes through consistently: The world they are in looks just like the world they left. They speak of nature as we know it, of sunlight and of vast distances filled with beauty. They speak of buildings, too, and of libraries and great forums. And they speak of music, and the sweet sounds of the life we know here. They also speak of villages of mud huts, and of tents pitched in desert sands. And, once in a while, they speak of storms, and black voids, and noise, and great fires.

Can all of these be true? Can the life beyond be so like our own, so full of nature's beauty, yet with accents of nature's terrors? In a world unbounded by time, a world that no longer need afford protection to frail physical bodies, can there be buildings, ancient and modern, shelters for beings who need no shelter? Why does one being describe a scene much like the one he departed in 1970 and another tell us of village huts he knew as a child in the twelfth century? Can they both be describing the same place?

Long ago, when I first began reading widely the many accounts of the hereafter that have reached us through mediums, I was struck by these great differences in description of the physical surroundings, and by what seemed to me to be the absurdity of the reports of buildings and other appurtenances of earthly man. All of this seemed just as improbable as were the streets paved with gold and the heavenly, harp-laden choirs robed in white. I knew those were false because they were so purposeless and illogical. The world beyond could not possibly be a tinseled place, decorated with the dross of man's earthly greed.

But a world that looks like our own world, even though more beautiful, a world that still contains man's mark in buildings and shelter—is this any more believable? I didn't think so then. That doubt was one of the very great ones that my readings of spirit communication had raised in me. That doubt, more than any other, is what compelled me to look elsewhere, first, before I could ever hope to comprehend the world the mediums keep describing.

But now I am back in that world, knowing far more than I knew before, and able to understand how it can be exactly what the beings in that world tell us it is.

Each of them is seeing, and each of us will see, when his time comes, what his *mind* sees. And much of what each mind sees will be what it has learned to see by living this earthly life.

I remind you that it is not our eyes that give us the pictures we look at. They and the brain provide only the processed stimuli; our *minds* give us the pictures. When we dream, we receive no visual stimuli, yet the dream pictures our minds provide are just as real and vivid as those of our waking hours. We dream only of things we know. We rarely—perhaps never—dream of shapes or scenes that are totally foreign to our experience. What we dream may seem distorted or exaggerated, but we somewhere before have experienced a shape or scene like the one in our dream. Had you never seen a telephone, or a picture of one, or a shape anything like one, you would not dream of a telephone. We dream—our minds dream—what we know.

What our minds have known in this life is *all* they will know in the next, when we arrive. What we see there will be images our minds have learned to see here—nothing more. When we cross over, there is no instant infusion of a new awareness, no thirty-second course administered to fill our minds with knowledge or images we had never had before. We *transit,* that's all, from here to there, and we bring only what we had when we left. We bring what our minds know, the things they have been able to dream about. Nothing more.

Dreams are as close as most of us will ever get in this life to an intuitive glimpse of what the life beyond is like. Yet to call death a dream is to demean it. We look on dreams as frivolous and unsubstantial. We wake from them, promptly forget them, and pick up our lives where they were before we went to sleep. We don't feel responsible for the strange things that happen in our dreams. We don't control them: they control us. Psychologists don't understand dreams any more than anyone else does. They don't know why we have them. But each of us knows, from his own experience, that dreams are moments without time, without the press of gravity, without limits to our ability to move about, to transport ourselves instantly through a kaleidoscope of constantly changing scenes.

The next life is something like this. Our minds, which make us dream in this life, make us *live* in the next. They are *all* we are, there. No physical body exerts control over them, to waken us and subdue the inner mind. We will not waken, ever, in the old way. We *are* awake there, constantly, and we *are* in control of ourselves there, in a world very close to the kind of world we could only dream about before.

Does this sound insubstantial? Do I sound like I'm describing a next life which is not a life at all, one with no more reality than the dreams that slip away into the night? It mustn't, and it needn't if we but reflect again on what we call "reality." We think of our "real" world as one which is tangible, solid, actual. Yet we know beyond a shadow of doubt that the things we see and feel as "real" are nothing more than collections of atoms, each made of nothing, in the last analysis, but pure energy. When our physicists peel the last layer from the atomic onion, they will find nothing. Nothing but discrete forms of energy. We have no idea at all how or why our senses and our minds perceive these packages of energy as *real* trees and buildings and tin cans and people. We only know that we *do* see them and feel them, and that they make up the "reality" of this life.

We must admit of another reality, one also made of energy, and one that is equally "real" to the perceptions of that energy body that leaves us at death and continues its existence in an entirely new state. That energy body is still "us," and will always be, and it will contain the mind that we shaped in ourselves over here. It holds our memory, our certain knowledge of everything that has ever happened to us, and of everything we ever looked at, and touched, and heard, and tasted, and smelled. That may be *all* it holds. But all of those things will live on in boundless eternity. We will be conscious of all of them forever.

That's why each of us will see in the next world what we know and have known in this one. That's why there are as many descriptions of the world beyond as there are beings living there. Each of us is shaping right now, and has been shaping all his life, the nature of what he will "see" and find in the world beyond when he arrives.

Where is that world? It is anywhere we see it to be in our new state. It is in the cities we left behind, or in the untracked wilderness we once longed to know. It is anywhere in the universe, if we wish it to be. There is no travel time, no distance that fetters us. We are now mind, and thought, and we are as uninhibited as mind and thought always were. We take no space, as our bodies used to in our earlier life. Yet space is there, and all of it is ours. We are neither "up there" nor "down here."

We are something vaguely like the energy broadcast from a television tower, existing throughout all of the miles of space around the tower, yet assembled instantly into a vivid picture, anywhere, when the energy is organized correctly. We are like air that cannot be felt or sensed, existing everywhere, occupying the void but not filling it. We are wherever our minds will us to be, and wherever we are, everything is as real as it ever was. What is different is the absence of time, and of the boundaries of material space. We are free, timeless, unbounded, and so is the world in which we now exist.

LIFE ON THE OTHER SIDE

We bring to the other side everything we have made ourselves to be on this side—no more, no less. We can "bring" physical objects that are important to us, because if they are in our minds, they can be there with us, in form and substance as real as they are here. We will see, and have, and touch whatever our minds want to see, and have, and touch. If we desire clothing, we shall be clothed, elegantly or simply, as we choose. But these things will not mean to us what they meant in our previous life. When each can have whatever his mind wills him to have, life is vastly different. No one is impressed by fine raiment other than those who have always been impressed by fine raiment. No palace, no matter how grand, will make us somebody in a world where anybody can have any palace he wishes.

We will discover that we exist in a world of *beings,* just as we did in the world we left. But we won't relate to them as we formerly did. Most of the drives that shaped our lives then are missing now. We have no physical body to nourish or protect, no competition to wage with other beings to obtain a larger share of the world's treasure. We have no need to reproduce ourselves. We cannot lie or cheat, because we use thought, not speech, to communicate. Our minds are open, naked. Our thoughts are not private when we communicate with others. There is no such thing as trying to be truthful, or honest, because there is no falsehood, no dishonesty. We are truly as babes, entering a world we are largely unprepared for because we have had to spend much of our earthly lives meeting the basic necessities of that existence. Yet we have all eternity to spend here. What do we do with it?

There are at least three pursuits we shall find ourselves engaged in—perhaps more, but only three I can be certain of from what we can learn here in our earthly probings. The first will be that of learning how to exist with others in our new state. Though billions have preceded us, we shall not see masses of ghostly humanity filling the scene. It will not be like the streets of New York, where streams of faceless people pass us and abrade us each day.

No, we will know there are persons there, but we will see and know only those with whose minds and selves we wish to and are able to relate. Our minds make them visible and tangible to us, and their minds make us so to them. Where two minds fail to meet, contact is insubstantial, and we are alone. We will find that we cannot tune in Confucius, or Jesus, or William James at will. Nor will Hitler or Ghengis Kahn intrude on us unless we both will it. There must be a harmony of two life-forces, a certain strange matching of energy patterns, a true meeting of minds before we can know another intimately. Newly arrived, we will not know how to accomplish that, and it will cause us concern.

We are not stranded, though. We will meet the persons who greet us the moment we die, and they will help us learn how to communicate with more. We will assuredly meet with close friends and relatives who preceded us, perhaps to pick up the same closeness we once had, perhaps to discover that what we thought was closeness was nothing like that at all. More and more, we will find kindred souls who are like ourselves, beings whose energy patterns, earth lives, and mental development make them much the same as we are.

We will find that whatever we do takes energy, just as everything we did in the life we left took energy. We *have* energy—we *are* energy—but it is not boundless. We replenish it not with food, but by absorbing it into our energy bodies from the vast reservoir that surrounds us. In the earth world, we couldn't comprehend the nature of that energy. We knew only that an unidentified kind existed, one that operated through our minds and that powered things like psychokinesis and ESP. We wondered then at the possibility of its being the same energy we would use in the life beyond. Now we know.

It takes *will* to tap that source in our new world. We must expend energy to obtain the energy we need. Some of us will learn how to do that better than others, because of the more purposeful wills and the better disciplines instilled in their minds during the past life. Some of us will be tired in the new life, just as we were in the old one. The burdens haven't disappeared the way we had hoped they might.

But many things are profoundly better. We will begin to understand for the first time the true meaning of love, a total sharing of one's entire being with another. We will be surprised to learn that we still have sexual feelings. We still retain those deep drives, the same ones that gave us pleasure and pain before, the ones that gave us a measure of immortality through our children, and that provided hints of the ecstasy that can come with the true merging of two human beings.

We will love sexually in this new life, but not in mere physical coupling and the physical explosion that accompanies it. Here we will know the total ecstasy of the sexual merging of two souls, purposefully and unreservedly, as two become one. For some, our unions will be with those from whom death had separated us until now. The bonds created in our previous lives may still be the most powerful and satisfying we could seek. For others, the partners may be new, and may change.

There is no such thing as promiscuity here, and there are no strictures on our behavior. We shall love whom we shall love, and the search for souls who will love us will be part of what we feel driven to do in this new life.

We are free to do what we wish, but we learn that freedom is something not easy to get used to. We are free to hate. We will discover, though, that if we had been accustomed to feeling hatred and expressing rage and anger in our earlier life, such will be of no help to us here. Of what use is hate, and ill-wishing, when there is no physical or material harm we can possibly bring to another, nothing of which we can deprive him except our love? We will have to learn, if we have been haters, that hate and anger are useless here and only serve to make our bewilderment more intense.

But love, and the wonder at beauty—these will overcome us increasingly, as we learn to let them. In them we will find ways to serve, to help others through love. Some of us will seek out and try to reach those that are having continuing difficulty adjusting to their new lives. That adjustment is not an easy one. Many will not understand their new state, and will continue to view the new life just as they viewed the old one. They will still seek power, they will still cling to their vanities, they will still seek to collect things they think have value. Only slowly will they find these are of no use now. These souls are in some torment because they do not know how to escape from the cramped existence their minds restrict them to. Their communications are limited, confined largely to others whose minds are as theirs, and they will be anguished for a long while. Because their minds had not been well-tuned to the possibility of other values, they will yearn for a world structured just like the one they left. They will not find that world, and they will feel lost.

That would be hell, and it is.

REACHING BACK

Finding one's way in the new life is only one of the challenges that await us, and for some it may prove nearly endless and all-consuming. But there are other things to occupy us, forever, if we wish them to. One of them is to follow an urge to remain in touch with the world we left behind. We can never forget our life there. It is part of us. It made us as we now are, for better or for worse.

We will find we have the power to reach back into that life and even to affect its course for those still living it. Some of us will choose to try to stay much involved in that life, and will be willing to spend considerable energy to do it. But we will now have a very different view of life there, one changed dramatically by our new relationship with time.

Our new world is one without time. "Time," that mysterious force that our earthly senses told us flowed always from the future, relentlessly creating the past, does not exist any longer for us. We live in the eternal "now," and we understand at last the gropings of the physicists who tried to explain that to us when we were alive on earth. Our unbounded universe is without past, present, or future. We are in the past, we are in the present, we are in the future—it is all the same to us now.

Our "memories" are memories no longer. They are absolutely clear, complete, uninhibited perceptions of *everything* we ever did, everything that ever happened. We can no longer bury in our subconscious the things we would rather forget. Our subconscious is *us* now, and everything in it is as clear and fresh as an October morning. Parts of that now vivid past can make for us another kind of hell, one that can torment us terribly as we struggle to overcome past wrongs we have done, using a new love that is hard for us to acquire and understand.

We will learn to move easily in the time we used to call the future. We will find we can *know* what will happen on the earth we left behind. We will know what can be *made* to happen, what choices earthly man has for affecting his future. All of this we can know, if we choose to put our minds to it and spend the energy our new state constantly requires.

We will remain involved back there in different ways, according to our choosing. Many of us will stay in touch only briefly, trying to do what we can to reassure loved ones we left behind. We can readily be next to them, intimately close to them in our own familiar old surroundings. We can see them clearly, hear them, touch them, talk to them, but we cannot make them see or hear us. Sometimes, when our energy patterns and theirs mesh in momentary harmony, we will know they have had a sense of our presence. But just as most of us felt we could not penetrate the screen when we were alive on earth, so most of us cannot easily penetrate it from the other side now that we exist there ourselves.

That will puzzle us, and upset us. We can know so clearly everything that happens and will happen in the life we left, see so well the wasting lives and foolish choices of those still living their earthly lives. Why can't they know we are there with them? Why do they seem so unable to respond to the guidance we can give? We know we could reach into their minds, heal their sick bodies, if we could penetrate the conscious control that shuts off the awareness we wish them to have. We try— some for only a little while, some for a long time—to reach and guide the living. For all of us it is one way to ease the torment of the now remembered past, to balance the books by giving a love and service we never knew we could give before.

Not all of us, though, are driven by a new awareness of love and service. There are those who are still as they were in their former lives, unable yet to sense what has happened, and guided still by the cramped and petty values that marked their lives on earth. They, too, are in contact with lives still living there, and in their continuing ignorance of what the new life holds, they still counsel evil, still know anger and hate. They are the *other* side of the new life we now live, just as they were the other side of truth and beauty in the life they left.

All of us will find, in whatever way we seek to affect those still living on earth, that contact there is not easy to accomplish. Some of us will discover that if we try hard enough, we can make our energies manifest on earth in psychic ways. We can move material objects, and startle earthlings into a puzzled awareness of our reality. We can make ourselves visible to their minds, sometimes in their dreams, sometimes to their waking consciousness. All of this takes great effort, and does not usually accomplish what we had hoped for. Man does not believe in strange things easily, nor pay attention to what our bizarre signs might mean. We always knew that, when we were on the earth side. Yet now that we are here, we still seek to penetrate that veil and bring our proof of continued existence, if we can. We discover that, just as was true in our first life, there are some among us now who seem better able than we to bridge between the two worlds, and more and more we make our efforts through them. We understand now what earthly "mediums" are, and why they communicate with this new life through their controls that are with us here. We find these beings can get through more readily than we can, and most of us will use them when we feel we must reach back to the life we left.

In time, many will weary of even this kind of contact, and will do more of the other things the new life holds for us and asks of us. But we will never wholly abandon our concern for the life we left behind, nor our hopes of affecting it for those still living it. There are reasons other than nostalgia, and affection for loved ones, and expiation of earlier wrongs, that will make us want to stay involved.

Our lives began on earth, and our lives here are marked by those beginnings. On earth, there were "good" and "evil," values which have no meaning here. In our new life there is only *truth* and *ignorance.* There can be no evil here—no murder, or injury, or untruth, or stealing, or hate, here—none of these is possible. But *ignorance* of the uselessness of hate, of the pettiness of possessions, of the barrier of vanity—these are very present, still embodied in many souls who come here knowing no other values. We struggle against these, through love, but the results are never final. Ignorance persists here, and is constantly reinforced by the evil—now ignorance—of new souls that enter constantly.

And so we try, for all eternity, to guide earthly man in ways of truth, knowing that others like us are trying just as hard to guide him in ways of ignorance. The struggle we knew in our earth life continues here, we are sad to discover, and we will keep trying to do something about it. We know so well, now, what mankind must become, and we can never suppress the desire to try to guide him.

THE SEARCH FOR TRUTH

When we enter our new state, we enter it with only those expectations for it that we developed in our life on earth. We will see, when we arrive, what we had expected to see. If we knew we would cross the Jordan and find the golden city on the other side, we shall cross the Jordan and enter the golden city. If our vision of God was that of the old man with a long beard and a book in his lap, we shall see him that way, and think we have found him. Our minds can tell us nothing else, when we arrive. There is no sudden revelation awaiting us to make all of this new life crystal clear.

It is only as we begin to develop and grow in our new surroundings that we will come to know that our knowledge is hopelessly inadequate, our visions faulty and childish. It will eventually dawn on us that we have a long, long way to go before we shall know the truth that underlies the existence we have entered. We begin with only a dim comprehension that the life we have just entered is not the end point, not the instant fulfillment of our earth lives. Our new life is only the barest beginning of a search for truth that will never be completed. This, more than any other challenge placed before us, is what we must respond to if our new lives are to have rich meaning, to hold more for us than either bewilderment or boredom, each of which can become its own separate kind of hell.

This is the prime struggle of the next life: the unending search for truth and meaning, the overcoming of ignorance. Because we knew of good and evil in our earthly world, we tried to take our sides in that struggle. Here, there is no good, no evil. There is only what *is*—knowledge or ignorance. No laws bind us, no government compels us or regulates us. We are free—free to know or not know, free to search for truth or to remain ignorant. Free to help others in that search, or to turn them aside. Such freedom oppresses us, because we are so unused to it. Our lives on earth, though we called them free, were not like this. There, we knew what we could and could not do, what we should and should not do. We were guided, pressured, shaped by the society of which we were a part, and our decisions were somehow easier to make because of that.

But here, this freedom can be unnerving, because we don't know what we are supposed to do. Only slowly do we comprehend that we are not *supposed* to do anything. But we *may* do everything, and *everything* includes the gaining of understanding of all of the mysteries of life that still remain. How do we go about using this freedom? How do we make our search for truth?

We begin with only the awareness we brought from our earlier experience. For the rest of the way, we must do just what we tried to do before—to think, to learn, to exchange what we know with others at the same stage of development as we are. These are the only ones with whom we can share our minds. There is no university we can enter, no graduate program that will build on what amounts to our grade-school educations. We begin with what we had, and we spend our energies to move ahead as well as we can.

Our questions were just as they were before: What are these minds and bodies we have? What is music, and why? What makes us able to think, and to know? Why do we respond to beauty? Why doesn't everyone? What is the universe, and why does it exist? The answers do not lie in front of us, obvious and complete and satisfying. Only the questions, and we cannot put them aside. We will seek answers by doing what we know best.

Yes, we will think, and we will try to learn. But we will also be physicists there, or doctors, or musicians, or artists. We will be teachers, or students, or builders, or poets. We need all of these around us, to learn. Together, we will know the ecstasy of the creative spirit in a way we could not have dreamed of before. We will know the exhilaration of mind meeting inquiring mind. We will know again the excitement of learning, the thrill of discovery of new insights in a world where we see no end of the need for insight.

And we will progress, starting from wherever we start, moving as well as our minds, our wills, and the energy we spend will allow us. We will sense that there are ascending planes of mind achievement as our awareness grows and we will meet and know other minds that have been growing a little ahead of us. They are in higher realms than we are, and there are further realms that lie far beyond them, realms of even higher knowledge, purer intellect, more selfless love. Our glimpses of them are fleeting, tantalizing, and we know we must reach for them, though it is not easy.

We look for God in those distant realms, we ask about him, we seek to know him. *But we finally know he is not there.* We know, sooner or later, that there is no single being like ourselves named God, no one appointed unknown ages ago as the single highest example of the beings we are trying to become. No, there is no one mind, no individual selected by himself or by an even higher being as the single supreme mind, no omniscient One that has been placed in charge of all eternity.

We view God differently now. He is not a *person*—not a father, not a judge, not a rewarder or punisher. He is not a ruler, not a law giver, not an operator of all of the twinkling stars in boundless space. He doesn't exist as we had been taught he did. He doesn't step forward and answer us when we call out his name.

But what *is* there, in this unlimited world of ours, is more than we could ever have imagined God to be. Here is the energy that drives us in our new existence. Here is the power behind our search for truth. Here is the love and the ecstasy we find as we free ourselves increasingly of the petty habits of our minds. Here is the awe and wonder we feel as we come to understand more about this indescribable existence. *These* are God. And *God* is *us,* as we grow in strength of spirit and love. *God* is the billions like us who are in the same search, seeking the same growth.

God is all we are, and we are all *God* is. He is in his Heaven and in his Hell because *we* are in his Heaven and in his Hell. We still think of him as God because there is no other name we know how to use, no way to enclose this vast idea in any human word. We think "God," and that thought is now boundless, now summing everything we are and everything we know. We have found God by knowing what God is, though we shall never find a being named God.

That does not distress us, for instead of a *being* we have found purpose, and knowledge, and love. That is God, and that is all we shall ever need.

JUDGMENT

I have not talked of judgment. I have described no cosmic record books, no tribunal that awaits our arrival and determines what our fate shall be. I have talked of no winnowing of wheat from chaff, of no separate gates that open to lives of bliss or of damnation.

There is none of this. The bliss, the ecstasy, is there for those who prepare themselves and *will* themselves to find it. The damnation is there, too, in the separate hells with which vivid memories of earlier malice torment us, and in the tragedy that awaits those of us who cannot adjust to this new life. What hell could be worse than the living, unceasing knowledge of harm we have brought to others? What fire could singe our souls half as much as the dormant-lying spark of an unfit life, a life that is unable to learn the ecstasy of new discovery?

The judgment that awaits us is of our own making. In our daily lives on earth, we form that judgment, little by little. On earth, we are good, and we are evil, each in the measure we choose. Each will be with us when we step across that threshold, and each will affect the continuing lives we shall lead. Forgiveness awaits us, but not pardon. Forgiveness is there, as love is there, because it is part of love. But we must *learn* love, starting from where we left off, and only by learning love will we slowly find the forgiveness that will free each of us from the little hells of our own creation. We start our journey anew, but we carry with us all the baggage from the last one.

I will leave it there. I can describe no more. I could wish for more, but this is all I can know with the certainty I need. It is enough for now. I am satisfied that what I know now is *some* of what I shall know then, when I make my own step into eternity.

What if I'm wrong? What if it's not like that at all? I know I am not wrong, for me, and that is all I need to know. Others may disagree, and will, but that does not disturb me because I know what I need to know for me.

Please do not misunderstand me. I say only what *I* know, not what you know. I ask you not to agree or disagree. That is your own matter, and nothing I or anyone else might say can or should tell you what to know. Your own mind will bring you where it brings you, just as mine brought me where it did. My mind brought me here, and because my mind knows, I know. For me, that is enough.

PART II

After Discovery

"A little science estranges men from God, but much science leads them back to Him."
—Louis Pasteur

Chapter 24

The Differences, Now

All of what you have read is empty exercise unless there comes out of it some difference, some sense of purpose, some reason to think or behave differently because of this new knowledge. Are things different for me?

Let me give you an example by way of answer. During the early part of my life, when I was struggling to tie Christian beliefs in a next life to Christian strictures about behavior in this one, I kept hitting a stone wall. I couldn't quite believe the notion that we had better behave in this world or some next-world judge would consign us to hell.

Not that I objected so much to behaving most of the time. It's just that the whole process seemed faulty. Hell was obviously a terrible place, and eternity was a long time. Who operated that delicate scale that could tip toward hell with one more misdeed? And who righted it forever toward heaven—and how come he was allowed to—when a mere death-bed confession came through?

Well, it isn't that way at all. There isn't any scale, there isn't
any judge, there isn't any separate hell or heaven. But I now
know that what we do and how we think in this life does make
a difference—a vast difference—in the next life, which is simply a
continuation of this one. If we are at all in the habit of planning
for the tomorrow's of this life, we should be doing the same for
the next.

That conviction is much easier to gain, I must say, if one has
a dramatic contact with the life beyond, as I did with my eye
problem. That kind of thing happens, I'm sure, largely because
we *let* it happen by opening our minds a bit and then listening
when something comes through.

But these things are rare, at least the highly dramatic ones.
What is not rare at all, I now know, is a subtle and steady flow
of influence, of gentle suggestion, of odd coincidence, that tells
me that I am in tenuous touch with the other side.

I know that I have had plenty of instances of guidance just in
writing this book, things I would earlier have brushed aside as
just luck or coincidence. Like stumbling across references that I
did not know existed, or getting clues from friends that they
could not have known were clues at all. Or waking from a deep
sleep and strange dreams with insights I didn't know I had, or
with an awareness of the need for a new direction of research
that I had not known about or had ignored. All of these I
would earlier have chalked up to my subconscious at work, or to
a freaky bit of luck. But I don't do that anymore.

I know well, now, that the more I discipline myself to listen,
to believe, to act on what I feel, the more will come through,
the more I'll get done and the more I will enjoy the results. I
could wish for a more evident communication channel, a more
positive two-way contact that lets me know with more surety
that I am listening correctly and being heard adequately. I
know that some people say that, for them, that's just the way it
is—voice answering voice. Well, I'm not so lucky, and I don't
think most of us ever will be. I still have to talk to empty space,
and I don't hear clear, English-language answers booming back.
But I know that I *get* answers, that I receive guidance, that I

am in touch, even though I can't pin everything down. That's all I need.

Of one thing I am sure: I am far more observant now, far more conscious of the people around me, far more awake to the beauty and majesty of this world of ours. I am much more aware of the needs of others, and through that awareness I sense a love and a humanness in people that I never looked for before. I occasionally experience moments of sheer exhilaration—fleeting moments, to be sure—that remind me that my life, my mind, and my mood are closely knit to others, and theirs to mine. We *all* affect each other, for bad or good. When I stifle the bad and concentrate on the good, which I really try to do, the effects are remarkable. The response from others brings me a kind of joy I can't remember experiencing in the old days.

I look at things in new ways—at music, to see if I can sense what the composer was feeling; at paintings, to see if they hold special meaning for me; at flowers and plants, to try to tap the exuberance that makes them grow and please us with their blooms. I never used to do this, though I thought I enjoyed them all. But I never really *looked* before, and looking makes a difference.

These are *conscious* things I do, though I still have to remind myself about them. I do them because I want to try to sense everywhere I can the harmony that pervades our world. I want my mind to be a fuller part of the one mind that binds us all. It is hard for me to tell you what all this means and what it does for me. I know the poets can do it better, and I wish I were one. All I can say is that I'm different in the way I look at the world and at others, and for an analytical, technical mind to recognize that surely means something.

I'm happy most of the time, in that I'm not sad. Happiness, for me, is the occasional spike of exhilaration, the overpowering and momentary feeling of being alive, of feeling just great. Happiness is no steady state of bliss, at least not for me. It's spurts, flashes, reminders that life is to be enjoyed, not railed against because it doesn't always go as I would have it.

Fear has left me, and certain kinds of fears used to be around a lot. Not fear of death, particularly—just an assortment of various worries that used to bother me. I suppose I had an unconscious fear of death—the psychiatrists tell us we all do at times. When I was younger I never thought about death much, one way or the other. But for the last few years, death has not been, for me, the end of life and thus has been nothing to be feared. I know I'll feel a little cheated if it comes before I'm ready, because there is so much to be learned and gained from this life. And I'll dislike having to leave those closest to me, placing on them the added burden of having to go it alone. If it comes when it should, when this old machine is worn-out and can go no further, I shall face it with excitement and expectation.

One thing the conviction of a life beyond has done is ease greatly the grief that comes when a loved one dies. I've faced that several times now, with sister, parents, other close relatives, and some very good friends. The sadness is still there, particularly when death comes too soon to a life not yet fulfilled. But mine is not an angry, bitter, puzzled grief that cuts deep and lasts a long time, as it used to be. I know that the life that has left us still lives on, still is aware of us, still loves us. All that has changed is the physical presence, and I know I shall meet that very presence when my own turn comes.

Those other fears I used to have, the ones that used to distress me when I was younger—those have disappeared. I've wondered many times why that should be, whether there is a real connection between a deep faith and the absence of fear. I believe there is, and it has little to do with the mere removal of the fear of death. It has to do with a better definition of success and failure.

What I used to fear was *failure*—failure to get where I wanted to get in my professional life, failure to gain the recognition I thought was a most important part of this life, failure to be respected or liked by people I wanted to have respect and like me.

Failure, I now know, is not that, nor is success found in the attainment of those things. Failure is neglecting to enjoy this life to the fullest. Failure is being blind to love and to the needs of others. Failure is not to wonder at the hidden meanings of life, and not to use one's mind and hands to search for those meanings. Failure is not to try to explain life or to make it better for all people by our creative acts. Those kinds of failure a deep faith can overcome, and with that, fear disappears.

As I say, these things are different for me now, and I know that is because of what I believe. Not that my life is serene, without disappointment or loneliness or worry or some pain. They are all still there. I still set expectations that don't work out—but I no longer get in a state over them. I still worry about whether I am doing what I ought to be doing, or serving and relating as well as I should serve and relate. I don't think I get clear answers, from anywhere.

But I am not morose about these things. I somehow have the feeling that as long as I'm not too lazy, as long as I don't stop trying to think and to learn and to help, things will continue to work out pretty well. I still get depressed at times—I think something about our cyclical chemistry does that to all of us on a regular basis. Not that I get sick, deep, endless depressed—just an occasional weariness, one which I now know will soon go away, one whose departure I can always hasten by a little upbeat thinking.

I know I am far from perfect. I know I have not shed my vanity nor my selfishness. But I know now what it is to be more perfect, and why I should continue to try. That makes a big difference in the way the days go.

Do I pray now? Yes. Do I pray to God? Yes, I frequently use the word, but as you saw, it doesn't ring the same in my mind as it used to. I no longer have to fight a vision of some ethereal giant cocking his head and straining to hear my small voice in the darkness. The word to me now means a power around me, a power with an intimate knowledge of who I am and what I need. I sometimes just call to "you out there" or "you around me," instead of to God, knowing in my heart that I am talking to beings who are of God.

They are trying to guide me, and I am trying to listen.

How do I pray? I usually close my eyes, but not always.

Sometimes I can be looking at the sea, or sitting in Symphony Hall, or simply lying in bed, and I will think a quick and simple thought: Thank you for awakening me to this majesty; or, Help me do what I must do; or, Tell me of a need I can fill; or, Bring wisdom or courage or strength to one I feel needs help. One thought at a time, repeated over and over. That's how I pray.

Are my prayers answered? I don't know, really. I think they sometimes are, because I see wonderful things happening, when I remember to look. I see things happen that seem tragic, too, though I am no longer so certain what tragedy is. I don't try to pinpoint results—I don't ask for particular, pinpointed results. I pray because I have to, because I know I am part of a larger life, and that I must try to make that life as much better and more useful as my tiny efforts are able to.

Don't get me wrong. I don't go around praying all the time. I have not become an ascetic or a monk. Far from it. I will go for quite long periods—days, even weeks—without praying or even thinking hard about life's mysteries. Life is too full of daily demands to permit every-hour-on-the-hour prayer or contemplation. I pray, I contemplate, when the spirit moves me, and it does, now, fairly frequently. But I'm by no means disciplined in it.

Church is a good time for prayer, because the mood is there, and at times during a service still cluttered with theater I find time for prayer and contemplation on my own.

Church doesn't trouble me anymore. I know what I know, and even though what I hear is a lot different from what I now think, we're all reaching for the same thing. I still find myself arguing mentally with the Scriptures and the prayers and the sermons, but not in the old upsetting way. I know now where the legends came from. I know about Osiris, and the Stoics, and about the possible origins of what I used to call pure superstition. I know the church is on the right track, if we would all but pay attention.

What I now find upsetting is an occasional smugness I sense in myself, a feeling that I know something the rest of these people don't and wouldn't it be nice if the church taught things the way they *really* are. But I stifle that simply by reminding myself that the way I think is only the way *I* think, and needn't at all be the way everybody is supposed to think. The last thing I want to become is some kind of evangelist.

I find I enjoy, in church, reflecting on the Jesus I now feel I know better. I have little trouble anymore with his miracles or his reappearances after death, and I now know why his tiny band of followers gave their lives to his teachings. Jesus did die, did reappear, and it was not an hallucination. It can happen, and it has happened, and it will happen again. I know that Jesus is still alive, still communing with beings in the next world who have achieved his same high state of knowledge and perfection, the state that Jesus already seemed to possess in his short life on earth.

When my mind wanders in church, as it still does, I sometimes steer it into speculation about others who might well be on the same plane, the same stage of spiritual knowledge and growth as Jesus. Who might they be? Mohammed, surely? Gandhi? Socrates? William James? A witch doctor who served his African village with love and insight and passed on to continue to grow in the next life? I don't really know, of course, but what I'm in church for now has a lot to do with this kind of reflection.

I don't go to church as much as I used to, mostly because we now live at some distance from our former church home. But I have a warm feeling about church and the people I know there, and church is a place I enjoy. Obviously, the change has been in me, not in the church, and that is certainly the best way to have it. I hate to think how badly we'd fail if we tried to tailor every church to fit exactly what each of us thinks it should be.

My health? I haven't consciously tried to use faith as a key to health, although I'm sure it can be done. I think the Christian Scientists succeed in that more often than most of us admit. I believe faith healing can work, too, and I'm sure some health benefits flow from the kinds of mental and bodily disciplines entailed in the more mystical religions.

I haven't gotten into those things because I haven't had reason to. I'm in good health, and have been for a number of years, as my doctor will attest. Sure, I'm slowing down, and I'm as creaky as we're expected to be in our fifties. But I'm not ill, and I haven't been for a long time—oddly enough, since about the time I was beginning to find my way through all I have told you. Before that I had plenty of problems. My doctor used to refer to me as a medical zoo.

I know there is a connection between faith and health, but it's not one I worked consciously to bring about. I think the connection comes quite naturally as one learns what it is to begin to enjoy life more fully and to sense in it the excitement which it holds—and learns as well not to waste himself in petty fears and angers and in the conflicts that accompany the pursuit of position and possessions.

If I do get very sick—and I suppose I shall at some point—I will not be at all bashful about praying to be cured, and I won't spurn acupuncture or faith healing or any other approach that might possibly do some good. Whether any of these will work or not, I have no idea. Well, yes, I have a pretty good hunch they might, but I also know that nothing is quite as predictable and reliable as we'd like it to be. So I'll have expectations for help and improvement, but I won't be painfully disappointed if they are not fulfilled. If nothing works, and I have to go, I'll go—expectantly.

Chapter 25

Reincarnation

I didn't mention reincarnation earlier. That doesn't mean I didn't think about it a great deal, because I did. Even the most cursory reading of religious or psychic literature reminds us that the idea of rebirth is as old as man, with millions of adherents throughout the world—Thoreau, Tolstoy, Henry Ford, and General Patton, to name a few.

I didn't just brush it aside. For me, the idea of reincarnation as a standard part of the afterlife simply didn't have a place in the heaven I finally understood. But the subject should be included in a book like this, for readers who are curious about it and interested to know why I can't believe in it.

There seem to be as many shadings of belief in reincarnation as there are in religious thought itself. Basically, all hold that the soul at death, or sometime after death, enters a new body, usually of a child in the womb, and begins life all over again. The new being has no memory of earlier lives, at least none that can be recalled consciously. But through hypnotism, or through the powers of psychically gifted persons, memories of previous existences can be summoned past the barrier of the conscious mind. That summoning is what has kept the idea alive over the centuries.

Underlying most of the reincarnation beliefs is the basic idea of purification of the soul. Life, say the believers, is the only place in which a soul can learn, can grow in knowledge of good and evil and be tempered to withstand adversity. Only when the soul is finally pure can it have eternal peace and need be reincarnated no more. Some cults also view reincarnation as the ultimate means of punishment for sins committed in earlier lives. Even the Bible says, "an eye for an eye, a tooth for a tooth," promising that everything will be evened up in time.

Because it's quite clear that the evening-up does not always take place in this life, some theologians interpret the biblical maxim as prime evidence supporting the reincarnation idea. Eastern religions have their "karma," the destiny of every human being, representing the sum total of all of the actions, and their consequences, of all of the existences that each life has been through.

There is much to recommend a belief in reincarnation. For one thing, it does carry out the promise of judgment, a promise that every human being instinctively hopes for. Without some kind of final judgment, life would seem to be unfair, and if life is unfair there can be no faith. It's comforting to know that the bad guys of this world will catch it the next time around. It's also nice to contemplate that the poor may be rich on the next trip, and that the failure in this life may have been a prince in the last one.

The evidence supporting the idea of rebirth is very impressive. For thousands of years, and continuing today, there have occurred instances of post-cognition—knowledge of past events completely outside of one's experience—that seem to be explainable only by reincarnation. Some of the stories are widely known, like the classic case of Bridey Murphy. Bridey was a nineteenth century Irish lass the world would never have heard of but for a Colorado housewife, Virginia Tighe. In 1952, under hypnosis, Mrs. Tighe revealed that in a former life she had been Bridey Murphy, and she described her life—in rich Irish brogue—

back in County Cork in amazing detail. Old Irish records were checked; old-timers from Bridey's village were questioned. Mrs. Tighe's descriptions held up with uncanny accuracy. She seemed to be describing Bridey Murphy's life of seventy years earlier in extraordinary and faultless detail.

Or was she? Was this reincarnation—or hoax? The controversy raged for years, as many investigators sought to explain Mrs. Tighe's flashbacks simply as the result of some excellent coaching. Whatever the true explanation, the simplest one, and the one still believed by many people, is reincarnation: Mrs. Tighe *was* Bridey Murphy in an earlier life.

The Bridey Murphy story is but one of thousands of similar previous-life reports. Edgar Cayce, an American medium and psychic healer of the twenties and thirties, probably did as much as anyone in America to spread the reincarnation gospel. Cayce was an extraordinary medium, one who accomplished some well-authenticated healings by using his psychic powers, healings that dumbfounded reputable physicians who attested to his cures. Though his healings probably accounted for most of the fame he achieved, he acquired a sizable band of followers through his clairvoyant readings of their past lives. He did not rely on hypnosis to regress patients back through former existences, as did Mrs. Tighe's mentor, but simply went into trance and carried his sitters back with him through their previous incarnations. Many times, by doing this, he was reportedly able to provide great help to disturbed people by explaining their present difficulties in terms of their "karma," their destiny derived from earlier lives.

In spite of all of the writings that suggest earlier lives, I cannot believe that reincarnation is the repeated, inescapable destiny of souls who depart this life. Not that I disbelieve the vast number of reports of this eerie post-cognition. I think there have been many authentic instances of detailed knowledge of lives far back in history, knowledge that could only have been gained by paranormal means. But I believe there is a much simpler explanation for these things than reincarnation, one which does not do violence to my belief in a simple and beautiful transition from this life to the next.

The eerie—and convincing—accounts of former lives are real,

but I do not think they are based on recall of previous existences. They are simply the efforts of departed souls to speak to the living, and through the living to make themselves heard. This is a brief form of *possession*—the dominance of a living mind by a mind on the other side. The beings themselves are part of what we call past, but they are in a present which is real over there: they are simply seeking to make themselves heard and felt on this side.

There is some persuasive evidence about this topic being gathered in a few experimental psychology laboratories. Subjects who are susceptible to deep hypnosis are put into trance and told by the hypnotist that they have now become someone else, some historic person like Fritz Kreisler, or the painter Raphael, or some other talented figure from the past. They are urged to play music, or draw, or paint, because they are now the great master himself. Some of the results, with some of the subjects, have been surprising. Hitherto untalented persons have demonstrated remarkable skills, with styles strongly suggestive of those of the master himself. Throughout the trance, the language, the attitudes, indeed the whole personality of the subject becomes altered in ways that seem in keeping with the earlier time and with the known facts about the person whose life the subject has assumed.

As with all other psychic investigations, this one has not unfailingly produced results such as I have described. But it has produced enough to convince some serious investigators that very deep hypnotic states do open the human mind to influences which are authentically those of persons who have gone beyond. The technique is called "artificial reincarnation," but it resembles the real thing in every detail.

I don't rule out reincarnation as a choice open to beings in the next life who wish to re-enter this world by their own choosing, in order to gain from it something they failed to gain in a former life. The evidence for possession, for radical changes in personality that occur from time to time, is too compelling to be ignored, and I can surmise that there exists a means whereby a human body can be literally taken over—probably quite readily, while a child is still unborn—by a departed mind who wishes to live again on earth.

But I should think this would not be a usual choice. It is one perhaps to be made by someone whose earlier time on earth was very short, or by one who had reached a very high stage of spiritual development and wished to return as teacher or artist. Or even as a force of evil.

I can't know about all this, of course, but it doesn't make any difference in my faith. What would make a difference, one so huge I could find no faith at all, would be reincarnation as an inevitable, regular, interminable part of the life after death. That would require *judgment*—omniscient, all-powerful, frequently cruel judgment. And that would demean the heaven I know, which has no room for the needed karmic record books and for vast queues of souls lined up awaiting instant dispatch to a human womb the moment egg and sperm collide. No, I don't think that's what this life or the next one are about, even though the idea of reincarnation may make some people happy and some even good.

Chapter 26

Implications for Issues

One of the effects of acquiring a firm set of beliefs is that they form a new and far more comfortable context within which to examine the issues that modern life poses and on which society seems to expect us to take stands. The Billy Grahams of this world have always had it a little easier than the agnostics because an informed student can find in the Bible an answer (usually a choice of answers) to any question or issue society might pose. The Bible approves of both war and peace, love and vengeance, fecundity and celibacy, wealth and poverty. Small wonder there has been a certain amount of confusion over the centuries as to exactly how man should behave.

The agnostic is obliged to take refuge in pure analytic intellect in order to find his position on complex issues. He usually winds up favoring the side which seems to be least worst for a number of people—usually people rather like himself. And he frequently finds himself in a lonely minority, because the Bible-driven Christian society we live in makes some pretty strange choices from time to time.

Now that I am not an agnostic, it's much easier to sort out my thoughts and feelings on any issue and to feel comfortable with where I come out. I still find myself in the minority more often than not, but I no longer have to re-examine endlessly the reasons for the positions I take. I also feel good about how I feel, and the only thing I worry about is that same sense of smugness that bothers me from time to time in church. I suspect my old friends view me as just as opinionated as I ever was, and until they read this book they will not know that I now have a different reason—a much better one, I think—for sounding as positive as I probably have always sounded about some of the issues of the day.

Let me give you two brief examples of how a changed frame of reference affects the views we hold.

SAMPLE ISSUE: EARLY DEATH AND ABORTION

The saddest death of all and the one hardest for us to understand is that of the very young—the infant, the child, the vigorous adolescent. We have been taught for so long that death is a form of judgment—God's will being expressed, God's wish to have a life returned to him being fulfilled—that we can only be puzzled by a God so cruel to his little children.

That idea of a child's death being God's will was one of the most vexing of all the teachings that used to upset me so in church. Equally distressing was the idea of an eternal state of rest, a static preservation for all time of the soul that reached the beyond, a beyond that would be heaven or hell depending on how the soul was judged by God. The church never said how infants get judged, or how they ever lived as anything but infants in their eternal resting place.

I now know that it's not that way at all. The mind, the energy-body, the soul—call it what you will—that transits at death is exactly as it was the moment before. It is a complete body, a complete spirit, differing from the eighty-year-old arrival only in the sum of earthly knowledge acquired before death.

The infant begins the next life with none of the wisdom that can be gained in this one. He also begins with none of the malice, the falsehoods, the misconceptions that we all absorb in this earthly struggle.

Is he better or worse off when he dies than an adult who has led a full life? Neither. He just begins from a different starting point, and will learn in the life to come whatever he chooses to learn. He has some advantages and some disadvantages. But he is a total being, not a mindless infant.

He was not called because someone wanted him there. He arrived because of the will or carelessness of someone in this life, or because his body was imperfect for the task of this life, or because his death was already part of his future. Any of these alone, or all of them together, led to his early death—and to his early start in the next life. That's really all that happened to him, sad as the occasion of his death may be.

And that's all that happens to a fetus that dies as a result of spontaneous or induced abortion. The *means* makes no difference. The physical life that began at the moment of conception has been ended. The mind, the spirit life, the energy-body that formed when sperm met egg, is now released. It is released whether the cause of death was natural or surgical.

We can make all the judgments we want to about the morality of abortion, but we must include the natural kind as well. We will find, if we do, that this is really not a moral issue at all. Death is not "wrong" and life "right." There can be no right or wrong in a transition that does not destroy life itself. The moral question, if there is one, is whether the physical life that was aborted would have had a fair chance to live and grow in healthy and productive fashion in this world and would be able to progress without torment in the next.

Viewed this way, the rightness or wrongness of an abortion decision depends on the validity of the forecast of the probable life situation for the child. I think there are some kinds of circumstances where the outlook can quite accurately be seen as a gloomy one, and both the fetus and society would be better served if the next life began sooner rather than later. In any case, the decision should be an individual, personal one, and society can play no helpful role by resolving the issue by law.

SAMPLE ISSUE: GENIUS AND GENES

I have known two authentic geniuses in my life, one recognized widely in the world and one known hardly at all. But they had one thing in common: an invincible trust in their minds. No nay-saying by others, no logical argument showing unquestionably that something could not be done or would not work, seemed to cause the slightest deviation in their course or make their self-confidence waver by so much as a millimeter. They both accomplished extraordinary things. Neither, of course, ascribed his success to any kind of divine intervention. They both would tell me they did what they did because they had faith in their minds. They relied confidently on the insights their minds brought them—flashes, hunches, intuitions, call it what you will. They *acted* on these—with zeal—to accomplish what they set out to do.

A less awesome word for the things that geniuses possess in such abundance is *creativity,* and that's something that most of us feel we have in at least some measure. When the results of creativity seem to be of great significance or the skills transcend what the rest of us can accomplish, we use the word genius. A Mozart composing extraordinary works at age four, an Einstein pressing back the limits of knowledge for all time—these are so unusual that we call them genius. Yet the basis of that genius is still the same spark of creativity that exists in all of us.

Genius is a matter of scale, and the scale, I believe, has but two determinants: the power of the unseen forces that seek to influence human minds, and the open-ness of those minds to that power.

Not all genius is "good" genius, as the history books so frequently remind us. There have been and will continue to be political, military, criminal and other personages whom we deem evil, yet who merit the term "genius" just as much as the noble minds of science and the arts. They are just as extraordinary, just as reliant on their minds and intuitions as the "good" geniuses. They differ only in how we judge their accomplishments. *We* call them evil. They are responding to forces on the other side which are viewed there simply as ignorance. In the other-world struggle for men's minds here on earth, ignorance opposes the forces of truth and knowledge, and mankind is the loser when ignorance gains the upper hand. Both forces are powerless, in themselves, with any human mind. Their power, whether for good or evil here on earth, depends on our willingness to hear one voice more clearly than the other.

I believe there are two reasons, and only two, why we don't see many more geniuses than we do. The external influence, the "power" needed from unseen minds to stimulate responses of genius proportions is not commonplace. Summoning such power over there, sustaining it, penetrating men's minds here with it seems to be no easier than communicating with and trusting that power over here.

But even when the power, influence, commitment, and persistence of needed magnitude centers on a human mind here, there must still be receptivity. There must be listening, and trusting by that mind, followed by unrelenting pursuit of the idea, if genius is to result. Geniuses are merely people whose minds are wide open, people who trust what their minds tell them and are energetic enough to go all the way. Some geniuses have indeed acknowledged a feeling of a "presence," of a guidance from beyond the world of their senses. Most have not, nor do they know they should.

There's some scientific and philosophic argument taking place these days about the possibility—nay, the certainty—that soon we'll be able to alter man's genes. Some geneticists believe we can learn not only how to make man healthier, but how to make him intellectually sharper, more creative, more genius-like in his ability to exist in and shape the world. That sounds like an exciting prospect until we remember that people like Hitler have lived in this world, and that science isn't always able to control the uses to which its major discoveries are put.

Thus there is concern in some quarters that science may someday be able to produce a breed of super-intellects, of geniuses who in the wrong hands or with the wrong motivations might conceivably do us all in. This is not the only worry that is expressed about genetic tinkering. There is a fairly good basis for believing that manipulation of the chromosomes could occasionally lead to unintended and distressing mutations of the human species, and that society would then have on its hands the terrible problem of what to do with the unfortunate creatures that result. And on top of all the other voices urging suppression or state control of mutation research are heard some strident ones from folks who believe passionately that it is a violation of God's will to monkey around with such basic life processes.

What all of these voices are asking is that we fetter science because for various reasons we fear it. That's just what we tried to do not so many years ago with Galileo, and for some of the same reasons. The issue we face here is a terribly important one. I'm not at all sure our political leaders, or even our scientific spokesmen, know enough about God's will or human genius and intellect to make decisions like this. But I'm very sure that mankind will be the loser if it tries to draw a line that tells science: *this far, and no farther.*

We need not fear that malevolent genius will rise from the test tube. Genius—good or evil—does not stem from chemistry. It stems from the power outside of us. What we should fear is knowledge not gained, and ignorance preserved.

Chapter 27

Ending . . . and Beginning

I wrote this book mostly to get my own head in order. That it has done. I also wanted to share these thoughts with anyone else who might have the same kind of doubts I used to have. That it has done, too, doubt for doubt, fact for fact, thought for thought. Though in many places it must have looked as though I were trying to persuade you of something or other, that has not been my intent. When the argument got heavy, it was *me* arguing with *me,* not with you.

I would like to think you learned something new as you went along, and perhaps became more comfortable musing about mysteries most of us don't talk about very much. I think I can promise you that the facts I cited are true. Most of them could be checked from more than one source, and where they seemed less positive than I would wish, I have tried to note that. Overall, I think the best indication of credibility lies in the very large number of constantly similar reports of all of the phenomena I have described, reports that come from all over the world and go back many years in history. To keep the book in bounds, I was obliged to confine myself to but a very few kinds of unexplained phenomena and could use only limited illustrations. There is much to be learned and to be gained, if you find you are curious about these things, from reading extensively and sifting these reports yourself.

I certainly don't expect you to accept the God and heaven I described—not from one reading, not from several, maybe never. Indeed, if you were to feel I am right about everything I have concluded, I shall have done you a disservice. You run a risk, if you should find yourself agreeing with everything I have told you, of thinking you now believe the same things. You may even feel that you have acquired some new convictions that will help you to understand life's mysteries and to cope better with life's difficulties. Quite possibly, you will be wrong.

Unless your own beliefs were already almost unshakable, you probably have a long, long way to go. Though you may have reached an intellectual, rational agreement with some of what I have described—and that's a great start—that is a far different thing from holding a belief. In my own case, many years had to pass before I truly knew that what my intellect told me was what I *believed*. During all those years I still found myself questioning endlessly, always testing the hand life was dealing me against what I thought I believed. I slid back, picked up, slid back again. Many times. I still do, too often, when I forget to look and to listen.

Faith, I now know, is not something we acquire once and for all, like a shiny new knife. The knife is of no value unless it is used. We must cut things with it, carve things with it. A knife will get dulled from time to time and must frequently be honed if it is to cut and carve as beautifully as it can. But only by cutting and carving will it be of value, and only by cutting and carving will the hand that guides it learn to understand what it can do. So with faith.

This book is but a starting point. All it can do, all it should do, is let you feel more comfortable about trying to carve your own belief. Your mind is all you have to work with, and it is all you need. If you learn to trust it, learn to listen to it as it

questions things you never thought to question before, you will
be at the beginning of your own search. You will not know
where that search will lead you when you begin. But if you do
begin, if you do observe, and think, and listen, and read, and
talk openly and comfortably with friends around you, you will
surely build your own belief, and you will finally come to trust
it. None of this is easy, none comes naturally. But it comes.

I leave you now with a wish. I wish for you the will to find a
faith, if you are at all as I was when this all began. I know now
what it was that lay inside the people I admired, the people I
envied because they seemed to have something I did not. I can
think of nothing we can do for ourselves that can possibly
compare with the impress on our lives that an abiding faith will
have. If you are even the slightest bit inclined to examine your
own faith or to make it stronger, I can urge only that you *begin*.
Begin in any way you choose, but begin, and begin a hundred
times more, until something inside you tells you that you now
believe. For me, beginning was reading and thinking, and then—
slowly—came awareness. *Believing* starts with awareness, and
grows as we question, and as we search for answers.

Look. Listen. Question. And, yes, love. Belief will come.

Suggested Further Reading

For those who are interested in probing a little more deeply, I recommend any of the books listed in the Acknowledgments section at the front of this book, as well as these:

The Roots of Coincidence—Arthur Koestler (Random House, 1972). An excellent science writer pokes at the unknown in a scientifically disciplined way.

An Historian's Approach to Religion—Arnold Toynbee (Oxford University Press, 1956). The thorough historian looks at religion as an historical rather than revelatory process.

The Varieties of Psychedelic Experience—R. E. Masters and L. Houston (Dell Publishing Co., 1966). Some instances of what the mind can do when LSD and other drugs upset control mechanisms.

The Universe and Dr. Einstein—Lincoln Barnett (Bantam, 1974). Understandable Einstein, conveying a sense of the universe and a helpful feeling of awe about this great intellect.

New World of the Mind—J. B. Rhine (Morrow, 1971). A fairly early book about the ESP experiments, more readable than many.

The Unexplained—Allen Spraggett (New American Library, 1967). A Canadian minister turned journalist cites wide personal experience with things supernatural. One of the better books of its kind.

You Do Take It With You—R. DeWitt Miller (Citadel Press, 1955). One of the most diligent investigators in the paranormal field touched all the bases to give a thorough and very readable sampling of all that's supernatural.

Noted Witnesses for Psychic Occurrences—Walter Franklin Prince (Reprinted 1967 by University Books from 1928 edition published by Boston Society for Psychical Research). An anthology of carefully documented cases of psychic experiences of well-known, hence presumably responsible, men and women, mostly American.

Let Us In—John Revere Burke (E. P. Dutton, 1931). The verbatim transcripts of communications said to have come through from William James many years after his death. Mostly useful to James fans. James' life and writings are highly recommended to survival inquirers.

The Betty Book—Stuart Edward White (E. P. Dutton, 1937). One of the classic documentaries of communications with the next world. Somewhat tedious, but worth it as a springboard for speculation.

The Case for Astral Projection—Sylvan J. Muldoon (Aries Press, 1936; reprinted Wehman, New Jersey, 1969). One of the best accounts of this strange phenomenon, written by one who claims to have mastered the technique.

Mind-Reach—Russell Targ and Harold Puthoff (Delacorte Press, 1977). Two Stanford Research Institute physicists employ rigorous scientific method to prove in new ways the existence of ESP. Useful if you want impressive and very recent documentation, including some interesting support for Uri Geller.

About the Author

Robert C. Casselman obtained his Bachelor of Science degree at MIT and has had a distinguished career as corporate executive, teacher, public servant, and now museum administrator. He joined fledgling Polaroid Corporation thirty-five years ago, and for many years served as Vice-President. Largely because of what this book is about, he made a mid-career change at forty-five and began doing whatever looked interesting. In succession, he taught at MIT, led a Massachusetts government reorganization, headed a large electro-optical and chemical research laboratory, and is presently administrative director of the Museum of Fine Arts, Boston.

Index